Microsoft® Office Specialist Exam Reference for Microsoft Office 2003

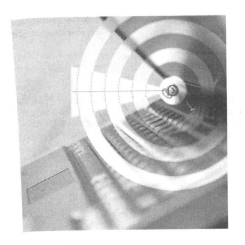

THOMSON
COURSE TECHNOLOGY

Australia • Canada • Mexico • Singapore • Spain • United Kingdom • United States

THOMSON
COURSE TECHNOLOGY

Microsoft® Office Specialist Exam Reference for Microsoft Office 2003
is published by Course Technology.

Executive Editor:
Nicole Jones Pinard

Developmental Editor:
Marjorie Hunt

Product Manager:
Emilie Perreault

Composition House:
GEX Publishing Services

Editorial Assistant:
Shana Rosenthal

QA Manuscript Reviewers:
Ashlee Welz, Danielle Shaw

Production Editor:
Kelly Robinson

Book Designer:
GEX Publishing Services

Contributing Author:
Jennifer Campbell

ISBN 0-619-27328-3

BRIEF TABLE OF CONTENTS

TABLE OF CONTENTS

ABOUT THIS BOOK

HOW TO USE THIS BOOK

Microsoft® Office Specialist Exam Reference for Office 2003 is a reference tool designed to prepare you for the Microsoft Office Specialist exams. This book assumes that you already understand the concepts that are the basis for the skills covered in this book, and, therefore, the book can be used as a study companion to brush up on skills before taking the exam, or as a desk reference when using Microsoft Office programs.

The Structure of this Book

There are six chapters in this book. The first chapter, Exam Tips, provides some background information on the Microsoft Office Specialist Certification program, the general process for taking an exam, and some helpful hints for preparing for and successfully passing the exams.

The remaining five chapters each cover a different Office program: Word, Excel, Access, PowerPoint, and Outlook. Each program-specific chapter begins by covering program basics in a brief Getting Started section. This section covers the basic skills that are not specifically covered in the Microsoft Office Specialist or Expert exams, but that are essential to being able to work in the program. Each Getting Started section is followed by the complete set of skills tested by the Microsoft Office Specialist Certification exams, starting with the Specialist exam, and then followed by the Expert exam where applicable. These sections are labeled and ordered to exactly match the Skill Sets and Skill Activities tested in the Microsoft Office Specialist and Expert Certification Exams. Bulleted steps containing clear instructions are provided for each skill.

Because there are often different ways to complete a task, the book provides multiple methods where appropriate for each skill or activity, including Menu, Button, Keyboard, Mouse, and Task Pane methods. The Microsoft Office Specialist and Expert exams allow you to perform the skills using any one of these methods, so you can choose the method with which you are most comfortable to complete the task.

Technical Concerns

This book assumes the following regarding your installation of Office 2003 and your computer's setup:

- ☐ You have installed Office 2003 using the Typical installation.
- ☐ You have a document open and ready to use when required to work within a specific document. Also, if the steps instruct you to format an Excel worksheet or a Word document, you can format the open document or worksheet in any way you want, choosing options that are appropriate for your needs.

☐ You have the correct toolbar(s) open. All toolbars are referenced in this book, and in each Getting Started section there is information about how to display specific toolbars. However, the steps to display a certain toolbar are not repeated for every skill.

☐ You have an Internet connection to complete certain steps, and you are familiar with how to connect to the Internet.

ACKNOWLEDGMENTS

Thank you to all of the people who contributed to the process of this book. I specifically want to thank the team at Course Technology: Emilie Perreault, Ashlee Welz, and Kelly Robinson. I am also grateful to Marjorie Hunt for her expertise and suggestions. Lastly, I thank my family: Lucy, Emma, and Mike, for all you bring to my life. This book is dedicated to my father, the best teacher I know.

Jennifer T. Campbell

EXAM TIPS

- ☐ What is Microsoft Office Specialist Certification?
- ☐ Certification benefits
- ☐ The Microsoft Office Specialist Certification process
- ☐ Choosing an exam
- ☐ Preparing for the exam
- ☐ Finding a testing center
- ☐ Taking the exam
- ☐ Receiving exam results

WHAT IS MICROSOFT OFFICE SPECIALIST CERTIFICATION?

Certification is a growing IT industry trend whereby a software or hardware company devises and administers exams for users that will demonstrate their abilities to use the software or hardware in an effective manner. By passing a Certification exam, users prove their abilities and knowledge of the software or hardware to prospective employers and colleagues.

The Microsoft Office Specialist program is the only comprehensive, performance-based certification program approved by Microsoft to validate desktop computer skills using the Microsoft Office programs:

- ☐ Microsoft Word
- ☐ Microsoft Excel
- ☐ Microsoft Access
- ☐ Microsoft PowerPoint®
- ☐ Microsoft Outlook®

The Microsoft Office Specialist program provides computer program literacy, measures proficiency, and identifies opportunities for skills enhancement. Successful candidates receive a Micorosoft Office Specialist certificate that sets them apart from their peers in the competitive job market. The certificate is a valuable credential recognized worldwide as proof that an individual has the desktop computing skills needed to work more productively and efficiently.

By encouraging individuals to develop advanced skills with Microsoft business desktop software, the Microsoft Office Specialist program is helping to fill the demand for qualified, knowledgeable people in the workplace. Microsoft Office Specialist also helps satisfy an organization's need for a qualitative assessment of employee skills.

Exam Tips

The Microsoft Office Specialist exams are developed, marketed, and administered by Certipoint, Inc., a company that has an exclusive license from Microsoft. The exams are available in 17 different languages and in more than 100 countries. Exams must be taken at an authorized Microsoft Office Specialist testing center called an iQcenter. In order to become an iQcenter, a facility must have a quiet room with the proper hardware and software, as well as trained personnel to manage the exams.

CERTIFICATION BENEFITS

Achieving Microsoft Office Specialist Certification in one or several of the Microsoft Office 2003 programs can be beneficial to you and your current or prospective employer. Earning Microsoft Office Specialist certification acknowledges you have the expertise to work with Microsoft Office programs. Microsoft Office Specialist-certified individuals report increased competence and productivity with Microsoft Office programs as well as increased credibility with their employers, co-workers, and clients. Microsoft Office Specialist certification sets you apart in today's competitive job market, bringing employment opportunities, greater earning potential and career advancement, in addition to increased job satisfaction.

For example, if you have passed the Microsoft Word 2003 Certification exam and you are interviewing for a job that requires knowledge and use of Word to complete business-related word processing tasks, Microsoft Office Specialist Certification in Microsoft Word will indicate to your prospective employer that you have the necessary skills to perform that aspect of the job. It also indicates not only that you have a certain level of skill, but that you also have the initiative to prepare for, sign up for, pay for, and take an exam. Microsoft Office Specialist Certification can help you to increase your productivity within your current job and is a great way to enhance your skills without taking courses to obtain a new degree.

THE MICROSOFT OFFICE SPECIALIST CERTIFICATION PROCESS

There are five steps to successfully completing Microsoft Office Specialist certification, as outlined in Table ET-1 and discussed in the remainder of this introductory chapter.

Table ET-1 Microsoft Office Specialist Certification Process

Action	Description
Choose an Exam	Choose from one of the following exams, based on your skills and interests: Word Specialist Word Expert Excel Specialist Excel Expert Access Specialist PowerPoint Specialist Outlook Specialist
Prepare for the exam	Select the method that is appropriate for you, including taking a class or purchasing self-study materials
Find a testing center	Find a site close to you using the iQcenter locator on *http://www.microsoft.com/learning/mcp/officespecialist/ officespecialist_locator.asp*, and either make an appointment or verify that the center accepts walk-ins
Take the exam	Bring payment and a valid picture ID (driver's license or valid passport); be sure to read the exam directions before starting the exam
Receive Exam Results	You will find out your results immediately. If you pass, you will receive your certificate two to three weeks after the exam

Choose an Exam

The Microsoft Office Specialist Certification program offers exams for the five main programs of Microsoft Office 2003: Word, Excel, Access, PowerPoint, and Outlook. For Word and Excel, there are two exams available, a Specialist exam that covers basic skills and an Expert exam that covers more advanced skills. The Specialist exam covers basic skills such as formatting and using graphics that will help you demonstrate your proficiency in the application. The Expert exam focuses on more advanced features of the application such as collaborating with other users, working on the Web, and importing and exporting data. The Expert exams assume that you know the Specialist skills, but includes no coverage of skills covered in the Specialist exams. The Access, PowerPoint, and Outlook exams have only one level each, covering both basic and advanced skills. Choose an application and an exam that will help you in your current position or job search, or one that tests skills that match your abilities and interests. You can find the list of skills covered in each exam on the Microsoft Office Specialist exam Web site *http://www.microsoft.com/learning/mcp/ officespecialist/requirements.asp#office2003*. You can also find more information on the exams at *www.certcities.com/certs/mous* and at *http:// www.microsoft.com/learning/mcp/officespecialist/requirements.asp*.

About the Office Master Certification

Master Certification Candidates must successfully complete three required exams and one elective exam. Required exams include Word 2003 Expert, Excel 2003, Expert, and PowerPoint 2003 Specialist. Elective exams include Access 2003 Specialist or Outlook 2003 Specialist.

PREPARE FOR THE EXAM

How you choose to prepare for an exam depends on your current skill level, which you can determine by reading through the objectives for the exam. As stated earlier, a list of skills covered in each exam is provided on the official Microsoft Office Specialist exam web site *http://www.microsoft. com/learning/mcp/officespecialist/requirements.asp#office2003.* Preparing for a Certification exam might be as involved as taking an introductory class and learning the program in its entirety. If you are already familiar with the program, preparation may only entail purchasing study materials and learning on your own all of the skills or those with which you feel you are not as familiar. If you have been using the program on a regular basis, you may need simply to review the skills on the objectives list for the exam you choose and brush up on those few that are problem areas for you.

Take a Class

Taking a class is a good way to help prepare you for a certification exam. If you are a complete beginner, enrolling in a class can help you prepare for a Specialist exam. If you are an experienced user and know the basics, an advanced class can help you prepare for an Expert exam. The benefits of taking a class include having an instructor as a resource, having the support of your classmates, and receiving study materials such as a lab book. Some classes are even geared specifically towards taking and passing a certification exam, and are taught by instructors who have passed the exam themselves. Your local community college, career education center, or community/continuing education programs will most likely offer such courses. Classes range from one day to several weeks in duration. You could also take a distance learning class from an online university or through one of the local options listed above; distance learning offers the flexibility of learning from home on your own time, but teaches the same skills as a traditional classroom course.

Purchase Materials for Self-Study

You can prepare on your own to take an exam by purchasing materials at your local bookstore or from an online retailer. To ensure that the study materials you are purchasing are well-suited to your goal of passing a certification exam, you should consider the following: favorable reviews (reviews are often available when purchasing online); a table of contents that covers the skills you want to master; and the Microsoft Office Specialist seal. The Microsoft Office Specialist or Expert seal indicates that Microsoft has confirmed that the book accurately covers all of the skills for particular Microsoft Office Specialist or Expert exam and that it provides esting material on these skills. The seal certifies that Microsoft recognizes he book as being an adequate tool for Certification preparation. Because his book is designed as a reference guide and does not contain material hat tests your knowledge of skills, it does not have the Microsoft Office Specialist or Expert seal. Depending on your abilities, you might want to purchase a book that will teach you the skills and concepts step-by-step and then test your knowledge. If you only require a refresher, this book is all that you need.

Here is a list of suggested products published by Course Technology that you can use for self-study. You can purchase these books online at www.course.com.

☐ **Illustrated Series:** For detailed information on this Course Technology book series, visit www.course.com/illustrated/

For Specialist Exam preparation:
Microsoft Office Access 2003 – Illustrated Introductory
(ISBN: 0-619-18807-3)
Microsoft Office Excel 2003 – Illustrated Introductory
(ISBN: 0-619-18804-9)
Microsoft Office Word 2003 – Illustrated Introductory
(ISBN: 0-619-19901-4)
Microsoft Office PowerPoint 2003 – Illustrated Introductory
(ISBN: 0-619-18810-3)
Microsoft Office 2003 – Illustrated Introductory (ISBN: 0-619-05789-0) &
Microsoft Office 2003 – Illustrated Second Course (ISBN: 0-619-18826-X)

For Expert Exam preparation:
Microsoft Office Excel 2003 – Illustrated Complete (ISBN: 0-619-18805-7)
Microsoft Office Word 2003 – Illustrated Complete (ISBN: 0-619-18802-2)

For Master Level Preparation:
Microsoft Office Word 2003 – Illustrated Complete (ISBN: 0-619-18802-2)
& Microsoft Office Word 2003 – Illustrated Complete (ISBN: 0-619-18802-2)
& Microsoft Office PowerPoint 2003 – Illustrated Introductory
(ISBN: 0-619-18810-3) & Microsoft Office Access 2003 – Illustrated
Introductory (ISBN: 0-619-18807-3)

☐ **New Perspectives Series:** For detailed information on this Course Technology book series, visit www.course.com/newperspectives/

For Specialist Exam preparation:
New Perspectives on Microsoft Access 2003 Comprehensive
(ISBN: 0-619-20672-1)
New Perspectives on Microsoft Excel 2003 Introductory
(ISBN: 0-619-20664-0)
New Perspectives on Microsoft Word 2003 Introductory
(ISBN: 0-619-20668-3)
New Perspectives on Microsoft PowerPoint 2003 Comprehensive
(ISBN: 0-619-21376-0)

New Perspectives on Microsoft Outlook 2003 Second Course
(ISBN: 0-619-20659-4)
New Perspectives on Microsoft Office 2003 First Course
(ISBN: 0-619-24358-9) & New Perspectives on Microsoft Office 2003
Second Course (ISBN: 0-619-20659-4)

For Expert Exam preparation:
New Perspectives on Microsoft Excel 2003 Comprehensive
(ISBN: 0-619-206650-9)
New Perspectives on Microsoft Word 2003 Comprehensive
(ISBN: 0-619-20668-3)

For Master Level Preparation:
New Perspectives on Microsoft Word 2003 Comprehensive
(ISBN: 0-619-20668-3) & New Perspectives on Microsoft Excel 2003
Comprehensive (ISBN: 0-619-206650-9) & New Perspectives on Microsoft
PowerPoint 2003 Comprehensive (ISBN: 0-619-21376-0) & New
Perspectives on Microsoft Access 2003 Comprehensive
(ISBN: 0-619-20672-1) & New Perspectives on Microsoft Office 2003
Second Course (ISBN: 0-619-20659-4)

☐ **Shelly Cashman Series:** For detailed information on this Course
Technology book series, visit *www.scseries.com*
For Specialist Exam Preparation:
Microsoft Office Access 2003 Complete Concepts and Techniques
(ISBN: 0-619-20039-1)
Microsoft Office Excel 2003 Complete Concepts and Techniques
(ISBN: 0-619-20033-2)
Microsoft Office Word 2003 Complete Concepts and Techniques
(ISBN: 0-619-20036-7)
Microsoft Office PowerPoint 2003 Complete Concepts and Techniques
(ISBN: 0-619-20042-1)
Microsoft Office Outlook 2003 Introductory Concepts and Techniques
(ISBN: 0-619-25537-4)
Microsoft Office 2003 Introductory Concepts and Techniques
(ISBN: 0-619-25574-9) & Microsoft Office 2003 Advanced Concepts
and Techniques (ISBN: 0-619-20025-1)

For Expert Exam Preparation:
Microsoft Office Excel 2003 Comprehensive Concepts and Techniques
(ISBN: 0-619-20034-0)
Microsoft Office Word 2003 Comprehensive Concepts and Techniques
(ISBN: 0-619-20037-5)

☐ **SAM 2003:** Visit *www.samcentral.course.com* for more information
SAM 2003 Assessment Student Tutorial, Version 2.0
(ISBN: 0-619-17259-2)
SAM 2003 Training Student Tutorial, Version 2.0
(ISBN: 0-619-17369-6)

SAM 2003 Assessment and Training Student Tutorial, Version 2.0
(ISBN: 0-619-17366-1)
SAM 2003 Instructor Resources Assessment and Training, Version 2.0
(ISBN: 0-619-17253-3)

For Master Level Preparation:
Microsoft Office 2003 Introductory Concepts and Techniques
(ISBN: 0-619-25574-9) & Microsoft Office 2003 Advanced Concepts
and Techniques (ISBN: 0-619-20025-1) & Microsoft Office 2003 Post-
Advanced Concepts and Techniques (ISBN: 6-619-20027-8)

FIND A TESTING CENTER

As previously stated, you must sign up to take Microsoft Office Specialist
or Expert certification exams at an authorized testing center, called an
iQcenter. iQcenters are often located in educational institutions, corporate
training centers, and even some computer stores.

You can find a listing of iQcenters in your area by logging onto *http://
www.microsoft.com/learning/mcp/officespecialist/officespecialist_
locator.asp*. Once you locate a center near you, you will need to call the
iQcenter and schedule a time to take the exam or find a center that allows
walk-in exams. Exams are offered in multiple languages and in several
countries, although each site might not offer all languages. If you require a
specific language, you should check with the iQcenter before registering for
the exam.

You will be expected to pay for the exam on the day of the exam, regardless
of whether or not you pass.

TAKE THE EXAM

The day of the exam you will want to be prepared by ensuring you have
slept well the previous night, have eaten, and that you are dressed com-
fortably. Arrive at the test site approximately a half an hour before the
scheduled exam time to ensure you have plenty of time to complete the
log-on information, pay for the exam, and acquaint yourself with your
surroundings.

You will need to bring payment for the exam and a valid picture ID (driver's
license or valid passport). You may not bring any study or reference materials into the exam. As the exam is administered on a computer, you may
not bring writing implements, calculators, or other test-taking materials.

If you do not pass the exam the first time, you can sign up to retake it as
many times as needed to pass, but you will be charged each time you take
it. No refunds will be given if you do not pass, and you may also be charged
for a missed exam appointment depending on the iQcenter's policies.

Each exam is administered within a functional copy of the Microsoft application corresponding to the exam that you are taking. The exam tests your knowledge of the program by requiring you to complete specific tasks in the program. You may use all the features within the program including Help and Wizards.

Exam Specifics

☐ The first step is to log onto the exam. You will be asked to complete the candidate information section, which includes the necessary information for completing and mailing your certificate. Then the exam administrator will assist you in starting the exam.

☐ The first screens you see after you log on are directions and test-taking tips. You should read all of these, as this information will help you become familiar with the exam environment. The timed portion of the exam does not include these start-up directional screens, so take your time and make sure you understand the directions before starting the exam.

☐ The overall exam is timed, although there is no time limit for each question. Most exams take an hour or less, but the allotted time depends on the subject and level. If you do not complete all of the exam questions within the given timeframe, you will lose points for any unanswered questions.

☐ There is an exam clock on the screen that can be turned on or off. The exam clock starts and stops while each question is loading, so the speed with which each question is loaded is not a factor in the time you have to complete the questions (In other words, if you are completing the test on a slow computer you will not be penalized,) The total time you spend taking the exam will vary based on the speed of your computer, but the actual time you have to complete the exam will be consistent with anyone else taking the exam.

☐ Because you have to complete the exam in a certain amount of time, you will want to take into consideration the amount of time you have per question. You will not be graded on your efficiency (i.e., the time you take per question), but you will need to keep in mind that if you spend a lot of time on one question, that leaves you with less time for other questions. If you are truly stuck, you may want to skip a question.

☐ The exam is "live in the application," which means that you will work with an actual document, spreadsheet, presentation, etc. and must perform tasks on that document.

☐ Each question is comprised of several tasks listed in a pane at the bottom of the screen. You should complete the tasks in the order listed and make sure that you complete all of the tasks in a question. You may need to scroll the pane to read all of the tasks in a question. It is a good idea to reread the entire question before advancing to the next question to ensure that you have completed all tasks. You will receive only partial credit for any question you do not complete in its entirety.

☐ The end result of your actions is what is scored when you advance to the next question. You will not lose points for any extra mouse clicks or movements as they relate to the task. You should undo any additional changes that are not part of the task that you might accidentally apply to the document. Because you will be marked down for any additional tasks that you perform, you can use the Reset button to return the document to its original state and redo the question from the beginning. Keep in mind that if you click the Reset button, all of your work on that question will be erased, and the clock will not restart.

☐ You cannot go back to a previous question. Be sure you have completed as much of the question as possible before advancing to the next question and that you have closed all dialog boxes that you might have opened during the course of completing a task.

☐ If the task requires typing, you will lose points for spelling mistakes.

☐ You can use any valid method available in the program to complete a task. For example, if asked to center text in a Word document, you can click a button on the Formatting toolbar or press [Ctrl][E]. If you press the [Spacebar] repeatedly to move the text to the center of the document, however, you will lose credit, as this is not an appropriate way to center text.

☐ You can use Office Help or any available Wizards during the exam. This will not count against you, but the time spent using Help or a Wizard might mean that you run out of time to complete later tasks.

☐ If something happens to the exam environment, for instance, if the program freezes or if there is a power failure, contact the exam administrator. He or she will restart the exam where you were before the exam was interrupted. Such interruptions will not count against you.

eceive Exam Results

☐ Exam results are displayed as soon as you complete the exam.

☐ You will be given a printout of your score to take with you. If you pass the exam, you will receive an official certificate in the mail in approximately two to three weeks.

☐ The exam results are confidential.

☐ If you do not pass, keep in mind that the exams are challenging. Do not become discouraged. Remember, you can retake the exam as many times as you want, although you will need to pay for each test you take. However, candidates who wish to retake the exam a second or subsequent time must wait a minimum of seven days before retaking the exam.

MICROSOFT OFFICE WORD 2003
EXAM REFERENCE
Getting Started with Word 2003

The Microsoft Word Office Specialist exams assume a basic level of proficiency in Word. This section is intended to help you reference these basic skills while you are preparing to take the Word Specialist or Expert exams.

☐ Starting and exiting Word
☐ Viewing the Word window
☐ Using toolbars
☐ Using task panes
☐ Opening, saving, and closing documents
☐ Navigating in the document window
☐ Using smart tags

START AND EXIT WORD

Start Word

Button Method
☐ Click the **Start button** 🏁 **start** on the Windows taskbar
☐ Point to **All Programs**
☐ Point to **Microsoft Office**
☐ Click **Microsoft Office Word 2003**
OR
☐ Double-click the **Microsoft Office Word 2003 program icon** 🔲 on the desktop

Exit Word

Menu Method
☐ Click **File** on the menu bar, then click **Exit**

Button Method
☐ Click the **Close button** ✖ on the Word window title bar

Keyboard Method
☐ Press **[Alt][F4]**

VIEW THE WORD WINDOW

Figure WD-1   Word Window

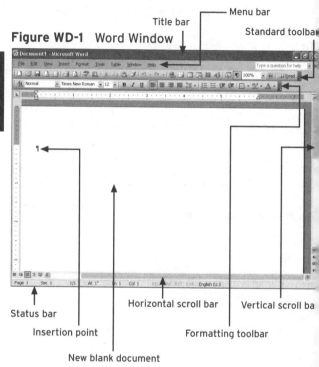

USE TOOLBARS

Display Toolbars

Menu Method

☐ Click **View** on the menu bar, point to **Toolbars**, then click the toolbar you want to display

OR

☐ Right-click any toolbar, then click the toolbar you want to display on the shortcut menu

ustomize Toolbars

Menu Method

☐ Click **Tools** on the menu bar, then click **Customize**, or click **View** on the menu bar, point to **Toolbars**, then click **Customize**, or right-click any toolbar, then click **Customize** on the shortcut menu

☐ In the Customize dialog box, select the appropriate tab and options, then click **Close**

Button Method

☐ Click the **Toolbar Options button** ⬚ or ⬚ of the toolbar to customize

☐ Point to **Add or Remove buttons**, then click **Customize**

☐ In the Customize dialog box, select the appropriate tab and options, then click **Close**

eposition Toolbars

Mouse Method

☐ Place the mouse pointer over the Toolbar Move handle ⦙ at the left end of any docked toolbar, or over the title bar of any floating toolbar

☐ When the pointer changes to ↔, press and hold the mouse button

☐ Drag the toolbar to the desired location, then release the mouse button

SE TASK PANES

splay Task Panes

Menu Method

☐ If no task pane is open, click **View** on the menu bar, then click **Task Pane** or right-click any toolbar, then click **Task Pane** on the shortcut menu

☐ Click the **Other Task Panes list arrow** ▼ on the task pane title bar, then click the name of the appropriate task pane

☐ Click the **Back button** ⬅ on the task pane title bar to return to the previously displayed task pane

ose Task Panes

Menu Method

☐ Click **View** on the menu bar, then click **Task Pane** or right-click any toolbar, then click **Task Pane** on the shortcut menu

Button Method

☐ Click the **Close button** ✕ on the task pane title bar

OPEN, SAVE, AND CLOSE DOCUMENTS

Open a New Document

Menu Method
☐ Click **File** on the menu bar, then click **New**
☐ In the New Document task pane, click **Blank Document** under **New**

Button Method
☐ Click the **New Blank Document button** 🗋 on the Standard toolbar

Keyboard Method
☐ Press **[Ctrl][N]**

Open an Existing Document

Menu Method
☐ Click **File** on the menu bar, then click **Open**
☐ In the Open dialog box, navigate to the appropriate drive and folder
☐ Click the file you want, then click **Open**

Task Pane Method
☐ Click a document name under the Open section in the Getting Started task pane or click **More** under the Open section, then follow the second and third bullets in the Open an Existing Document Menu Method above

Button Method
☐ Click the **Open button** 📄 on the Standard toolbar
☐ Follow the second and third bullets in the Open an Existing Document Menu Method above

Keyboard Method
☐ Press **[Ctrl][O]**
☐ Follow the second and third bullets in the Open an Existing Document Menu Method above

Use Save As

Menu Method
☐ Click **File** on the menu bar, then click **Save As**
☐ In the Save As dialog box, click the **Save in list arrow**, and navigate the drive and folder where you want to store the document
☐ Type an appropriate document name in the File name text box, then click **Save**

Keyboard Method
☐ Press **[F12]**
☐ Follow the steps in the second and third bullets of the Use Save As Menu Method above

ave a Document

Menu Method

☐ Click **File** on the menu bar, then click **Save** to save changes to a previously saved document

Button Method

☐ Click the **Save button** 🔲 on the Standard toolbar to save changes to a previously saved document

Keyboard Method

☐ Press **[Ctrl][S]**

ose a Document

Menu Method

☐ Click **File** on the menu bar, then click **Close**
☐ If prompted to save the file, click **Yes, No, or Cancel** as appropriate

Button Method

☐ Click the **Close Window button** ⊠ on the menu bar
☐ If prompted to save the changes to the document, click **Yes**, **No**, or **Cancel** as appropriate

Keyboard Method

☐ Press **[Ctrl][W]** or **[Alt][F4]**
☐ If prompted to save the file, click **Yes, No, or Cancel** as appropriate

---

AVIGATE IN THE DOCUMENT WINDOW

Keyboard Method

Use Table WD-1 as a reference

Table WD-1 Navigation Keyboard Shortcuts

Keyboard shortcut	Moves the insertion point
[Ctrl][Home]	To the beginning of the document
[Ctrl][End]	To the end of the document
[Home]	To the beginning of the current line
[End]	To the end of the current line
[Page Down], [Page Up]	Down or up one screen at a time
[→], [←]	To the right or left one character at a time
[Ctrl][→], [Ctrl][←]	To the right or left one word at a time
[↓], [↑]	Down or up one line at a time

Scroll Bar Method

☐ Drag the scroll box in the scroll bar to move in the document without moving the insertion point

☐ Click above the scroll box in the vertical scroll bar to move up a screen without moving the insertion point
☐ Click below the scroll box in the vertical scroll bar to move down a screen without moving the insertion point
☐ Click the **up scroll arrow** ▲ in the vertical scroll bar to move up one line
☐ Click the **down scroll arrow** ▼ in the vertical scroll bar to move down one line
☐ Click the **Next Page button** ⯯ or the **Previous Page button** ⯭ on the vertical scroll bar to move to the next or previous page

Word

USE SMART TAGS

Button Method

☐ Move the pointer over text underlined with a purple dotted line until the **Smart Tag Actions button** ⑤ appears

☐ Click ⑤ to view a menu of actions you can perform, then click an action

Word **SPECIALIST** Exam
Reference

Skill Sets:

1. Creating content
2. Organizing content
3. Formatting content
4. Collaborating
5. Formatting and managing documents

ORD **SPECIALIST** SKILL SET 1: **CREATING** CONTENT

SERT AND EDIT TEXT, SYMBOLS, AND SPECIAL HARACTERS

sert Text

Keyboard Method

❑ Click where you want to insert text
❑ Type the words to insert, making sure to press **[Spacebar]** where appropriate to insert spaces between words and **[Enter]** to begin a paragraph on a new line

sert Symbols and Special Characters

Menu Method

❑ Click where you want to insert a symbol
❑ Click **Insert** on the menu bar, then click **Symbol**
❑ In the Insert Symbol dialog box, select the appropriate tab, then select the character or symbol you want to insert
❑ Click **Insert**, then click **Close**

de Text

Menu Method

❑ Select text you want to hide
❑ Click **Format** on the menu bar, then click **Font**
❑ In the Font dialog box, click the **Font tab**
❑ Click the **Hidden check box**, then **click OK**

it Text

Keyboard Method

❑ Select the text you want to delete or replace, or place the insertion point where you want to edit, then use the methods in Table WD-2 to delete text.

Table WD-2 Deleting and Editing Text

Method	Effect
Press [Backspace]	Deletes selected text or the character immediately to the left of the insertion point
Press [Delete]	Deletes selected text or the character immediately to the right of the insertion point
Select the text to delete, then type replacement text	The characters you type will replace the selected text

Cut and Paste Text

Menu Method

☐ Select the text to cut
☐ Click **Edit** on the menu bar, then click **Cut**, or right-click, then click **Cut** on the shortcut menu
☐ Click where you want to paste the text
☐ Click **Edit** on the menu bar, then click **Paste**

Button Method

☐ Select the text to cut
☐ Click the **Cut button** 🔏 on the Standard toolbar
☐ Click where you want to paste the text
☐ Click the **Paste button** 🔏 on the Standard toolbar

Keyboard Method

☐ Select the text to cut
☐ Press **[Ctrl][X]**
☐ Click where you want to paste the text
☐ Press **[Ctrl][V]**

Copy and Paste Text

Menu Method

☐ Select the text to copy
☐ Click **Edit** on the menu bar, click **Copy**, or right-click, then click **Copy** on the shortcut menu
☐ Click where you want to paste the text
☐ Click **Edit** on the menu bar, then click **Paste**

Button Method

☐ Select the text to copy
☐ Click the **Copy button** 🔏 on the Standard toolbar
☐ Click where you want to paste the text
☐ Click the **Paste button** 🔏 on the Standard toolbar

Keyboard Method

☐ Select the text to copy
☐ Press **[Ctrl][C]**
☐ Click where you want to paste the text
☐ Press **[Ctrl][V]**

;e the Paste Special Command

Menu Method

- ☐ Select text you want to copy
- ☐ Click **Edit** on the menu bar, then click **Copy**
- ☐ Click where you want to paste the text
- ☐ Click **Edit** on the menu bar, then click **Paste Special**
- ☐ In the Paste Special dialog box, select the appropriate pasting and file type options, then click **OK**

;e the Office Clipboard

Menu Method

- ☐ Click **Edit** on the menu bar, then click **Office Clipboard** or click the **Other Task Panes list arrow** ▼ on the task pane title bar, then click **Clipboard**
- ☐ Copy or cut items from the document to add them to the clipboard
- ☐ Click where you want to insert an item from the clipboard
- ☐ In the Clipboard task pane, click an item to paste it into the document at the insertion point

rrect Spelling and Grammar Errors

Menu Method

- ☐ Click **Tools** on the menu bar, then click **Spelling and Grammar**
- ☐ In the Spelling and Grammar dialog box, choose to ignore or change misspelled words, add words to the dictionary and accept or ignore grammar suggestions as appropriate
- ☐ When the spelling and grammar check is complete, click **OK** in the message box

Button Method

- ☐ Click the **Spelling and Grammar button** 📝 on the Standard toolbar
- ☐ Follow the steps in the second and third bullets in the Correct Spelling and Grammar Errors Menu Method above

Keyboard Method

- ☐ Press **[F7]**
- ☐ Follow the steps in the second and third bullets in the Correct Spelling and Grammar Errors Menu Method above

;e the Thesaurus

Menu Method

- ☐ Select the word for which you want to find a synonym
- ☐ Click **Tools** on the menu bar, point to **Language**, then click **Thesaurus**
- ☐ In the Research task pane, point to the appropriate synonym, click the down arrow that appears, then click **Insert**

OR

- ☐ Right-click the word for which you want to find a synonym
- ☐ Point to **Synonyms** on the shortcut menu, then click the appropriate synonym, or click **Thesaurus**, then in the Research task pane, point to the appropriate synonym, click the down arrow that appears, then click **Insert**

Word

Keyboard Method

☐ Select the word for which you want to find a synonym
☐ Press **[Shift][F7]**
☐ In the Research task pane, point to the appropriate synonym, click the down arrow that appears, then click **Insert**

INSERT FREQUENTLY USED AND PREDEFINED TEXT

Create AutoText Entries and Use AutoComplete

Menu Method

☐ Select the text for which you want to create an AutoText entry
☐ Click **Insert** on the menu bar, point to **AutoText**, then click **New**
☐ In the Create AutoText dialog box, click **OK**
☐ Click where you want to insert the AutoText entry, then type the first few letters of the new AutoText entry
☐ When the AutoComplete ScreenTip appears, press **[Enter]** or **[Tab]** to complete the AutoText entry

Keyboard Method

☐ Select the text for which you want to create an AutoText entry, then press **[Alt][F3]**
☐ Follow the steps in the third through fifth bullets in the Create AutoText Entries and Use AutoComplete Menu Method above

Use AutoCorrect

Menu Method

☐ Click **Tools** on the menu bar, then click **AutoCorrect Options**
☐ On the AutoCorrect tab of the AutoCorrect dialog box, enter the text you want AutoCorrect to replace in the Replace text box
☐ Type the replacement text you want in the With text box, then click **Add**
☐ Click the appropriate check boxes to correct formatting and typing mistakes, then click **OK**

Insert a Date Field

Menu Method

☐ Click **Insert** on the menu bar, then click **Date and Time**
☐ In the Date and Time dialog box, click the appropriate date format, click the **Update automatically check box** to select it if necessary, then click **OK**

Keyboard Method

☐ Press **[Alt][Shift][D]**

Modify a Date Field

Menu Method

☐ Right-click the date field, then click **Edit Field** on the shortcut menu
☐ In the Field dialog box, select the appropriate formatting under Date formats, then click **OK**

NAVIGATE TO SPECIFIC CONTENT

Find Text

Menu Method

☐ Click **Edit** on the menu bar, then click **Find** to open the Find and Replace dialog box with the Find tab displayed
☐ Type the text you want to find in the Find what text box, then click **Find Next** repeatedly to view all instances
☐ Click **Yes** if prompted to search the document from the beginning
☐ Click **OK** in the message box, then click **Cancel** in the Find and Replace dialog box

Keyboard Method

☐ Press **[Ctrl][F]**
☐ Follow the steps in the second through fourth bullets in the Find Text Menu Method above

Replace Text

Menu Method

☐ Click **Edit** on the menu bar, then click **Replace** to open the Find and Replace dialog box with the Replace tab displayed
☐ Type the text you want to replace in the Find what text box
☐ Type the replacement text you want in the Replace with text box, then click **Replace** to replace current instance, **Replace All** to replace every instance, or **Find Next** to select the next instance
☐ Click **Yes** if prompted to search the document from the beginning
☐ Click **OK**, then click **Close** in the Find and Replace dialog box

Keyboard Method

☐ Press **[Ctrl][H]** to open the Replace tab in the Find and Replace dialog box
☐ Follow the steps in the second through fifth bullets in the Replace Text Menu Method above

Navigate to Specific Content

Menu Method

☐ Click **Edit** on the menu bar, then click **Go To**
☐ On the Go To tab of the Find and Replace dialog box, select the appropriate options, click **Next** to move to the specified element, then click **Close**

Button Method

☐ Click the **Select Browse Object** 🔘 on the vertical scroll bar
☐ Click the appropriate button on the Browse palette (such as Browse by Page) to move to the next instance of the specified item (such as the next page, comment, or section)
☐ To go to the next or previous item of the same type, click the **Next button** ⬇ or the **Previous button** ⬆ on the vertical scroll bar

Keyboard Method

☐ Press **[Ctrl][G]**
☐ On the Go To tab of the Find and Replace dialog box, select the appropriate options
☐ To go to the next item of the same type, click **Next** or press **[Ctrl][Page Down]**; to go to the previous item of the same type, click **Previous** or press **[Ctrl][Page Up]**

INSERT, POSITION, AND SIZE GRAPHICS

Insert an Image Using the Clip Art Task Pane

Menu Method

☐ Set the insertion point in the document where you want the image to appear
☐ Click **Insert** on the menu bar, point to **Picture**, then click **Clip Art**
☐ In the Clip Art task pane, type the search criteria in the **Search for** text box, then click **Go**
☐ Position 🔖 over the image you want, click the **list arrow**, then click **Insert**

Insert an Image from a File

Menu Method

☐ Click in the document where you want the image to appear
☐ Click **Insert** on the menu bar, point to **Picture**, then click **From File**
☐ In the Insert Picture dialog box, click the **Look in list arrow**, navigate t the drive and folder where the image is located, click the image filename, then click **Insert**

Create Graphics in a Document

Button Method

☐ Click the appropriate button on the Drawing toolbar, using Table WD-3 as a reference
☐ Use ➕ to drag the shape to the size you want
☐ To create a perfectly proportional shape, click the appropriate button using Table WD-4 as a reference, then press and hold **[Shift]** while dragging ➕ on the Drawing Canvas

Table WD-3 Drawing Shapes

Drawing toolbar button	Shape
⬛ Line button	Straight line
⬜ Rectangle button	Square or rectangle
⬭ Oval button	Circle or oval
⬛ Arrow button	Straight arrow

Creating WordArt

Menu Method

☐ Click **Insert** on the menu bar, point to **Picture**, then click **WordArt**
☐ In the WordArt Gallery, click the WordArt shape, then click **OK**
☐ In the Edit WordArt Text dialog box, enter the text and select the appropriate formatting options, then click **OK**

Button Method

☐ Click the **Insert WordArt button** 🄰 on the Drawing toolbar, then follow the second and third bullets of the Creating WordArt Menu Method

Creating AutoShapes

Menu Method

☐ Click **Insert** on the menu bar, point to **Picture**, then click **AutoShapes**
☐ Click the appropriate AutoShape button on the AutoShape toolbar, then draw the object using the $+$ pointer

Button Method

☐ Click the **AutoShapes button** AutoShapes ▾ on the Drawing toolbar, point to an AutoShape category, then click the appropriate AutoShape
☐ Draw the object using the $+$ pointer

Modify Graphics in a Document

Menu Method

☐ Select the object you want to modify, click **Format** on the menu bar, then click **[Object]** where [Object] is the element you are modifying, or right-click the object, then click **Format [Object]**
☐ In the Format [Object] dialog box, make the appropriate selections, then click **OK**

Button Method

☐ Select the object you want to modify, click the **Draw button** Draw ▾ on the Drawing toolbar, then use Table WD-4 as a reference to modify the graphic

OR

☐ Click the object to rotate, position the pointer over the green rotate handle ⥁ so that it changes to ⥀ then drag the handle to rotate the object as desired

Table WD-4 Methods for Modifying Graphics

Effect	Method using Draw menu commands
Group multiple objects together	Click Group
Ungroup objects	Click Ungroup
Order	Point to Order, then click the appropriate option
Grid	Click Grid. In the Drawing Grid dialog box, click the appropriate options, then click OK
Nudge	Point to Nudge, then click the appropriate option
Align or Distribute	Point to Align or Distribute, then click the appropriate option
Rotate or Flip	Point to Rotate or Flip, then click the appropriate option on the Rotate or Flip submenu
Text Wrap	Point to Text Wrapping, then click the appropriate option on the Text Wrapping submenu
Reroute Connectors	Click Reroute Connectors
Edit Points	Click Edit Points

Add Text to Graphics in a Document

Button Method

☐ Click the **Text Box button** 🔲 on the Drawing toolbar

☐ Using ┼, drag to create the text box

☐ Type the text to appear in the text box

Position Graphics in a Document

Keyboard Method

☐ Click the graphic to select it

☐ Using ┼, drag the graphic to the location you want

Button Method

☐ Click the **Draw button** Draw ▾ on the Drawing toolbar, then click the appropriate option, using Table WD-4 as a reference

Resize a Graphic

Mouse Method

☐ Click the graphic to select it

☐ Move the pointer over any sizing handle on the graphic until it changes to the appropriate pointer, using Table WD-5 as a reference

☐ Drag the sizing handle until the graphic is the size you want, then release the mouse button

Table WD-5 Resize Pointers

Pointer	Appears over	Used to
↗ or ↘	Corner sizing handle	Resize proportionally
↔	Side sizing handle	Resize horizontally
↕	Top or bottom sizing handle	Resize vertically

Word

CREATE AND MODIFY DIAGRAMS AND CHARTS

Create a Chart

Menu Method

☐ Click **Insert** on the menu bar, point to **Picture**, then click **Chart**
☐ Click **Chart** on the menu bar, then click **Chart Type**
☐ In the Chart Type dialog box, select the appropriate chart type, then click **OK**
☐ Edit the placeholder data in the datasheet as appropriate, then click the **Close button** on the datasheet

Create Charts Using Data from Other Applications

Menu Method

☐ Click **Insert** on the menu bar, then click **Object**
☐ In the Object dialog box, click **Microsoft Graph Chart** in the Object type list box, then click **OK**
☐ Select all of the cells in the datasheet
☐ Click **Edit** on the menu bar, then click **Import File**
☐ In the Import File dialog box, navigate to the appropriate drive and folder, click the **file**, then click **Open**
☐ In the Import Data Options dialog box, click the worksheet in the workbook that contains the data to import, make sure the **Overwrite existing cells check box** is selected, then click **OK**

OR

☐ Click **Insert** on the menu bar, point to **Picture**, click **Chart**, then follow the steps in the second through sixth bullets in this Menu Method

Modify a Chart

Menu Method

☐ Double-click the chart to open it in Microsoft Graph, if necessary
☐ Click **Chart** on the menu bar, click **Chart Options**, make the modifications you want in the Chart Options dialog box as appropriate, then click **OK**

Add and Format Objects in a Chart

Menu Method

☐ Double-click the chart to open it in Microsoft Graph, if necessary

☐ Right-click any chart object, then click **Format [Chart Object]** on the shortcut menu

☐ In the Format [Chart Object] dialog box, choose the appropriate options to format the selected object or add additional objects, then click **OK**

Resize a Chart

Mouse Method

☐ Double-click the chart to open it in Microsoft Graph, if necessary

☐ Move the pointer over any sizing handle on the chart until it changes to the appropriate pointer, using Table WD-5 on page 25 as a reference

☐ Drag the appropriate sizing handle to resize the chart to the dimensions you want, then release the mouse button

Change a Chart Type

Menu Method

☐ Double-click the chart to open it in Microsoft Graph

☐ Click **Chart** on the menu bar, then click **Chart Type**, or right-click the white area in the chart, then click **Chart Type** on the shortcut menu

☐ In the Chart Type dialog box, make the appropriate selections, then click **OK**

Format Charts and Chart Text

Menu Method

☐ Click the appropriate chart object to select it (in the following steps, [Object] refers to the object you are formatting)

☐ Click **Format** on the menu bar, then click **Selected [Object]**, or right-click the object, then click **Format [Object]**

☐ In the Format [Object] dialog box, select the appropriate options, then click **OK**

Mouse Method

☐ Double-click the chart to open it in Microsoft Graph, if necessary

☐ Double-click the appropriate chart object to select it

☐ In the Format [Object] dialog box, select the appropriate options, then click **OK**

Create an Organization Chart

Menu Method

☐ Position the insertion point where the diagram is to appear in the document

☐ Click **Insert** on the menu bar, then click **Diagram**

☐ In the Diagram Gallery dialog box, click the **Organization Chart icon** if necessary, then click **OK**

☐ Click a chart shape, then type the text you want it to contain

OR

☐ Click **Insert** on the menu bar, point to **Picture**, then click **Organization Chart**

Button Method

☐ Click in the location where you want the organization chart to appear to set the insertion point
☐ Click the **Insert Diagram or Organization Chart button** 🔲 on the Drawing toolbar
☐ Follow the steps in the third and fourth bullets in the Create an Organization Chart Menu Method above

Modify an Organization Chart

Button Method

☐ Select the organization chart
☐ Use the Organization Chart toolbar buttons to modify shapes as appropriate using Table WD-6 as a reference

Table WD-6 Organization Chart Toolbar Buttons

Button	Used to
Insert Shape list arrow Insert Shape ▾	Insert Subordinate, Coworker, or Assistant chart shapes
Layout list arrow Layout▾	Change the specified layout
Select button Select▾	Select levels, branches, or lines in the chart
Autoformat button 🔲	Open the Organization Chart Style Gallery dialog box where you can apply predefined formatting to an entire chart
Text Wrapping button 🔲	Change the way text flows around the chart

LOCATE, SELECT, AND INSERT SUPPORTING INFORMATION

Get Help

Menu Method

☐ Click **Help** on the menu bar, then click **Microsoft Word Help**
☐ Use Table WD-7 as a reference to select the most appropriate way to search for help using the Word Help task pane

Word

Button Method

□ Click the **Microsoft Word Help button** 🔞 on the Standard toolbar
□ Use Table WD-7 as a reference to select the most appropriate way to search for help using the Word Help task pane

OR

□ Click the **Type a question for help box** on the menu bar
□ Type a question or keywords, then press **[Enter]**
□ Read the Help information relating to the question or keywords you typed in the Word Help task pane, using Table WD-7 as a reference

Keyboard Method

□ Press **[F1]** to open the Word Help task pane
□ Use Table WD-7 as a reference to select the most appropriate way to search for help using the Word Help task pane

Table WD-7 Word Help Task Pane Options

Option	To use
Table of Contents	Click Table of Contents in the task pane, click the Expand indicator next to each topic you want to explore further, then click the topic you want and read the results in the task pane
Search for text box	Type a keyword in the Search for text box, click the Start Searching button ➡️, then click the blue hyperlinked text to read more in the Microsoft Office Word Help Window, or click the grayed text to view the topic in the Table of Contents
Assistance	Returns to the main Help task pane and opens a Web site from which you can search for Help topics
Training	Opens a Web site that offers tutorials on different subjects
Communities	Opens a Web site from which you can join different discussion groups
Downloads	Opens a Web site from which you can download add-ins and updates

Use the Research Task Pane

Menu Method

□ Click **Tools** on the menu bar, then click **Research**
□ Type a word or words your want to research in the Search for text box
□ Choose the reference material you want to search in the Research task pane, then click the **Start Searching button** ➡️

Button Method

□ Click the **Research button** 🔳 on the Standard toolbar
□ Choose a search method and reference material in the Research task pane, then click the **Start Searching button** ➡️

Keyboard Method

☐ Press and hold **[Alt]**, then click a word you want to research in the document
☐ Read the search results in the Research task pane

WORD SPECIALIST SKILL SET 2: ORGANIZING CONTENT

INSERT AND MODIFY TABLES

Insert Tables

Menu Method

☐ Click **Table** on the menu bar, point to **Insert**, then click **Table**
☐ In the Insert Table dialog box, specify the desired number of columns and rows, then click **OK**
☐ To enter text in a table, click a cell then type the text you want; press **[Tab]** or the arrow keys to navigate between cells

OR

☐ Click **Table** on the menu bar, then click **Draw Table**
☐ Drag using ✐ to draw rows and columns

Button Method

☐ Click the **Insert Table button** ▦ on the Standard toolbar
☐ Drag to select the number of rows and columns you want on the Table palette

OR

☐ Click the **Draw Table button** ▨ on the Tables and Borders toolbar, then use ✐ to drag a table border and row and column gridlines

Convert Text to Tables

Menu Method

☐ Select the text you want to convert to a table
☐ Click **Table** on the menu bar, point to Convert, then click **Text to Table**
☐ In the Convert Text to Table dialog box, select the appropriate options, then click **OK**

Button Method

☐ Select the text you want to convert to a table
☐ Click the **Insert Table button** ▦ on the Standard toolbar

Apply AutoFormats to Tables

Menu Method

☐ Select the table
☐ Click **Table** on the menu bar, then click **Table AutoFormat**
☐ In the Table AutoFormat dialog box, click the desired option(s) under Table styles, then click **Apply**

Button Method

☐ Select the table
☐ Click the **Table AutoFormat button** ▨ on the Tables and Borders toolbar
☐ In the Table AutoFormat dialog box, click the desired option(s) under Table styles, then click **Apply**

Add or Modify Table Borders

Menu Method
- ☐ Select the table
- ☐ Click **Format** on the menu bar, then click **Borders and Shading**, or right-click the **table**, then click **Borders and Shading** on the shortcut menu
- ☐ In the Borders and Shading dialog box, select the desired border options on the Borders tab, then click **OK**

Button Method
- ☐ Select the table
- ☐ Click the **Border list arrow** on the Formatting toolbar, then click the desired border option from the palette

Add or Modify Table Shading

Menu Method
- ☐ Select the cells you wish to shade
- ☐ Click **Format** on the menu bar, then click **Borders and Shading**, or right-click the **table**, then click **Borders and Shading** on the shortcut menu
- ☐ In the Borders and Shading dialog box, select the appropriate shading options on the Shading tab, then click **OK**

Button Method
- ☐ Select the cells you wish to shade
- ☐ Click the **Fill Color list arrow** on the Drawing toolbar, then select the desired color

Insert Rows and Columns in a Table

Menu Method
- ☐ Select the column next to where you want the new column to appear, or select the row above or below where you want the new row to appear
- ☐ Click **Table** on the menu bar, then point to **Insert**
- ☐ Click the appropriate option

OR
- ☐ Select the column to the right where you want the new column to appear, or click the row below where you want the new row to appear
- ☐ Right-click, then click **Insert Columns** or **Insert Rows** as appropriate on the shortcut menu

Button Method
- ☐ To add a column at the end of a table, select the row or column below or to the left of where you want to add a row or column
- ☐ Right-click, then click **Insert Row** or **Insert Column** on the shortcut menu

Keyboard Method
- ☐ To insert a new row at the bottom of the table, click the far-right cell in the last row
- ☐ Press **[Tab]**

Delete Rows and Columns in a Table

Menu Method

☐ Select the row(s) or column(s) to delete
☐ Click **Table** on the menu bar, then point to **Delete**
☐ Click the appropriate option

OR

☐ Select the column or row to delete
☐ Right-click, then click **Delete Columns** or **Delete Rows** on the shortcut menu

Keyboard Method

☐ Select the row(s) or column(s) to delete
☐ Press **[Ctrl][X]**

Modify Cell Formats in a Table

Menu Method

☐ Select the cell(s) to modify
☐ Click **Table** on the menu bar, then click **Table Properties**
☐ In the Table Properties dialog box, click the **Cell tab**
☐ Set the appropriate width options or click an alignment option, then click **OK**

Button Method

☐ Select the cell(s) to modify
☐ Click the cell **Alignment list arrow** 🔲 on the Tables and Borders toolbar
☐ Click the appropriate option

Modify Tables

Menu Method

☐ Click anywhere in the table you want to modify, click **Table** on the menu bar, then click **Table Properties**
☐ In the Table Properties dialog box, select the desired formatting options, using Table WD-8 as a reference

Table WD-8 Table Properties Dialog Box Tabs

Tab	Used to
Table	Set size of table, alignment of table on page, text wrapping options, borders and shading, cell margins
Row	Set row height, and specify how to break table over multiple pages
Column	Set column width
Cell	Set cell width and specify vertical alignment of cell contents

Button Method

☐ Click the appropriate button on the Tables and Borders toolbar to modify the table, using Table WD-9 as a reference.

Table WD-9 Tables and Borders Toolbar Buttons for Modifying Tables

Button	Used to
Merge Cells button 🔲	Merge selected cells
Split Cells button 🔲	Split selected cells
Change Text Direction button 🔲	Rotate cell text of selected cells 90°
Distribute Columns Evenly button 🔲	Make columns the same width
Distribute Rows Evenly button 🔲	Make rows the same height

Mouse Method

☐ Position the pointer over a row or column edge the until the pointer changes to ↕ or ↔, then drag the pointer in the appropriate direction to resize the table

CREATE BULLETED LISTS, NUMBERED LISTS, AND OUTLINES

Create a Bulleted List

Menu Method

☐ Select the text to which you want to apply bullets, or click where you want to start a new bulleted list
☐ Click **Format** on the menu bar, then click **Bullets and Numbering**, or right-click, then click **Bullets and Numbering** on the shortcut menu
☐ In the Bullets and Numbering dialog box, click the **Bulleted tab**, select the appropriate option(s), then click **OK**
☐ To add a bullet to a new list, type the text, then press **[Enter]**
☐ To add a bullet to an existing list, click at the end of the last item in the bulleted list to set the insertion point, press **[Enter]**, then type the text for the new bullet item

Button Method

☐ Select the text to which you want to apply bullets, or click where you want to start a new bulleted list
☐ Click the **Bullets button** 🔲 on the Formatting toolbar
☐ Follow the steps in the fourth and fifth bullets in the Create a Bulleted List Menu Method above

Keyboard Method
- □ Select the text to which you want to apply bullets, or click where you want to start a new bulleted list
- □ Press **[Ctrl][Shift][L]**
- □ Follow the steps in the fourth and fifth bullets in the Create a Bulleted List Menu Method

Create a Numbered List

Menu Method
- □ Select the text to which you want to add numbers, or click where you want to start a new numbered list
- □ Click **Format** on the menu bar, then click **Bullets and Numbering**, or right-click, then click **Bullets and Numbering** on the shortcut menu
- □ In the Bullets and Numbering dialog box, click the **Numbered tab**, select the appropriate option, then click **OK**
- □ To add an item to a new list, type the text, then press **[Enter]**
- □ To add an item to an existing list, click at the end of the last numbered item in the list to set the insertion point, press **[Enter]**, then type the text for the new numbered item

Button Method
- □ Select the text to which you want to add numbers, or click where you want to start a new numbered list
- □ Click the **Numbering button** on the Formatting toolbar
- □ Follow the steps in the fourth and fifth bullets in the Create a Numbered List Menu Method above

Create a Custom Bulleted or Numbered List

Menu Method
- □ Select the bulleted or numbered list to customize, or click where you want to start a new list
- □ Click **Format** on the menu bar, then click **Bullets and Numbering**, or right-click, then click **Bullets and Numbering** on the shortcut menu
- □ In the Bullets and Numbering dialog box, click the **Bulleted tab** or the **Numbered tab**, click any style, then click **Customize**
- □ In the Customize Numbered List or Customize Bulleted List dialog box, choose the appropriate bullet character, bullet position, and text position, then click **OK**
- □ To add a customized bullet or number to a new list, type the text, then press **[Enter]**
- □ To add a customized bullet or number to an existing list, click at the end of the last numbered item in the list to set the insertion point, press **[Enter]**, then type the text for the new bulleted or numbered item

Button Method
- □ Select the bulleted or numbered list to customize, or click where you want to start a new list
- □ Click the **Numbering button** or the **Bullets button** on the Formatting toolbar
- □ Follow the steps in the third through sixth bullets in the Create a Custom Bulleted or Numbered List Menu Method above

Create an Outline

Menu Method

☐ Select the text you want to format as an outline
☐ Click **Format** on the menu bar, then click **Bullets and Numbering**, or right-click, then click **Bullets and Numbering** on the shortcut menu
☐ In the Bullets and Numbering dialog box, click the **Outline Numbered tab**, click the appropriate style, then click **OK**
☐ To move an outline item up a level in the outline, click anywhere in the item you want to move, click the **Promote button** ⬆ on the Outlining toolbar or click at the beginning of the line to set the insertion point, then press **[Shift][Tab]**
☐ To move an outline item down a level in the outline, click anywhere in the item you want to move, then click the **Demote button** ⬇ on the Outlining toolbar, or click at the beginning of the line to set the insertion point, then press **[Tab]**

Button Method

☐ To demote an outline item, click anywhere in the item to set the insertion point, then click the **Increase Indent button** 📝
☐ To promote an outline item, click anywhere in the item to set the insertion point, then click the **Decrease Indent button** 📝 to promote an outline text item

Keyboard Method

☐ Click at the end of a numbered list to set the insertion point
☐ Press **[Enter]** to type a new outline item at the same level on a new line
☐ Press **[Tab]** at the beginning of an outline item to demote the item to the next level, or press **[Shift][Tab]** to promote the item

---

INSERT AND MODIFY HYPERLINKS

Insert Hyperlinks

Menu Method

☐ Select the text you want to become a hyperlink
☐ Click **Insert** on the menu bar, then click **Hyperlink** or right-click, then click **Hyperlink** on the shortcut menu
☐ In the Insert Hyperlink dialog box, specify the appropriate options, using Table WD-11 as a reference

Button Method

☐ Select the text you want to become a hyperlink
☐ Click the **Insert Hyperlink button** 🔗 on the Standard toolbar
☐ In the Insert Hyperlink dialog box, specify the appropriate options, using Table WD-11 as a reference

Keyboard Method

☐ Select the text you want to become a hyperlink
☐ Press **[Ctrl][K]**
☐ In the Insert Hyperlink dialog box, click the appropriate options, using Table WD-10 as a reference

OR
- [ ] Click where you want the hyperlink to a Web site to appear
- [ ] Type the URL of the Web page to which you want to link, then press **[Enter]** or **[Spacebar]** to automatically convert the text to a hyperlink to the specified Web address

Table WD-10 Inserting Hyperlinks Using the Insert Hyperlink Dialog Box

To link to another place in the document	To link to another document	To link to a Web page	To add an e-mail link
Click Place in This Document, select a location in the Select a place in this documet list, then click OK	Click Existing File or Web Page, click the Look in list arrow, navigate to the appropriate drive and folder, click the filename in the list, then click OK	(*Note*: Make sure you are connected to the Internet.) Click Existing File or Web Page, click the Address text box, then type the URL, then click OK	Click E-mail Address, type the address and any other text to display, then click OK

Modify Hyperlinks

Menu Method

- [ ] Right-click the hyperlink, then click **Edit Hyperlink** on the shortcut menu
- [ ] In the Edit Hyperlink dialog box, make the appropriate modifications using Table WD-10 as a reference, then click **OK**

OR

- [ ] Right-click the hyperlink, then click **Remove Hyperlink** on the shortcut menu

WORD SPECIALIST SKILL SET 3: FORMATTING CONTENT

FORMAT TEXT

Apply and Modify Character Formats

Select the text to which you want to apply a character format, then use Table WD-11 as a reference to apply the character formatting you want.

Table WD-11 Applying and Modifying Character Formats

Format	Formatting toolbar button	Menu	Keyboard
Bold	Bold button **B**	Click Format on the menu bar, click Font, click Bold under Font style, then click OK	Press [Ctrl][B]
Underline	Underline button **U**	Click Format on the menu bar, click Font, click Underline under Font style, then click OK	Press [Ctrl][U]
Italic	Italic button *I*	Click Format on the menu bar, click Font, click Italic under Font style, then click OK	Press [Ctrl][I]
Increase or decrease font size	Click the Font Size button `12 ▾`, then click the desired size	Click Format on the menu bar, click Font, click the desired font size under the Size section, then click OK	To increase: Press [Ctrl] [right bracket]; To decrease: Press [Ctrl][left bracket]
Font color	Click the Font Color button **A ▾**, then click the desired color	Click Format on the menu bar, click Font, click the Font color list arrow, click the desired color, then click OK	None

Use the Format Painter

Button Method

☐ Select the text with formatting you want to copy
☐ Click the **Format Painter button** 🖌 on the Standard toolbar
☐ Select the text to format
☐ To copy formatting and apply it to multiple text items in different locations, double-click 🖌, select each text item you want to format, then click 🖌 to turn the option off

Keyboard Method

☐ Select the text with formatting you want to copy
☐ Press **[Ctrl][Shift][C]**
☐ Select the text to format
☐ Press **[Ctrl][Shift][V]** for each instance

Create a New Style

Menu Method

☐ Click **Format** on the menu bar, then click **Styles and Formatting**
☐ In the Styles and Formatting task pane, click **New Style**
☐ In the New Style dialog box, type a name for the new style, choose the font and paragraph formatting options you want, then click **OK**

Button Method

☐ Click the **Styles and Formatting button** 🛦 on the Formatting toolbar
☐ In the Styles and Formatting task pane, select a style or click Clear Formatting from the Pick formatting to apply list, or click New Style to create a new style

Apply and Clear Styles

Menu Method

☐ Select the text, table, or list to which you want to apply a style
☐ Click **Format** on the menu bar, then click **Styles and Formatting**
☐ In the Styles and Formatting task pane, select a style or click **Clear Formatting** from the Pick formatting to apply list

Button Method

☐ Select the text, table, or list to format
☐ Click the **Styles and Formatting button** 🛦 on the Formatting toolbar
☐ In the Styles and Formatting task pane, select a style or click **Clear Formatting** from the Pick formatting to apply list

OR

☐ Select the text, table, or list to format
☐ Click the **Styles list arrow** `Normal ▾` on the Formatting toolbar
☐ Click a style, or click **Clear Formatting**

Apply Highlighting

Button Method

☐ Select the text to highlight
☐ Click the **Highlight list arrow** `✎ ▾` on the Formatting toolbar, then click the highlight color you want

OR

☐ Click the **Highlight list arrow** `✎ ▾` on the Formatting toolbar, then click the highlight color you want
☐ Use 🖉 to drag over the text to highlight, then click `✎ ▾` when highlighting is complete

Apply Character Effects

Menu Method

☐ Select the text to which you want to apply a character effect
☐ Click **Format** on the menu bar, then click **Font**, or right-click, then click **Font** on the shortcut menu
☐ In the Effects section of the Font dialog box, click the check boxes to apply appropriate formatting, then click **OK**

Keyboard Method

☐ Select the text to which you want to apply a character effect
☐ Press the keyboard combination to apply the appropriate character effect, using Table WD-12 as a reference

Table WD-12 Keyboard Methods for Applying Character Effects

Effect	Keyboard method
All Caps	[Ctrl][Shift][A]
Small Caps	[Ctrl][Shift][K]
Subscript	[Ctrl][=]
Superscript	[Ctrl][Shift][=]

Apply Text Animation

Menu Method

☐ Click **Format** on the menu bar, then click **Font**, or right-click, then click **Font** on the shortcut menu
☐ In the Font dialog box, click the **Text Effects tab**
☐ Click the animation style you want, then click **OK**

Modify Character Spacing

Menu Method

☐ Select the text you want to modify
☐ Click **Format** on the menu bar, then click **Font**, or right-click, then click **Font** on the shortcut menu
☐ Click the **Character Spacing tab** in the Format Font dialog box
☐ Specify the appropriate spacing options, then click **OK**

FORMAT PARAGRAPHS

Apply Borders to Paragraphs

Menu Method

☐ Select the text to which you want to apply a border
☐ Click **Format** on the menu bar, then click **Borders and Shading**
☐ In the Borders and Shading dialog box, click the **Borders tab** if necessary
☐ Select the appropriate option(s), then click **OK**

Word

Button Method

☐ Select the text you want to apply a border to
☐ Click the **Borders list arrow** ▦▾ on the Formatting toolbar
☐ Click the appropriate option(s) from the Borders palette

Apply Shading to Paragraphs

Menu Method

☐ Select the text to shade
☐ Click **Format** on the menu bar, then click **Borders and Shading**
☐ In the Borders and Shading dialog box, click the **Shading tab** if necessary
☐ Select the shading option(s) you want, then click **OK**

Set First-Line Indents

Menu Method

☐ Select the paragraphs to indent
☐ Click **Format** on the menu bar, then click **Paragraph**, or right-click, then click **Paragraph** on the shortcut menu
☐ In the Indentation section of the Indents and Spacing tab in the Paragraph dialog box, click the **Special list arrow**
☐ Click **First line**, then specify the appropriate indentation amount in the By text box
☐ Click **OK**

Button Method

☐ Select the paragraphs to indent
☐ Click the **Tab button** to the left of the ruler until you see the **First Line Indent marker** ▽
☐ Click the gray bottom border of the ruler where you want the First Line Indent marker to appear

Mouse Method

☐ Select the paragraphs to indent
☐ Position the pointer over the First Line Indent marker ▽ on the ruler until the ScreenTip appears
☐ Press and hold the left mouse button
☐ Drag the First Line Indent marker ▽ to the appropriate location on the ruler

Indent Entire Paragraphs

Menu Method

☐ Select the paragraph to indent
☐ Click **Format** on the menu bar, then click **Paragraph**, or right-click, then click **Paragraph** on the shortcut menu
☐ In the Paragraph dialog box, click the **Indents and Spacing tab**
☐ Specify the appropriate Left and Right indentations, then click **OK**

Button Method

☐ Click anywhere in the paragraph you want to indent
☐ Click the **Increase Indent button** ⁝≣ or the **Decrease Indent button** ≣⁝ on the Formatting toolbar to increase or decrease the indentation by .5" from the left margin

□ To indent from the right margin, position the pointer over the **Right Indent marker** ▽ on the right side of the ruler, then drag to the desired location on the ruler

Set Hanging Indents

Menu Method
□ Click anywhere in the paragraph you want to indent
□ Click **Format** on the menu bar, then click **Paragraph**, or right-click, then click **Paragraph** on the shortcut menu
□ In the Paragraph dialog box, click the **Indents and Spacing tab** if necessary
□ In the Indentation section, click the **Special list arrow**
□ Click **Hanging**, specify the indentation amount you want in the By text box, then click **OK**

Button Method
□ Click anywhere in the paragraph you want to indent
□ Point to the **Hanging Indent marker** 🖰 on the left side of the ruler until the ScreenTip appears, then drag it to the desired mark on the ruler

Keyboard Method
□ Click anywhere in the paragraph you want to indent
□ Press **[Ctrl][T]** as many times as necessary

Apply Paragraph Spacing

Menu Method
□ Click anywhere in the paragraph you want to to format
□ Click **Format** on the menu bar, then click **Paragraph**, or right-click, then click **Paragraph** on the shortcut menu
□ In the Paragraph dialog box, click the appropriate options in the Spacing section of the Indents and Spacing tab, then click **OK**

Button Method
□ Position the insertion point in the paragraph to format
□ Click the **Line Spacing list arrow** 📰▾ on the Formatting toolbar, then click the appropriate line spacing option

Modify Paragraph Alignment

Menu Method
□ Click anywhere in the paragraph you want to format
□ Click **Format** on the menu bar, then click **Paragraph**, or right-click, then click **Paragraph** on the shortcut menu
□ In the Paragraph dialog box, click the **Indents and Spacing tab**
□ Click the **Alignment list arrow** in the General section, then click the desired alignment using Table WD-14 as a reference

Button Method
□ Click anywhere in the paragraph you want to format
□ Click the appropriate alignment button on the Formatting toolbar, using Table WD-14 as a reference

Word

Keyboard Method
☐ Click anywhere in the paragraph you want to format
☐ Press the appropriate keyboard combination, using Table WD-13 as a reference

Table WD-13 Buttons and Keyboard Methods for Paragraph Alignment

Alignment	Formatting toolbar button	Keyboard
Left-aligned	Align Left button ▤	[Ctrl][L]
Right-aligned	Align Right button ▥	[Ctrl][R]
Centered	Center button ▥	[Ctrl][E]
Justified	Justify button ▤	[Ctrl][J]
Reset to previous		[Ctrl][Q]

Set Tabs

Menu Method
☐ Click **Format** on the menu bar, then click **Tabs**
☐ In the Tabs dialog box, select a tab stop position from the list, or type the ruler location where you want the tab to be placed in the Tab stop position text box
☐ Click the appropriate alignment option button and specify other options you want, then click **OK**

Button Method
☐ Click the **Tab button** to the left of the horizontal ruler until the appropriate tab symbol appears, using Table WD-14 as a reference, then click the horizontal ruler where you want to place the tab stop

Table WD-14 Tab Stop Icons

Icon	Creates this kind of tab
� L	Left
▲	Center
◢	Right
▲	Decimal
▮	Bar

Remove Tabs

Menu Method
☐ Click **Format** on the menu bar, then click **Tabs**
☐ In the Tabs dialog box, select the tab location to delete, click **Clear**, then click **OK**

Button Method

☐ Position the pointer over the tab stop you want to remove on the horizontal ruler

☐ Use ⌖ to drag the tab off the ruler to delete it, then release the mouse button

Modify Tabs

Menu Method

☐ Click **Format** on the menu bar, then click **Tabs**

☐ In the Tabs dialog box, choose the appropriate modification options, then click **OK**

Button Method

☐ Position the pointer over the tab stop you want to remove on the horizontal ruler

☐ Use ⌖ to drag the tab to a different location on the ruler, then release the mouse button

---

APPLY AND FORMAT COLUMNS

Format Existing Text as Columns

Menu Method

☐ Select the text to format as columns

☐ Click **Format** on the menu bar, then click **Columns**

☐ In the Columns dialog box, select the desired options, then click **OK**

Button Method

☐ Select the text to format as columns

☐ Click the **Columns button** 📰 on the Standard toolbar, then drag to select the desired number of columns

Modify Text Alignment in Columns

Menu Method

☐ Position the insertion point in the column to modify

☐ Click **Format** on the menu bar, then click **Columns**

☐ In the Columns dialog box, specify the appropriate width and spacing options for each column, then click **OK**

Create Columns Before Entering Text

Menu Method

☐ Click **Format** on the menu bar, then click **Columns**

☐ In the Columns dialog box, select the desired options, then click **OK**

☐ Start typing text in the document

☐ To insert a column break, click **Insert** on the menu bar, then click **Break**

☐ Click the **Column break option button** in the Break dialog box, then click **OK**

Button Method

☐ Click the **Columns button** 🏢 on the Standard toolbar, then drag to select the desired number of columns

☐ Follow the steps in the third through fifth bullets in the Create Columns Before Entering Text Menu Method

Revise Column Layout

Menu Method

☐ Select the column of text you want to modify

☐ Click **Format** on the menu bar, then click **Columns**

☐ In the Columns dialog box, specify the desired options, then click **OK**

Button Method

☐ Select the column of text to be modified

☐ Position the pointer over the **Move Column marker** 🏢 on the ruler until it changes to ◀—▶, then drag ◀—▶ to the desired location

INSERT AND MODIFY CONTENT IN HEADERS AND FOOTERS

Create and Modify Headers and Footers

Menu Method

☐ Click **View** on the menu bar, then click **Header and Footer**

☐ Type the text you want to appear at the top of each page in the Header text box

☐ Click the **Switch Between Header and Footer button** 🗐 on the Header and Footer toolbar

☐ Type the text you want to appear at the bottom of each page in the Footer text box

☐ To modify header and footer text, click in the Header or Footer text box, and make appropriate edits

☐ Click **Close** on the Header and Footer toolbar

Insert and Format Page Numbers

Menu Method

☐ Click **Insert** on the menu bar, then click **Page Numbers**

☐ In the Page Numbers dialog box, specify the desired position, alignment, and format for page numbers

☐ Click **OK**

MODIFY DOCUMENT LAYOUT AND PAGE SETUP

Insert Page Breaks

Menu Method

☐ Click to the right of where you want to insert the page break
☐ Click **Insert** on the menu bar, then click **Break**
☐ In the Break dialog box, click the **Page break option button** if necessary, then click **OK**

Keyboard Method

☐ Click to the right of where you want to insert the page break, then press **[Ctrl][Enter]**

Delete Page Breaks

Keyboard Method

☐ Click immediately after the page break, then press **[Backspace]**
OR
☐ Click immediately before the page break, then press **[Delete]**

Modify Page Margins

Menu Method

☐ Click **File** on the menu bar, then click **Page Setup**
☐ In the Page Setup dialog box, click the **Margins tab** if necessary
☐ Change the margin settings to the desired dimensions, then click **OK**

Button Method

☐ Click the margin marker you want to move on the ruler
☐ Using ◀▶ or ↕, drag the margin marker to the desired location, then release the mouse button

Modify Page Orientation

Menu Method

☐ Click **File** on the menu bar, then click **Page Setup**
☐ In the Page Setup dialog box, click the **Margins tab** if necessary
☐ Click either the **Portrait** or **Landscape icon**, then click **OK**

Word Specialist Skill Set 4: Collaborating

Circulate Documents for Review

Distribute Documents for Review via E-mail

Menu Method
☐ Make sure you are connected to the Internet
☐ Click **File** on the menu bar, point to **Send To**, then click **Mail Recipient (for Review)** or **Mail Recipient (as Attachment)** to open your e-mail program, displaying an e-mail message with the current document specified as an attachment
☐ In the e-mail message, type the e-mail address of a recipient in the To text box, then click the **Send button**

Send a Document as an E-mail Attachment

Menu Method
☐ Make sure you are connected to the Internet
☐ Open your e-mail program, type an e-mail address of a recipient in the To text box, then type an appropriate message in the message area
☐ Click the appropriate button to insert an attachment, browse to the appropriate drive and folder, select the document you want to attach, then click **OK**
☐ Click the **Send button**

Compare and Merge Documents

Compare Documents

Menu Method
☐ Click **Tools** on the menu bar, then click **Compare and Merge Documents**
☐ In the Compare and Merge Documents dialog box, browse to an appropriate drive and folder, then select a document to compare
☐ Click the **Merge list arrow**, then click the appropriate merge option, using Table WD-15 as a reference
☐ Click the **Display for Review list arrow** `Final Showing Markup` on the Reviewing toolbar, then click the appropriate option

Table WD-15 Methods for Merging Documents

Command	Results
Merge	Merges the changes into the original document, then opens the original document if it's not already open
Merge into current document	Merges the changes into the edited (current) document

Table WD-15 Methods for Merging Documents (continued)

Command	Results
Merge into new document	Merges the changes into a new document and leaves the original and edited documents unchanged; clicking the Legal blackline check box, then clicking Compare produces the same result

Merge Revisions

Menu Method

□ Open the revised document
□ Click **Tools** on the menu bar, then click **Compare and Merge Documents**
□ In the Compare and Merge Documents dialog box, navigate to the drive and folder that contains the original document, click the original document, then click **Merge**

INSERT, VIEW, AND EDIT COMMENTS

Insert Comments

Menu Method

□ Select text or click next to or select text about which you want to write a comment
□ Click **Insert** on the menu bar, then click **Comment**
□ Type the comment in the Comment text box

Button Method

□ Select text or click next to or select text about which you want to write a comment
□ Click the **Insert Comment button** on the Reviewing toolbar
□ Type the comment in the Comment text box

View Comments

Menu Method

□ Click **View** on the menu bar
□ Click **Markup**

Button Method

□ Click the **Show list arrow** Show ▾ on the Reviewing toolbar, then click **Comments**

Edit Comments

Keyboard Method

□ Make sure comments are displayed on your screen
□ Click the **Comment text box**, then modify the comment text

Word

TRACK, ACCEPT, AND REJECT PROPOSED CHANGES

Track Changes

Menu Method

☐ Click **Tools** on the menu bar, then click **Track Changes**
☐ Make text and formatting changes to the document

Button Method

☐ Click the **Track Changes button** 📄 on the Reviewing toolbar
☐ Make text and formatting changes to the document

Review Changes

Button Method

☐ In Normal view, position the insertion point over the marked change or text in brackets to see the registered user's name and the current date appear in a ScreenTip, along with a brief description of the change
☐ Click the appropriate button on the Reviewing toolbar to navigate through and display changes and comments, using Table WD-16 as a reference

OR

☐ In Print Layout view, position the insertion point over the ScreenTip in the right margin to see the registered user's name and the date the change or comment was made
☐ Click the appropriate button on the Reviewing toolbar to navigate through and display changes and comments, using Table WD-16 as a reference

Table WD-16 Reviewing Toolbar Navigation Buttons

Button	Effect
Next button 📄	Move to the next comment or change
Previous button 📄	Move to the previous comment or change
Show button Show ▾	Can change display options: comments, text insertions and deletions, formatting changes, select reviewers to display, and display the reviewing pane at the bottom of the window

Respond to Changes

Menu Method

☐ Right-click the tracked edit to which you want to respond
☐ Click **Accept Deletion**, **Reject Deletion**, **Accept Insertion**, or **Reject Insertion** on the shortcut menu as appropriate

Button Method

☐ Select the change to which you want to respond, then click the appropriate button on the Reviewing toolbar, using Table WD-17 as a reference

able WD-17 Reviewing Toolbar Response Buttons

Button	Use
Accept Change button	To accept a change
Accept Change list arrow	To choose to accept a change, all changes, or all shown changes
Reject Change/Delete Comment button	To reject a change or delete a comment
Reject Change/Delete Comment list arrow	To choose to reject the change or delete the comment; to reject all changes; or to delete all comments
New Comment button	To insert a new comment

Word

WORD SPECIALIST SKILL SET 5: FORMATTING AND MANAGING DOCUMENTS

CREATE NEW DOCUMENTS USING TEMPLATES

Find a Template Online

Menu Method

☐ Click **File** on the menu bar, then click **New**
☐ In the New Document task pane, type a keyword in the Search online text box, click **Go**, then click a template in the Search Results task pane
☐ In the Template Preview dialog box, click **Previous** and **Next** to preview the available templates, choose the template you want, then click **Download** to open a new document with the template applied
☐ Click **No** if asked for help with the template

Use a Template from Your Computer

Menu Method

☐ Click **File** on the menu bar, then click **New**
☐ In the New Document task pane, click **On my computer**
☐ In the Templates dialog box, click the template you want, then click **OK** to open a new document with the template applied
☐ Click **No** if asked for help with the template

REVIEW AND MODIFY DOCUMENT PROPERTIES

Review the Document Summary

Menu Method

☐ Click **Tools** on the menu bar, then click **AutoSummarize**
☐ In the Autosummarize dialog box, click the appropriate option using Table WD-18 as a reference, then click **OK** if necessary

Table WD-18 AutoSummarize Options

Option	Reviewing the summary
Highlight key points	Key document points are highlighted in yellow; other text is grayed out; navigate through the key points or close the summary view by using the buttons on the Autosummarize toolbar
Create a new document and put the summary there	A new Word document opens, and the key points are outlined; other text does not appear; save the document as a new file
Insert an executive summary or abstract at the top of the document	Key document points are outlined and appear at the top of the document

able WD-18 AutoSummarize Options (continued)

Option	Reviewing the summary
Hide everything but the summary without leaving the original document	Key document points appear in outline form; other text is hidden; navigate through the key points or close the summary view by using the buttons on the AutoSummarize toolbar

odify the Document Summary

Menu Method

☐ Review the document summary where it appears to make sure that it includes the key points
☐ Edit the summary text as appropriate

se Word Count

Menu Method

☐ Click **Tools** on the menu bar, then click **Word Count**
☐ In the Word Count dialog box, choose the appropriate options, click **Show Toolbar**, then click **Close**
☐ Make any text edits or additions to the document as necessary, then click **Recount** on the Word Count toolbar to view the modified recount total

Keyboard Method

☐ Press **[Ctrl][Shift][G]**
☐ Follow the steps in the second through fourth bullets of the Use Word Count Menu Method above

RGANIZE DOCUMENTS USING FILE FOLDERS

reate Folders for Document Storage

Menu Method

☐ Click **File** on the menu bar, then click **Save As**
☐ In the Save As dialog box, click the Save in list arrow, then navigate to the folder where you want to create the new folder
☐ Click the **Create New Folder button**
☐ In the New Folder dialog box, type the folder name, then click **OK**
☐ In the Save As dialog box, type the document name in the File name text box
☐ Click **Save**

Keyboard Method

☐ Press **[F12]**
☐ Follow the steps in the second through sixth bullets of the Create Folders for Document Storage Menu Method above

Use Folders for Document Storage

Menu Method

☐ Click **File** on the menu bar, then click **Save As**
☐ In the Save As dialog box, navigate to the folder where you want to store your document
☐ Type the document name in the File name text box
☐ Click **Save**

Keyboard Method

☐ Press **[F12]**
☐ Follow the steps in the second through fourth bullets of the Use Folders for Document Storage Menu Method above

Rename Folders

Note: You cannot rename a folder that includes an open document.

Menu Method

☐ Click **File** on the menu bar, then click **Save As**
☐ In the Save As dialog box, navigate to the folder you want to rename
☐ Right-click the folder name, click **Rename** on the shortcut menu, then type the new folder name, then press **[Enter]**

Keyboard Method

☐ Press **[F12]**
☐ Follow the steps in the second through third bullets of the Rename Folders Menu Method above

SAVE DOCUMENTS IN APPROPRIATE FORMATS FOR DIFFERENT USES

Save a Document with a Different File Format

Menu Method

☐ Click **File** on the menu bar, then click **Save As**
☐ In the Save As dialog box, click the **Save as type list arrow**, then select the appropriate file format
☐ Click the **Save in list arrow** then navigate to the drive and folder where you want to save your document
☐ Type the document name in the File name text box, then click **Save**

Keyboard Method

☐ Press **[F12]**
☐ Follow the steps in the second through fourth bullets of the Save a Document with a Different File Format Menu Method above

Save a Document as a Web Page

Menu Method

☐ Click **File** on the menu bar, then click **Save as Web Page**
☐ In the Save As dialog box, type the filename in the File name text box
☐ Click **Save**

PRINT DOCUMENTS, ENVELOPES, AND LABELS

Print a Document

Menu Method
☐ Click **File** on the menu bar, then click **Print**
☐ In the Print dialog box, select the desired print settings, then click **OK**

Button Method
☐ Click the **Print button** 🖨 on the Standard toolbar

Keyboard Method
☐ Press **[Ctrl][P]**
☐ In the Print dialog box, select the desired print settings, then click **OK**

Print Envelopes and Labels

Menu Method
☐ Click **Tools** on the menu bar, point to **Letters and Mailings**, then click **Envelopes and Labels**
☐ In the Envelopes and Labels dialog box, click the **Envelopes tab** or the **Labels tab**, type the text you want and specify the appropriate settings
☐ Make sure you have the envelope or label paper in the manual feed tray of your printer, then click **Print**

PREVIEW DOCUMENTS AND WEB PAGES

Preview a Document

Menu Method
☐ Click **File** on the menu bar, then click **Print Preview**

Button Method
☐ Click the **Print Preview button** 🔍 on the Standard toolbar

Keyboard Method
☐ Press **[Ctrl][F2]**

Preview Documents as Web Pages

Menu Method
☐ Click **File** on the menu bar, then click **Web Page Preview**

Word

CHANGE AND ORGANIZE DOCUMENT VIEWS AND WINDOWS

Reveal Formatting

Menu Method

☐ Click **Format** on menu bar, then click **Reveal Formatting**
☐ In the Reveal Formatting task pane, click the **Font** and/or the **Paragraph Expand indicators**, if necessary
☐ View the formatting options displayed in the task pane

Menu Method

☐ Press **[Shift][F1]**
☐ Follow the steps in the second and third bullets of the Reveal Formatting Menu Method above

Reveal Hidden Text

Button Method

☐ Click the **Show/Hide ¶ button** ¶ on the Standard toolbar

Use Views

Use Table WD-19 to change the view.

Table WD-19 Document Views

View	Button (located to the left of the horizontal scroll bar)	What you see	On View menu, click this item
Normal	☰	Formatted text, but not headers, footers, or some graphics	Normal
Web Layout	🗔	Document as it would appear when published to a Web page	Web Layout
Print Layout	▣	Document as it would appear when printed	Print Layout
Outline view	🖹	Document with headings indented to display the document structure	Outline

Table WD-19 Document Views (continued)

View	Button (located to the left of the horizontal scroll bar)	What you see	On View menu, click this item
Reading Layout	🕮	The document optimized for on-screen reading, with most toolbars hidden and the font in ClearType	Reading Layout
Full Screen	`100%` ▾ (on the Standard toolbar)	Document without any toolbars, task bars, or title bars	Full Screen
Zoom		Document magnified or shrunk to see more or less	Zoom, in the Zoom dialog box select the settings you want, then click OK
Document Map	🔲 (on the Standard toolbar)	The Document Map on the left side of the screen with links to headings	Document Map
Thumbnails		The Thumbnails pane on the left side of the screen with miniature icons for each page	Thumbnails

Show or Hide White Space

Button Method

☐ In Print Layout view, position the pointer between two pages until it changes to either the **Show White Space pointer** ⬍ or the **Hide White Space pointer** ⬍, then simply click

Split Windows

Menu Method

☐ Click **Window** on the menu bar, then click **Split**
☐ Using the ⬍ pointer, position the split bar where you want to split the document
☐ Double-click the **split bar** to remove the split

Button Method
☐ Point to the split box at the top of the vertical scroll bar
☐ Follow the steps in the second and third bullets of the Split Windows Menu Method

Arrange Panes

Menu Method
☐ Restore all minimized Word documents
☐ Click **Window** on the menu bar, then click **Arrange All** to tile all open Word documents

MICROSOFT OFFICE WORD 2003
EXPERT EXAM REFERENCE

Skill Sets:
1. Formatting content
2. Organizing content
3. Formatting documents
4. Collaborating
5. Customizing Word

WORD EXPERT SKILL SET 1: FORMATTING CONTENT

CREATE CUSTOM STYLES FOR TEXT, TABLES, AND LISTS

Create Styles

Menu Method

- [ ] Click **Format** on the menu bar, then click **Styles and Formatting**
- [ ] In the Styles and Formatting task pane, click **New Style**
- [ ] In the New Style dialog box, type the name of the style in the Name text box, click the **Style type list arrow**, then click **Character**, **Paragraph**, **Table**, or **List**
- [ ] Select the appropriate formatting options using Table WD-20 as a reference, then click **OK**

Button Method

- [ ] Click the **Styles and Formatting button** 🔠 on the Formatting toolbar
- [ ] Follow the second through fourth bullets in the Creating Custom Styles for Text, Tables, and Lists Menu Method above

Table WD-20 Formatting Options in the New Style Dialog Box

Button	Used to	Applies to
Font Type list arrow Times New Roman ▾	Change the font type	Paragraphs, Characters, Lists, and Tables
Font Size button 12 ▾	Increase or decrease the font size	Paragraphs, Characters, Lists, and Tables
Bold button **B**	Make text appear as **bold**	Paragraphs, Characters, Lists, and Tables
Italic button *I*	Make text appear as *Italic*	Paragraphs, Characters, Lists, and Tables

Table WD-20 Formatting Options in the New Style Dialog Box (continued)

Button	Used to	Applies to
Underline button	Make text appear as <u>underlined</u>	Paragraphs, Characters, Lists, and Tables
Font Color button	Change the font color	Paragraphs, Characters, Lists, and Tables
Align Left button	Align text with the left margin	Paragraphs only
Center button	Align text so it is centered between left and right margins	Paragraphs only
Align Right button	Align text with the right margin	Paragraphs only
Justify button	Align text with both the left and right margins	Paragraphs only
Single Space button	Space the lines so that largest font fits plus a small amount of space	Paragraphs only
1.5 Space button	Adjust the spacing so that it is 1.5 times that of single spacing	Paragraphs only
Double Space button	Adjust the spacing so that it is 2 times that of single spacing	Paragraphs only
Increase Paragraph Spacing button	Increase space between paragraphs; click as many times as necessary until sample box matches desired spacing	Paragraphs only
Decrease Paragraph Spacing button	Decrease space between paragraphs; click as many times as necessary until sample box matches desired spacing	Paragraphs only
Decrease Indent button	Move the paragraph closer to the left margin in half-inch increments	Paragraphs only
Increase Indent button	Move the paragraph away from the left margin in half-inch increments	Paragraphs only

CONTROL PAGINATION

Control Page Breaks within Paragraphs

Menu Method

- ☐ Select the text to which you want the page breaks to apply, or deselect all text to apply the page break settings to the entire document
- ☐ Click **Format** on the menu bar, then click **Paragraph**, or right-click, then click **Paragraph** on the shortcut menu
- ☐ In the Paragraph dialog box, click the **Line and Page Breaks tab**

☐ Click the appropriate options, using Table WD-21 as a reference, then click **OK**

Table WD-21 Page Break Options in the Paragraph Dialog Box

Option	Effect
Widow/Orphan control	Prevents the last line of a paragraph from appearing at the top of a page (widow) or the first line of a paragraph from appearing at the bottom of a page (orphan)
Keep lines together	Prevents a page or column break from occurring within the selected paragraphs
Keep with next	If necessary, inserts a page break before the selected line(s), object, or paragraphs in order to keep them with the subsequent text
Page break before	Inserts a page break before each new paragraph

Word

Control Page Breaks Between Paragraphs

Menu Method

☐ Select the text to which you want the page breaks to apply, or deselect all text to apply the page break settings to the entire document
☐ Click **Format** on the menu bar, then click **Paragraph**, or right-click, then click **Paragraph** on the shortcut menu
☐ In the Paragraph dialog box, click the **Line and Page Breaks tab**
☐ Click the **Keep with next check box**, then click **OK**

Control Line Breaks

Menu Method

☐ Select the text you want to hyphenate, or deselect all text to apply the hyphenation options to the entire document
☐ Click **Tools** on the menu bar, point to **Language**, then click **Hyphenation**
☐ In the Hyphenation dialog box, click the **Automatically hyphenate document check box**

OR

☐ Select the text you want to hyphenate, or deselect all text to apply the hyphenation options to the entire document
☐ Click **Tools** on the menu bar, point to **Language**, then click **Hyphenation**
☐ In the Hyphenation dialog box, click **Manual**
☐ If the Manual Hyphenation message box appears, click **Yes** or **No** as appropriate for each instance, then click **OK** when the manual hyphenation is complete

OR

☐ Click **Format** on the menu bar, then click **Paragraph**, or right-click, then click **Paragraph** on the shortcut menu
☐ In the Paragraph dialog box, click the **Line and Page Breaks tab**
☐ Click the **Don't hyphenate check box**, then click **OK**

FORMAT, POSITION, AND RESIZE GRAPHICS USING ADVANCED LAYOUT FEATURES

Wrap Text around Graphics

Menu Method

☐ Click the graphic to select it, click **Format** on the menu bar, then click **Picture**
☐ In the Format Picture dialog box, click the **Layout tab** if necessary, then click **Advanced**
☐ In the Advanced Layout dialog box, click the **Text Wrapping tab** if necessary, click the appropriate Wrapping style icon, then click **OK**
☐ In the Format Picture dialog box, click **OK**

Button Method

☐ Click the graphic to select it
☐ Click the **Text Wrapping button** 🖼 on the Picture toolbar
☐ Click the appropriate text wrapping option from the menu

Crop Graphics

Menu Method

☐ Click the graphic to select it, click **Format** on the menu bar, then click **Picture**
☐ In the Format Picture dialog box, click the **Picture tab** if necessary
☐ Enter the values in the Crop from section of the dialog box
☐ In the Format Picture dialog box, click **OK**

OR

☐ Right-click the graphic, then click **Format Picture** on the shortcut menu
☐ Follow the steps in the second through fourth bullets in the Crop Graphics Menu Method above

Mouse Method

☐ Double-click the graphic to open the Format Picture dialog box
☐ Follow the steps in the second through fourth bullets in the Crop Graphics Menu Method above

Button Method

☐ Click the graphic to select it
☐ Click the Crop button 🔖 on the Picture toolbar
☐ Use the 🔖 pointer to drag any of the crop marks around the graphic inward to crop unwanted sections of the graphic, then release the mouse button
☐ Click outside the graphic to deactivate the cropping feature

Rotate Graphics

Menu Method

☐ Click the graphic to select it, click **Format** on the menu bar, then click **Picture**

☐ In the Format Picture dialog box, click the **Size tab** if necessary
☐ In the Size and rotate section of the dialog box enter an appropriate value in the **Rotation text box**
☐ Click **OK**

OR

☐ Right-click the graphic, then click **Format Picture** on the shortcut menu
☐ Follow the steps in the second through fourth bullets in this Rotate Graphics Menu Method

Mouse Method

☐ Double-click the graphic to open the Format Picture dialog box
☐ Follow the steps in the second through fourth bullets in the Rotate Graphics Menu Method

Button Method

☐ Click the graphic to select it
☐ Position the pointer over the **green rotation handle** ⌿ at the top of the graphic
☐ Use the **⟳ pointer** to rotate the graphic to the desired angle

Control Image Contrast and Brightness

Menu Method

☐ Click the graphic to select it, click **Format** on the menu bar, then click **Picture**
☐ In the Format Picture dialog box, click the **Picture tab** if necessary
☐ Specify the appropriate settings in the Image control section of the dialog box
☐ Click **OK**

OR

☐ Right-click the graphic, then click **Format Picture** on the shortcut menu
☐ Follow the steps in the second through fourth bullets in the Control Image Contrast and Brightness Menu Method above

Mouse Method

☐ Double-click the graphic to open the Format Picture dialog box
☐ Follow the steps in the second through fourth bullets in the Control Image Contrast and Brightness Menu Method above

Button Method

☐ Click the graphic to select it
☐ Click the appropriate button on the Picture toolbar to achieve the desired effect using Table WD-22 as a reference

Table WD-22 Image Contrast and Brightness Buttons on the Picture Toolbar

Button name	Button
More Contrast	◑
Less Contrast	◑
More Brightness	▦
Less Brightness	▦

Word

Scale and Resize Graphics

Menu Method

- ☐ Click the graphic to select it, click **Format** on the menu bar, then click **Picture**
- ☐ In the Format Picture dialog box, click the **Size tab** if necessary
- ☐ Enter appropriate values in the Height and Width text boxes in the Size and rotate and Scale sections of the dialog box
- ☐ Click **OK**

OR

- ☐ Right-click the graphic, then click **Format Picture** on the shortcut menu
- ☐ Follow the steps in the second through fourth bullets in the Scale and Resize Graphics Menu Method above

Mouse Method

- ☐ Double-click the graphic to open the Format Picture dialog box
- ☐ Follow the steps in the second through fourth bullets in the Scale and Resize Graphics Menu Method above

Button Method

- ☐ Click the graphic to select it
- ☐ Position the pointer over a **sizing handle** on the graphic until the pointer changes, using Table WD-6 on page 27 as a reference
- ☐ Drag the sizing handle to resize the graphic to the size you want, then release the mouse button

INSERT AND MODIFY OBJECTS

Inserting and Modifying New Objects

Menu Method

- ☐ Click where you want to insert the object, click **Insert** on the menu bar, then click **Object**
- ☐ In the Object dialog box, click the Create New tab if necessary, select the file type from the Object type list box, then click **OK**
- ☐ In the program window for the new object, create the object using the toolbars as necessary, then click outside of the object to restore Word

Inserting and Modifying Objects from a File

Menu Method

- ☐ Click where you want to insert the object, click **Insert** on the menu bar, then click **Object**
- ☐ In the Object dialog box, click the **Create from File tab**, then click **Browse**
- ☐ In the Browse dialog box, navigate to the drive and folder that contains the object, click the object, then click **Insert**
- ☐ Click **OK** in the Object dialog box

CREATE AND MODIFY DIAGRAMS AND CHARTS USING DATA FROM OTHER SOURCES

Creating a Chart Using Data from Excel

Menu Method

☐ Click where you want to insert the chart, click **Insert** on the menu bar, point to **Picture**, then click **Chart**

☐ Click **Edit** on the menu bar, then click **Import File**

☐ In the Import File dialog box, navigate to the drive and folder that contains the Excel file containing the data you want, click the Excel file, then click **Open**

☐ In the Import Data Options dialog box, select the sheet and range for the chart data, then click **OK**

☐ Modify the chart as necessary, then click outside of the chart to return to Word

Modify a Chart

Menu Method

☐ Double-click the chart to open it in Microsoft Graph

☐ Click **Chart** on the menu bar, click **Chart Options**, make the modifications you want in the Chart Options dialog box as appropriate, then click **OK**

Linking and Embedding an Excel Chart

Menu Method

☐ Open Excel, open the file where the chart is stored, click the chart, click **Edit** on the menu bar, then click **Copy**

☐ Click in the Word document where you want to insert the chart, click **Edit** on the menu bar, then click **Paste Special**

☐ In the Paste Special dialog box, click the **Paste option button** or the **Paste link option button**, then click **OK**

Word

WORD EXPERT SKILL SET 2: ORGANIZING CONTENT

SORT CONTENT IN LISTS AND TABLES

Menu Method

☐ Select the list or table
☐ Click **Table** on the menu bar, then click **Sort**
☐ In the Sort Text or the Sort dialog box, select the column by which you want to sort and any other appropriate options, then click **OK**

Button Method

☐ To sort one column in a table, click in the column you want to sort; or to sort all data in a table select the entire table
☐ Click the **Sort Ascending button** [↓↑] or the **Sort Descending button** [↓↑] on the Tables and Borders toolbar

PERFORM CALCULATIONS IN WORD TABLES

Use Formulas in Tables

Menu Method

☐ Click the table cell where you want the formula to appear, click **Table** on the menu bar, then click **Formula**
☐ In the Formula dialog box, make sure an equal sign (=) appears in the Formula text box, click the **Paste function list arrow**, click the appropriate function, then type the rest of the formula as appropriate
☐ Click the Number format list arrow, click an appropriate format, then click **OK**

Button Method

☐ To calculate the sum total of a row or column, click the table cell where you want the total to appear
☐ Click the **AutoSum button** [Σ] on the Tables and Borders toolbar

MODIFY TABLE FORMATS

Merge Table Cells

Menu Method

☐ Select the cells to merge
☐ Click **Table** on the menu bar, then click **Merge Cells**

Button Method

☐ Select the cells to merge
☐ Click the **Merge Cells button** [▦] on the Tables and Borders toolbar

Split Table Cells

Menu Method

☐ Select the cell(s) to split
☐ Click **Table** on the menu bar, then click **Split Cells**

☐ In the Split Cells dialog box, enter the number of rows and columns, then click **OK**

Button Method

☐ Select the cell(s) to split
☐ Click the **Split Cells button** 🔳 on the Tables and Formatting toolbar
☐ In the Split Cells dialog box, enter the number of rows and columns, then click **OK**

Modify Text Position in a Cell

Menu Method

☐ Select the cell(s) to align, or select the entire table
☐ Click **Table** on the menu bar, then click **Table Properties**
☐ In the Table Properties dialog box, click either the **Cell tab** or the **Table tab**
☐ Click the appropriate alignment option, then click **OK** to close the dialog box

OR

☐ Select the cell(s) to align, or select the entire table
☐ Right-click the table, then click **Table Properties** on the shortcut menu
☐ Follow the steps in the third and fourth bullets in the Modify Text Position in a Cell Menu Method above

OR

☐ Select the cell(s) to align, or select the entire table
☐ Right-click the table, then point to **Cell Alignment** on the shortcut menu
☐ Click the appropriate alignment option from the submenu

Button Method

☐ Select the cell(s) to align, or select the entire table
☐ Click the appropriate alignment button on the Formatting toolbar using Table WD-14 on page 42 as a reference

OR

☐ Select the cell(s) to align, or select the entire table
☐ Click the **Alignment button list arrow** on the Tables and Borders toolbar. (*Note*: The Alignment button shown on the toolbar will vary depending on last usage.)
☐ Click the appropriate option from the drop-down menu

Modify Text Direction in a Cell

Menu Method

☐ Select the cell(s) to format
☐ Right-click the selected cells or table, then click **Text Direction** on the shortcut menu
☐ Click the appropriate option in the Text Direction-Table Cell dialog box, then click **OK**

Button Method

☐ Select the cell(s) to format, or select the entire table

Word

☐ Click the **Text Direction button** 📊 on the Tables and Borders toolbar repeatedly until the text is positioned in the direction you want (*Note*: the button will vary depending on last usage)

Modify Table Properties

Menu Method

☐ Select the cell(s) to format, or select the entire table
☐ Click **Table** on the menu bar, then click **Table Properties**
☐ In the Table Properties dialog box, make the appropriate modifications, then click **OK**

Insert and Modify Fields

Menu Method

☐ Click where you want to insert a field, click **Insert** on the menu bar, point to **Field**
☐ In the Field dialog box, select a category, click a field in the field name list, specify appropriate properties for the selected field, then click **OK**

SUMMARIZE DOCUMENT CONTENT USING AUTOMATED TOOLS

Use AutoSummarize

Menu Method

☐ Click **Tools** on the menu bar, then click **AutoSummarize**
☐ In the AutoSummarize dialog box, click the appropriate option using Table WD-18 on page 50 as a reference, then click **OK** if necessary

Display Content Readability

Menu Method

☐ Click **Tools** on the menu bar, then click **Spelling and Grammar**
☐ In the Spelling and Grammar dialog box, click **Options**
☐ In the Spelling and Grammar dialog box, click the **Show readability statistics check box**, then click **OK**

OR

☐ Click **Tools** on the menu bar, then click **Options**
☐ In the Options dialog box, click the Spelling and Grammar tab
☐ Click the **Show readability statistics check box**, then click **OK**

Analyze Content Readability

Menu Method

☐ Click **Tools** on the menu bar, then click **Spelling and Grammar**
☐ When the Spelling and Grammar check is complete, the Readability Statistics dialog box opens
☐ Read the information, then click **OK**

Button Method

☐ Click the **Spelling and Grammar button** 🦜 on the Standard toolbar
☐ Follow the steps in the second and third bullets in the Analyze Content Readability Menu Method

Keyboard Method

☐ Press **[F7]**
☐ Follow the steps in second and third bullets in the Analyze Content Readability Menu Method

Word

USE AUTOMATED TOOLS FOR DOCUMENT NAVIGATION

Create Bookmarks

Menu Method

☐ Select the text to bookmark
☐ Click **Insert** on the menu bar, then click **Bookmark**
☐ In the Bookmark dialog box, type the bookmark name (without using spaces and beginning the bookmark name with a letter), then click **Add**

Use Bookmarks

Menu Method

☐ Click **Edit** on the menu bar, then click **Go To**
☐ In the Go To tab of the Find and Replace dialog box, click **Bookmark** in the Go to what list box
☐ Click the **Enter bookmark name list arrow**, then click the name of the bookmark you want to go to
☐ Click **Go To**, then click **Close**

Keyboard Method

☐ Press **[Ctrl][G]**
☐ Follow the steps in the second through fourth bullets in the Use Bookmarks Menu Method above

Use the Document Map

Menu Method

☐ Click **View** on the menu bar, then click **Document Map**
☐ In the left pane of the Document Map, click a heading to jump to that location in the right pane
☐ Right-click the Document Map, then click the appropriate option on the shortcut menu to display, expand, or collapse headings

Button Method

☐ Click the **Document Map button** 🔍 on the Standard toolbar
☐ Click the **Expand indicator** ➕ next to a header in the Document Map to display the subheadings
☐ Click the **Collapse Indicator** ➖ next to a header in the Document Map to collapse the subheadings

Use Thumbnails

Menu Method

☐ Click **View** on the menu bar, then click **Thumbnails**
☐ In the left pane, click the appropriate thumbnail to jump to that screen in the document

Button Method

☐ Click the **Reading Layout button** 📖 to the left of the horizontal scroll bar
☐ Click the **Thumbnails button** 🔲 Thumbnails on the Reading Layout toolbar
☐ In the left pane, click the appropriate thumbnail to jump to that screen in the document

Keyboard Method

☐ Press **[Alt][R]**
☐ Follow the steps in the second and third bullets in the Use Thumbnails Button Method above

---

MERGE LETTERS WITH OTHER DATA SOURCES

Complete a Mail Merge Using Data from Word, Excel, or Access

Menu Method

☐ Click **Tools** on the menu bar, point to **Letters and Mailings**, then click **Mail Merge**
☐ Make sure the **Letters option button** is selected in the Mail Merge task pane, click **Next: Starting document** at the bottom of the task pane, make sure the **Use the current document option button** is selected, then click **Next: Select recipients**
☐ Make sure the **Use an existing list option button** is selected, then click **Browse**
☐ In the Select Data Source dialog box, navigate to the appropriate drive and folder, click the data source you want, then click **Open**
☐ If the Select Table dialog box opens, click the appropriate table or query, then click **OK**
☐ In the Mail Merge Recipients dialog box, specify the recipients you want, then click **OK**
☐ Click **Next: Write your letter** at the bottom of the task pane, then write your letter
☐ To insert a field from your data source, click in the document to set the insertion point, click **More items** in the task pane, select the field(s) in the Insert Merge Field dialog box, then click **Insert**
☐ If necessary, click **Match Fields** in the Insert Merge Field dialog box, make the appropriate modifications in the Match Fields dialog box, then click **OK**
☐ Click **Close** in the Insert Merge Field dialog box, then navigate through the rest of the Mail Merge task pane, making changes or accepting the defaults as appropriate to create the mail merge

Complete a Mail Merge Using Data from Outlook

Note: Outlook must be set as your default mail client in order to use it as a data source. To set Outlook as you default mail client, open Outlook, click Tools on the menu bar, then click Options. In the Options dialog box, click the Other tab if necessary, then click the Make Outlook the default program for E-mail, Contacts, and Calendar check box, if necessary.

Menu Method

- [ ] Click **Tools** on the menu bar, point to **Letters and Mailings**, then click **Mail Merge**
- [ ] In the Mail Merge task pane, select a document type, click **Next: Starting document**, select the appropriate options, then click **Next: Select recipients**
- [ ] Click the **Select from Outlook contacts option button**, then click **Choose Contacts Folder**
- [ ] In the Select Contacts List folder dialog box, make sure **Contacts** is selected in the list, then click **OK**
- [ ] In the Mail Merge Recipients dialog box, click **Clear All**, click the appropriate check boxes to select the Contacts folder recipients you want, then click **OK**
- [ ] Navigate through the rest of the Mail Merge task pane, making changes or accepting the defaults as appropriate to create the mail merge

MERGE LABELS WITH OTHER DATA SOURCES

Create Merge Labels

Menu Method

- [ ] Create a new blank document
- [ ] Click **Tools** on the menu bar, point to **Letters and Mailings**, then click **Mail Merge**
- [ ] In the Mail Merge task pane, click the **Labels option button**, click the **Next: Starting document**, make sure the **Change document layout option button** is selected, then click **Label options**
- [ ] In the Label Options dialog box, specify the appropriate options, then click **OK**
- [ ] Make sure the **Use the current document option button** is selected, then click **Next: Select recipients**
- [ ] Make sure the **Use an existing list option button** is selected, then click **Browse**
- [ ] In the Select Data Source dialog box, navigate to the drive and folder that contains your desired data source, click the data source you want, then click **Open**
- [ ] If the Select Table dialog box opens, click the table or query you want, then click **OK**
- [ ] In the Mail Merge Recipients dialog box, click **OK**
- [ ] Navigate through the rest of the Mail Merge task pane, making changes or accepting the defaults as appropriate to create the labels

STRUCTURE DOCUMENTS USING XML

Add Schemas, Solutions, and Settings in the Schema Library

Menu Method

- [ ] Click **Tools** on the menu bar, then click **Templates and Add-Ins**
- [ ] In the Templates and Add-Ins dialog box, click the **XML Schema tab**
- [ ] Click **Add Schema**, browse to the XML document you want using the Add Schema dialog box, then click **Open**
- [ ] In the Schema Settings dialog box, enter appropriate information in the URI and Alias text boxes, then click **OK**
- [ ] Click **OK** in the Templates and Add-Ins dialog box

Remove Schemas, Solutions, and Settings in the Schema Library

Menu Method

- [ ] Click **Tools** on the menu bar, then click **Templates and Add-Ins**
- [ ] In the Templates and Add-Ins dialog box, click the **XML Schema tab**
- [ ] Click **Schema Library**, then click the Schema you want to remove
- [ ] Click **Delete Schema**, click **Yes** in the message box, then click **OK** in the Templates and Add-Ins dialog box

Update Schemas, Solutions, and Settings in the Schema Library

Menu Method

- [ ] Click **Tools** on the menu bar, then click **Templates and Add-Ins**
- [ ] In the Templates and Add-Ins dialog box, click the **XML Schema tab**
- [ ] Click **Schema Library**, then click the Schema you want to update
- [ ] Click **Update Schema**, click **OK**, then click **OK** in the Templates and Add-Ins dialog box

Modify Schemas, Solutions, and Settings in the Schema Library

Menu Method

- [ ] Click **Tools** on the menu bar, then click **Templates and Add-Ins**
- [ ] In the Templates and Add-Ins dialog box, click the **XML Schema tab**
- [ ] Click **Schema Library**, then click the Schema you want to modify
- [ ] Click **Schema Settings**, make any modifications you want in the Schema Settings dialog box, click **OK**, then click **OK** in the Templates and Add-Ins dialog box

Add Schemas and Transforms to Documents

Menu Method

- [ ] Open the document to which you want to apply a schema
- [ ] Open the XML Structure task pane, then click **Templates and Add-Ins**
- [ ] In the Templates and Add-Ins dialog box, click the **XML Schema tab**

☐ Select the schema to add to the document in the Available XML schemas list or click Add Schemas, navigate to the folder that contains the schema you want, select the schema, specify appropriate settings in the Schemas Settings dialog box, click **Open**, then click **OK** in the Templates and Add-Ins dialog box

☐ Use the XML Structure task pane to apply elements to selected text

Delete Schemas to Documents

Menu Method

☐ Click **Tools** on the menu bar, then click **Templates and Add-Ins**
☐ In the Templates and Add-Ins dialog box, click the **XML Schema tab**
☐ Deselect the **Checked schemas are currently attached check box**, then click **OK**

Modify Schemas and Transforms

Menu Method

☐ Click **Tools** on the menu bar, then click **Templates and Add-Ins**
☐ In the Templates and Add-Ins dialog box, click the **XML Schema tab**
☐ Click **Schema Library**, select the schema you want, click **Schema Settings**, make the modifications you want in the Schema Settings dialog box, click **OK**, then click **OK** in the Schema Library dialog box, then click **OK** in the Templates and Add-Ins dialog box

Manage Elements and Attributes in XML documents

Menu Method

☐ Open the XML document and view the XML structure task pane
☐ Select the text to which you want to apply an XML tag
☐ Click the appropriate tag in the Choose an element to apply to your current select list box, then deselect the text

Define XML options

Menu Method

☐ Click **Tools** on the menu bar, then click **Templates and Add-Ins**
☐ In the Templates and Add-Ins dialog box, click the **XML Schema tab**
☐ Click **Schema Library**, then click the schema to which you want to associate a solution
☐ Choose an appropriate option in the Use solution with list box, then click **Add Solution**
☐ In the Add Solution dialog box, browse to the XSLT file you want, then click **Open**
☐ In the Solution Settings dialog box, select the appropriate options, then click **OK**

WORD EXPERT SKILL SET 3: FORMATTING DOCUMENTS

CREATE AND MODIFY FORMS

Create Forms

Button Method

☐ Click in the document to set the insertion point where you want to insert the form

☐ Click the appropriate field type button on the Forms toolbar, using the first three rows of Table WD-23 as a reference

☐ To specify settings for a field, click the field, then click the **Form Field Options button** 🔲 on the Forms tab, or right-click the field, then click **Properties** on the shortcut menu

☐ In the [Object] Form Field Properties dialog box, specify the settings you want for the selected field, then click **OK**

Table WD-23 Form Toolbar Buttons

Button	Used to
Text Form Field button 🔤	Add a text field form control
Check Box Form Field button ☑	Add a check box field form control
Drop-Down Form Field button 🔽	Add a drop-down list field form control
Form Field Options button 🔲	Open the Form Field Option dialog box
Draw Table button 📝	Draw a table for form fields using ✏
Insert Table button 📰	Insert a table
Insert Frame button 🔲	Draw a frame to contain form controls
Form Field Shading button 🔳	Turn shading off in the form fields
Reset Form Fields 🔲	Restore form fields to the default settings
Protect Form button 🔒	Protect forms so users can only type the data in the form fields

Modify Forms

Button Method

☐ Use Table WD-23 as a reference to modify the form

Set and Change Options on Form Fields and Check Boxes

Menu Method

☐ Double-click the field or check box

☐ In the Form Field Options dialog box, make the appropriate selections, then click **OK**

CREATE AND MODIFY DOCUMENT BACKGROUND

Create a Picture Watermark

Button Method
- [ ] Click **Format** on the menu bar, point to **Background**, then click **Printed Watermark**
- [ ] In the Printed Watermark dialog box, click the **Picture Watermark option button**, then click **Select Picture**
- [ ] In the Insert Picture dialog box, navigate to and select the appropriate graphic, then click **Insert**
- [ ] Click **OK** in the Printed Watermark dialog box

Create a Text Watermark

Button Method
- [ ] Click **Format** on the menu bar, point to **Background**, then click **Printed Watermark**
- [ ] In the Printed Watermark dialog box, click the **Text Watermark option button**
- [ ] Specify the appropriate text, font, color, and other options, then click **OK**

Apply a Theme

Button Method
- [ ] Click **Format** on the menu bar, then click **Theme**
- [ ] In the Theme dialog box, click the appropriate theme in the Choose a Theme list, then click **OK**

Create and Modify Document Background Colors

Menu Method
- [ ] Click **Format** on the menu bar, point to **Background**
- [ ] Click the color you want to apply on the color palette, or click **More Colors**, choose a color from the Colors dialog box, then click **OK**

Create and Modify Document Fill Effects

Menu Method
- [ ] Click **Format** on the menu bar, point to **Background**, then click **Fill Effects**
- [ ] In the Fill Effects dialog box, specify the fill effects you want in the Gradient, Texture, Pattern, and Picture tabs, then click **OK**

Word

CREATE AND UPDATE DOCUMENT INDEXES AND TABLES OF CONTENTS, FIGURES, AND AUTHORITIES

Create an Index

Menu Method

- ☐ Select the text you want to reference as a main or subentry in the inde
- ☐ Click **Insert** on the menu bar, point to **Reference**, then click **Index and Tables**
- ☐ In the Index and Tables dialog box, click the **Index tab** if necessary, then click **Mark Entry**
- ☐ In the Mark Index Entry dialog box, specify the appropriate options, click **Mark** or **Mark All**, then click **Close** in the Mark Index Entry dialog box
- ☐ Repeat for each word or phrase in the document that you want indexec then close the Index and Tables dialog box
- ☐ Position the insertion point where you want the index to appear
- ☐ Click **Insert** on the menu bar, point to **Reference**, then click **Index and Tables**
- ☐ In the Index and Tables dialog box, click the **Index tab** if necessary
- ☐ Select the appropriate options, then click **OK**

Keyboard Method

- ☐ Select the text you want to reference as a main entry or subentry in the index
- ☐ Press **[Alt][Shift][X]** to mark the text as an index entry
- ☐ Follow the steps in the fourth through ninth bullets in the Create an Index Menu Method above

Modify an Index

Keyboard Method

- ☐ Make changes to an index using Table WD-24 as a reference

Table WD-24 Modifying an Index

If you want to make this change	Do this
Delete an index entry	☐ Select the entry in the index, then press [Delete]
Change and update an index entry	☐ Edit the text in quotes following the reference in the text ☐ Right-click any field in the index, then click Update Field on the shortcut menu, or place the insertion point in the Index, then press [F9]

Word

Table WD-24 Modifying an Index (continued)

If you want to make this change	Do this
Add an index entry	☐ Follow the steps in the first through fifth bullets in the Create an Index Menu Method to add a new entry ☐ Right-click any field in the index, then click Update Field on the shortcut menu, or place the insertion point in the index, then press [F9]
Format an index entry	☐ Select an index entry ☐ Click Insert on the menu bar, point to Reference, then click Index and Tables or right-click an entry, click Edit Field on the shortcut menu, then click Index in the Field dialog box ☐ In the Index and Tables or Index dialog box, click Modify ☐ In the Style dialog box, select the style to apply, or click Modify, make the style modifications in the Modify Style dialog box, then click OK ☐ Click OK in the Style dialog box, then click OK in the Index and Tables or Index dialog box ☐ Click Yes in the message box to replace the existing index if necessary

Word

Insert a Table of Contents

Menu Method

☐ Make sure your document has heading styles applied to text that you want to appear in the table of contents
☐ Click in the document where you want the table of contents to appear to set the insertion point
☐ Click **Insert** on the menu bar, point to **Reference**, then click **Index and Tables**
☐ In the Index and Tables dialog box, click the **Table of Contents tab**
☐ Specify the formatting options you want, then click **OK**

Update a Table of Contents

Menu Method

☐ Make the appropriate modifications to the document
☐ Right-click any field in the table of contents, then click **Update Field** on the shortcut menu
☐ In the Update Table of Contents dialog box, click the appropriate option button, then click **OK**

Keyboard Method

☐ Make the appropriate modifications to the document
☐ Click any field in the Table of Contents to set the insertion point, then press **[F9]**
☐ In the Update Table of Contents dialog box, click the appropriate option button, then click **OK**

Insert a Table of Figures

Menu Method

□ Add captions to your figures as necessary
□ Click where you want the table of figures to appear
□ Click **Insert** on the menu bar, point to **Reference**, then click **Index and Tables**
□ In the Index and Tables dialog box, click the **Table of Figures tab**, click the appropriate options, then click **OK**

Update a Table of Figures

Menu Method

□ Make the changes you want to the document
□ Right-click a field in the Table of Figures, then click **Update Field** on the shortcut menu
□ In the Update Table of Figures dialog box, click the appropriate option button, then click **OK**

Keyboard Method

□ Make the changes you want to the document
□ Click in the Table of Figures to set the insertion point, then press **[F9]**
□ In the Update Table of Figures dialog box, click the appropriate option button, then click **OK**

Create a Table of Authorities

Menu Method

□ Select the text you want to cite
□ Click **Insert** on the menu bar, point to **Reference**, then click **Index and Tables**
□ In the Index and Tables dialog box, click the **Table of Authorities tab** then click **Mark Citation**
□ In the Mark Citation dialog box, click the appropriate options, click **Mark**, then click **Close** in the Mark Citation dialog box
□ For each additional word or phrase in the document that you want indexed, select the text, then repeat the first through fourth bullets above
□ Click in the document where you want the Table of Authorities to appear to set the insertion point
□ Click **Insert** on the menu bar, point to **Reference**, then click **Index and Tables**
□ In the Index and Tables dialog box, click the **Table of Authorities tab** if necessary, select the appropriate options, then click **OK**

Keyboard Method

□ Select the text you want to cite
□ Press **[Alt][Shift][I]** to mark the text as a citation
□ Follow the steps in the fourth through eighth bullets in the Create a Table of Authorities Menu Method above

pdate a Table of Authorities

Menu Method

☐ Make the appropriate modifications to the document
☐ Right-click any **field** in the table of authorities, then click **Update Field** on the shortcut menu

Keyboard Method

☐ Make the appropriate modifications to the document
☐ Click anywhere in the table of authorities to set the insertion point, then press **[F9]**

NSERT AND MODIFY ENDNOTES, FOOTNOTES, APTIONS, AND CROSS-REFERENCES

reate Footnotes and Endnotes

Menu Method

☐ Click in the document where you want the footnote to reference
☐ Click **Insert** on the menu bar, point to **Reference**, then click **Footnote**
☐ In the Footnote and Endnote dialog box, select the appropriate location and format options, then click **Insert**
☐ If you are in Normal view, type the text in the Footnotes or Endnotes pane, then click the **Close button** in the Footnotes or Endnotes pane; if you are in Print Layout view, type the footnote or endnote text

evise or Format Footnotes and Endnotes

Menu Method

☐ In Print Layout view, click **Edit** on the menu bar, then click **Go To**
☐ In the Find and Replace dialog box, click **Footnote** or **Endnote** in the Go to what list
☐ In the Enter footnote number or Enter endnote number text box, type the number of the footnote or endnote you want to modify
☐ Click **Go To**, double-click the **footnote** or **endnote** you wish to modify, then edit the footnote or endnote text as appropriate
☐ Click **Close** in the Find and Replace dialog box

OR

☐ In Normal view, click **View** on the menu bar, then click **Footnotes**
☐ If the Footnotes dialog box opens, click the appropriate option button
☐ Edit the text in the Footnotes or Endnotes pane, then click **Close** in the Footnotes or Endnotes pane

Keyboard Method

☐ In Normal view, double-click the footnote or endnote number
☐ Make the changes to the text in the Footnotes or Endnotes pane, then click the **Close button** in the Footnotes or Endnotes pane

Insert a Caption

Menu Method

☐ Click the figure to which you want to add a caption to select it
☐ Click **Insert** on the menu bar, point to **Reference**, then click **Caption**
☐ In the Caption dialog box, specify the appropriate options, then click **O**

Modify Captions

Menu Method

☐ Edit the caption as appropriate
☐ Right-click the table of figures, click **Update Field**, click the **Update entire table option button** in the Update Table of Figures dialog box, then click **OK**

Insert a Cross-Reference

Keyboard Method

☐ Click where you want the cross-reference to appear, then type the text for the reference
☐ Click **Insert** on the menu bar, point to **Reference**, then click **Cross-reference**
☐ In the Cross-reference dialog box, specify the appropriate options, click **Insert**, then click **Close**

Modify a Cross-Reference

Menu Method

☐ Right-click the cross-reference to modify, then click **Edit Field**
☐ Make the appropriate selections in the Field dialog box, then click **OK**

CREATE AND MANAGE MASTER DOCUMENTS AND SUBDOCUMENTS

Create a Master Document from an Existing Document

Menu Method

☐ Open an existing document, click **View** on the menu bar, then click **Outline**
☐ To apply heading styles to each heading in the document, select the heading text, then click the appropriate button on the Outlining toolbar to promote or demote headings as necessary to create the master document, using Table WD-25 as a reference

Button Method

☐ Click the **Outline View button** 📄
☐ Select the text, then click the appropriate button on the Outlining toolbar to promote or demote headings as necessary to create the master document, using Table WD-25 as a reference

Table WD-25 Outlining Toolbar Buttons

Button	Used to
Promote to Heading 1 button 🔼	Change the text to the highest heading level
Promote button 🔼	Change the text to the next highest heading level
Outline Level list arrow [Body text ▾]	Select the level by name
Demote button 🔽	Change the text to the next lowest heading level
Demote to Body Text button 🔽	Change the text to body text

Create a New Master Document

Menu Method

☐ Open a new, blank document, click **View** on the menu bar, then click **Outline**
☐ Type appropriate headings for the title and each subdocument, then click the appropriate button on the Outlining toolbar to promote or demote headings as necessary to create the master document, using Table WD-25 as a reference
☐ Save the document

Create Subdocuments

Menu Method

☐ Click **View** on the menu bar, then click **Outline**
☐ Select the text you want to make into a subdocument, then click the **Create Subdocument button** 📄 on the Outlining toolbar
☐ Save and close the master document

Close and Open Subdocuments

Button Method

☐ With the master document open, click the **Collapse Subdocuments button** ➖ on the Outlining toolbar to close all subdocuments
☐ Click the **Expand Subdocuments button** ➕ to open all subdocuments in the master document

Manage Master Documents and Subdocuments

☐ Use Table WD-26 as a reference to manage master documents and subdocuments

Table WD-26 Managing Master Documents and Subdocuments

Task	Method
Merge subdocuments	Select two subdocuments in the main document, then click the Merge Subdocument button 🔲 on the Outlining toolbar
Split an outlining level into its own subdocument	Click the Expand indicator next to the appropriate heading in the subdocument, then click the Split Subdocument button 🔲 on the Outlining toolbar
Move a subdocument	Drag the subdocument icon 🔳 in the master document until the vertical line indicator is below where you want it to appear. (*Note:* Moving it within a subdocument will create a subdocument within the subdocument.)
Remove a subdocument	Click the subdocument icon 🔳 for the subdocument, then click the Remove Subdocument button 🔳 on the Outlining toolbar to combine the text into the master document
Insert a new subdocument	Position the insertion point where you want the new subdocument to appear, click the Insert Subdocument button 🔲 in the Insert Subdocument dialog box, make sure that the appropriate drive and folder are listed in the Look in box, click the filename, then click Open

Word

WORD EXPERT SKILL SET 4: COLLABORATING

MODIFY TRACK CHANGES OPTION

Set Ink Colors and Balloon Options

Menu Method

☐ Click **Tools** on the menu bar, then click **Options**
☐ Click the **Track Changes tab** in the Options dialog box
☐ Set the ink color and balloon options, then click **OK**

Show and Hide Reviewers

Button Method

☐ Click the **Show button** Show ▾ on the Reviewing toolbar
☐ Point to **Reviewers**, then click a reviewer name or **All Reviewers** to select or deselect the check box

PUBLISH AND EDIT WEB DOCUMENTS

Create a Web Document

Menu Method

☐ Click **File** on the menu bar, click **New**
☐ In the New Document task pane, click **Web Page**

Edit Web Documents

Menu Method

☐ Click **File** on the menu bar, then click **Open**
☐ In the Open dialog box, navigate to the appropriate drive and folder, make sure the Files of type box lists **All Word Documents**, click the HTML file or MHTML file, then click **Open**
☐ Edit the document by adding, deleting, and modifying graphics, text, frames, and hyperlinks

Publish a Web Document

Note: You will need to have access to storage on a network or on the Internet in order to publish a document to the Web.

Menu Method

☐ Make sure that you are connected to the Internet
☐ Click **File** on the menu bar, then click **Save as Web Page**
☐ Click the Save in list arrow, then navigate to and click **My Network Places**
☐ If a Web server is listed in the dialog box, and if you have permission to post files to it, double-click it; if you have an MSN password, double-click **My Web Sites on MSN**, sign in, then choose the appropriate drive and folder
☐ Type the filename in the File name box, then click **Save**

Word

Set Web Options

Menu Method

□ Click **Tools** on the menu bar, then click **Options**

□ In the Options dialog box, click the General tab, then click **Web Option**

□ In the Web Options dialog box make the appropriate selections, click **OK**, then click **OK** in the Options dialog box

Add Frames to a Web Document

Menu Method

□ Click **Format** on the menu bar, point to **Frames**, then click **New Frames Page**

□ Click the appropriate button on the Frames toolbar to add a new fram to the Web document

Modify Frames in a Web Document

Menu Method

□ Click **Format** on the menu bar, point to **Frames**, then click **Frame Properties**

□ In the Frame Properties dialog box, specify the appropriate settings, then click **OK**

MANAGE DOCUMENT VERSIONS

Create a Document Version

Menu Method

□ Click **File** on the menu bar, then click **Versions**

□ In the Versions dialog box, click **Save Now**

□ In the Save Version dialog box, type any comments in the Comments on version text box, then click **OK**

□ In the Save As dialog box, type the filename in the File name text bo: then click **OK**

View a Document Version

Menu Method

□ Click **File** on the menu bar, then click **Versions**

□ In the Versions in [Filename] dialog box, click the appropriate version then click **Open**

Delete a Document Version

Menu Method

□ Click **File** on the menu bar, then click **Versions**

□ In the Versions in [Filename] dialog box, click the appropriate version then click **Delete**

□ Click **Yes** in the message box, then click **Close** in the Versions in [Filename] dialog box

PROTECT AND RESTRICT FORMS AND DOCUMENTS

Set Formatting Restrictions

Menu Method

☐ Click **Tools** on the menu bar, then click **Protect Document**
☐ In the Protect Document task pane, click the **Limit formatting to a selection of styles check box** to select it, then click **Settings**
☐ In the Formatting Restrictions dialog box, make the appropriate selections, then click **OK**

Set Editing Restrictions

Menu Method

☐ Click **Tools** on the menu bar, then click **Protect Document**
☐ In the Protect Document task pane, select the **Allow only this type of editing in the document check box** to place a checkmark in it, then click the appropriate option from the changes list box

Add Users Excepted from Restrictions

Menu Method

☐ Click **Tools** on the menu bar, then click **Protect Document**
☐ In the Protect Document task pane, select the **Allow only this type of editing in the document check box** to place a checkmark in it, then click the appropriate option from the changes list box
☐ Select the appropriate users from the Groups list box, or click **More users**, add individual names in the Add Users dialog box, then click **OK**

Set a Password

Menu Method

☐ Click **Tools** on the menu bar, then click **Protect Document**
☐ In the Protect Document task pane, select the appropriate options, then click the **Yes, Start Enforcing Protection button**
☐ In the Start Enforcing Protection dialog box, type and confirm the password, then click **OK**

ATTACH DIGITAL SIGNATURES TO DOCUMENTS

Attach Digital Signatures

Menu Method

☐ Click **Tools** on the menu bar, then click **Options**
☐ In the Options dialog box, click the **Security tab**, then click **Digital Signatures**
☐ In the Digital Signature dialog box, click **Add**, then click **OK** or **Yes** in any message boxes
☐ In the Select Certificate dialog box, make sure the registered user's name is listed and selected, then click **View Certificate**

Word

☐ Click **OK** in the Certificate dialog box, then click **OK** in the Select Certificate dialog box
☐ Click **OK** in the Digital Signature dialog box, then click **OK** in the Options dialog box

Use Digital Signatures to Authenticate Documents

Menu Method

☐ Click **Tools** on the menu bar, then click **Options**
☐ In the Options dialog box, click the **Security tab**, then click **Digital Signatures**
☐ In the Digital Signature dialog box, make sure the correct certificate is selected, then click **View Certificate**
☐ Note the names next to Issued to and Issued by, then make sure the certificate is still valid
☐ Click **OK** in the Certificate dialog box, click **OK** in the Digital Signature dialog box, then click **OK** in the Options dialog box

CUSTOMIZE DOCUMENT PROPERTIES

Insert and Edit Summary and Custom Information

Menu Method

☐ Click **File** on the menu bar, then click **Properties**
☐ In the [Filename] Properties dialog box, make the appropriate selections in the Summary and Custom tabs, then click **OK**

WORD EXPERT SKILL SET 5: CUSTOMIZING WORD

CREATE, EDIT, AND RUN MACROS

Create Macros

Menu Method
- [ ] Click **Tools** on the menu bar, point to **Macro**, then click **Record New Macro**
- [ ] In the Record Macro dialog box, type the macro name in the Macro name text box
- [ ] Click the **Store macro in list arrow**, then click the appropriate macro storage option
- [ ] To assign a keyboard shortcut to the macro, click the **Keyboard button** in the Customize Keyboard dialog box, press the appropriate keyboard shortcut to insert a shortcut key in the Press new shortcut key text box, click **Assign**, then click **Close**; or to assign a button to the macro, click the **Toolbars button** to open the Customize dialog box, click the **Commands tab**, select the appropriate command in the Commands section, drag it to the toolbar or to a menu, then click **Close**
- [ ] Perform the actions for the macro in the open document
- [ ] Click **Tools** on the menu bar, point to **Macro**, then click **Stop Recording**

Button Method
- [ ] Click the **Record Macro button** 🔘 on the Visual Basic toolbar
- [ ] Follow the second through sixth bullets in the Create Macros Menu Method above
- [ ] Click the **Stop Recording button** ◼ on the Stop Recording toolbar

Run Macros

Menu Method
- [ ] Click **Tools** on the menu bar, then click **Options**
- [ ] In the Options dialog box, click the **Security tab**, then click **Macro Security**
- [ ] In the Security dialog box, make sure the **Security Level tab** is selected, click the **Medium option button** or the **Low option button**, click **OK** in the Security dialog box, then click **OK** in the Options dialog box
- [ ] Open the file that contains the macro, click **Yes** to enable a macro if prompted
- [ ] Click **Tools** on the menu bar, point to **Macro**, then click **Macros**
- [ ] In the Macros dialog box, make sure the appropriate macro is selected in the macro list, then click **Run**

Button Method
- [ ] Follow the first through fourth bullets in the Run Macros Menu Method above
- [ ] Click the button on the toolbar for the macro you created

Keyboard Method

☐ Follow the first through fourth bullets in the Run Macros Menu Method
☐ Press the keyboard combination for the macro you created

Edit Macros

Menu Method

☐ Click **Tools** on the menu bar, point to **Macro**, then click **Macros**
☐ In the Macros dialog box, make sure the appropriate macro is selected in the macro list, then click **Edit**
☐ In the Microsoft Visual Basic Editor window, make the appropriate modifications
☐ Click **File** on the menu bar, then click **Close and Return to Microsoft Word**

CUSTOMIZE MENUS AND TOOLBARS

Create Menus

Menu Method

☐ Click **Tools** on the menu bar, then click **Customize**, or right-click any toolbar, then click **Customize** on the shortcut menu
☐ In the Customize dialog box, click the **Commands tab**, click the **Save in list arrow**, then click the appropriate option
☐ Click **New Menu** In the Categories list box, then drag the **New Menu command** from the Commands list to the menu bar and position it using
☐ Click the appropriate option in the Categories list box to display commands for that category in the Commands list box, drag the command(s) you want from the Commands list box on top of New Menu on the menu bar so that a box appears below New Menu, drag the command onto the box, then release the mouse button
☐ Right-click **New Menu** on the menu bar, select all of the text in the Name box on the shortcut menu, then type the menu name
☐ Click anywhere in the document to close the shortcut menu, then click **Close** in the Customize dialog box

Create Toolbars

Menu Method

☐ Click **Tools** on the menu bar, then click **Customize** or right-click a toolbar, then click **Customize** on the shortcut menu
☐ In the Customize dialog box, click the **Toolbars tab**, then click **New**
☐ In the New Toolbar dialog box, type the toolbar name in the Toolbar name text box, click the **Make toolbar available to list arrow**, click the appropriate option, then click **OK**
☐ Click the **Commands tab**, then click the appropriate option in the Categories list box

□ Use 🔧 to drag the command(s) you want from the Commands list box to the new toolbar, then release the mouse button
□ Click **Close** in the Customize dialog box

Add Buttons to Toolbars

Menu Method
□ Click **Tools** on the menu bar, then click **Customize** or right-click a toolbar, then click **Customize** on the shortcut menu
□ In the Customize dialog box, click the **Commands tab**, click the **Save in list arrow**, then click the appropriate option
□ Click the appropriate option in the Categories list box, use 🔧 drag the appropriate command to the appropriate location on the appropriate toolbar, then release the mouse button
□ Click **Close** in the Customize dialog box

Remove Buttons from Toolbars

Button Method
□ Click the **Toolbar options button** 🔧 on the toolbar from which you want to delete a button, point to **Add or Remove Buttons**, then point to the **toolbar name**
□ Click the **button** on the shortcut menu you want to remove so that it no longer has a check mark next to it

Keyboard Method
□ Press and hold **[Alt]**
□ Click the button you want to remove, then drag it off of the toolbar

MODIFY WORD DEFAULT SETTINGS

Change the Default File Location for Templates

Note: Only perform these steps if you want to permanently change the default location for workgroup templates and permanently add additional tabs to the Templates dialog box.

Menu Method
□ Click **Tools** on the menu bar, then click **Options**
□ In the Options dialog box, click the **File Locations tab**, click **Workgroup templates** in the File types list, then click **Modify**
□ In the Modify Location dialog box, click the Look in list arrow, navigate to and select the folder or drive that you want to specify as the new location for storing workgroup templates, then click **OK**
□ Click **OK** in the Options dialog box

Set the Default Dictionary

Note: Only perform these steps if you want to permanently change the default dictionary.

Menu Method

☐ Click **Tools** on the menu bar, then click **Options**
☐ Click the **Spelling & Grammar tab**, then click **Custom Dictionaries**
☐ In the Custom Dictionaries dialog box, select the dictionary, then click **Change Default**
☐ Click **OK** in the Custom Dictionaries dialog box, then click **OK** in the Options dialog box

Modify the Default Font Settings

Note: Only perform these steps if you want to permanently change the default font settings.

Menu Method

☐ Click **Format** on the menu bar, then click **Font**
☐ Make the appropriate formatting changes in the Font dialog box, click **Default**, then click **Yes** in the message box
☐ Click **OK** in the Font dialog box

Microsoft Office Excel 2003
Exam Reference
Getting Started with Excel 2003

The Microsoft Excel Office Specialist exams assume a basic level of proficiency in Excel. This section is intended to help you reference these basic skills while you are preparing to take the Excel Specialist or Expert exams.

☐ Starting and exiting Excel
☐ Viewing the Excel window
☐ Using toolbars
☐ Using task panes
☐ Opening, saving, and closing workbooks
☐ Navigating in the worksheet window
☐ Using views
☐ Using smart tags
☐ Getting Help

START AND EXIT EXCEL

Start Excel

Button Method
☐ Click the **Start button** ⚇ start on the Windows taskbar
☐ Point to **All Programs**
☐ Point to Microsoft Office, then click **Microsoft Office Excel 2003**
OR
☐ Double-click the **Microsoft Excel program icon** 🖾 on the desktop

Exit Excel

Menu Method
☐ Click **File** on the menu bar, then click **Exit**

Button Method
☐ Click the **Close button** 🗷 on the Excel program window title bar

Keyboard Method
☐ Press **[Alt][F4]**

VIEW THE EXCEL WINDOW

Figure EX-1

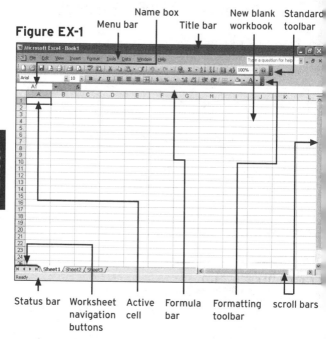

Status bar   Worksheet   Active   Formula   Formatting   scroll bars
              navigation   cell   bar   toolbar
              buttons

USE TOOLBARS

Display Toolbars

Menu Method

☐ Click **View** on the menu bar, point to **Toolbars**, then click the toolbar you want to display

OR

☐ Right-click any toolbar, then click the toolbar you want to display on the shortcut menu

Customize Toolbars

Menu Method

☐ Click **Tools** on the menu bar, then click **Customize**, or click **View** on the menu bar, point to **Toolbars**, then click **Customize**, or right-click any toolbar, then click **Customize** on the shortcut menu
☐ In the Customize dialog box, select the appropriate options, then click **Close**

Button Method

☐ Click the **Toolbar Options button** on the toolbar to customize
☐ Point to **Add or Remove buttons**, then click **Customize**
☐ Click the appropriate options in the Customize dialog box, then click **Close**

Reposition Toolbars

Mouse Method

☐ Position the pointer over the Toolbar Move handle at the left end of any docked toolbar, or over the title bar of any floating toolbar
☐ When the pointer changes to ↔, press and hold the mouse button
☐ Drag the toolbar to the desired location, then release the mouse button

---

USE TASK PANES

Display Task Panes

Menu Method

☐ If no task pane is open, click **View** on the menu bar, then click **Task Pane** or right-click any toolbar, then click **Task Pane** on the shortcut menu
☐ Click the **Other Task Panes list arrow** ▼ on the task pane title bar, then click the appropriate task pane
☐ Click the **Back button** on the task pane title bar to return to the previously displayed task pane

Close Task Panes

Menu Method

☐ Click **View** on the menu bar, then click **Task Pane** or right-click any toolbar, then click **Task Pane** on the shortcut menu

Button Method

☐ Click the **Close button** ✕ on the task pane title bar

OPEN, SAVE, AND CLOSE WORKBOOKS

Open a New Workbook

Menu Method

☐ Click **File** on the menu bar, then click **New**
☐ Click **Blank workbook** under New in the New Workbook task pane

Button Method

☐ Click the **New button** on the Standard toolbar

Keyboard Method

☐ Press **[Ctrl][N]**

Excel

Open an Existing Workbook

Menu Method

☐ Click **File** on the menu bar, then click **Open**
☐ In the Open dialog box, navigate to the appropriate drive and folder
☐ Click the file you want, then click **Open**

Task Pane Method

☐ Click a workbook under the Open a workbook section in the Getting Started task pane

OR

☐ Click **More** under the Open section in the Getting Started task pane, then follow the second and third bullets in the Open an Existing Workbook Menu Method above

Button Method

☐ Click the **Open button** 🖼 on the Standard toolbar
☐ Follow the second and third bullets in the Open an Existing Workbook Menu Method above

Keyboard Method

☐ Press **[Ctrl][O]**
☐ Follow the second and third bullets in the Open an Existing Workbook Menu Method above

Use Save As

Menu Method

☐ Click **File** on the menu bar, then click **Save As**
☐ In the Save As dialog box, click the **Save in list arrow**, then navigate to the drive and folder where you want to store the workbook
☐ Type an appropriate filename in the File name text box, then click **Save**

Keyboard Method

☐ Press **[F12]**
☐ Follow the steps in the second and third bullets of the Use Save As Menu Method above

Save an Existing Workbook

Menu Method

☐ Click **File** on the menu bar, then click **Save**

Button Method

☐ Click the **Save button** 🖫 on the Standard toolbar

Keyboard Method

☐ Press **[Ctrl][S]**

Close Workbooks

Menu Method

☐ Click **File** on the menu bar, then click **Close**
☐ If prompted to save the file, click **Yes** or **No** as appropriate

Button Method

☐ Click the **Close Window button** ☒ on the menu bar
☐ If prompted to save the file, click **Yes** or **No** as appropriate

Keyboard Method

☐ Press **[Ctrl][W]** or **[Alt][F4]**
☐ If prompted to save the file, click **Yes** or **No** as appropriate

NAVIGATE IN THE WORKSHEET WINDOW

Menu Method

☐ Click **Edit** on the menu bar, then click **Go To**
☐ In the Go To dialog box, select the appropriate options, then click **OK**

Keyboard Method

☐ Press **[Ctrl][G]**
☐ Follow the steps in the second bullet of the Navigate in the Worksheet Window Menu Method above

OR

☐ Use Table EX-1 as a reference to navigate through the worksheet using keyboard shortcuts

Table EX-1 Navigation Keyboard Shortcuts

Key	Moves the insertion point
[Ctrl][Home]	To the beginning of the worksheet (cell A1)
[Ctrl][End]	To the end of the worksheet
[Page Up]	One screen up
[Page Down]	One screen down
[Alt][Page Up]	One screen to the left
[Alt][Page Down]	One screen to the right

Scroll Bar Method

To change the view without moving the insertion point, do one of the following:

☐ Drag the **scroll box** in the scroll bar to move within the worksheet
☐ Click above the scroll box in the vertical scroll bar to jump up a screen
☐ Click below the scroll box in the vertical scroll bar to jump down a screen
☐ Click the **up scroll arrow** in the vertical scroll bar to move up one row
☐ Click the **down scroll arrow** in the vertical scroll bar to move down one row

Excel

USE VIEWS

Refer to Table EX-2 to change worksheet views.

Table EX-2 Workbook Views

View	What you see	Click this button on the Standard Toolbar	Menu Method
Normal view	Formatted worksheet, but not headers, footers, or some graphics; does not show worksheet as it would appear when printed		Click View on the menu bar, then click Normal
Page Break Preview	Same as Normal view, except with blue lines indicating page breaks; page breaks can be manually modified using the resize pointers		Click View on the menu bar, then click Page Break Preview
Print Preview	Worksheet as it would appear when printed	Print Preview button	Click File on the menu bar, then click Print Preview

USE SMART TAGS

Button Method

☐ Move the pointer over a cell with a purple triangle in the lower left corner until the **Smart Tag Actions button** ⑥ appears
☐ Click ⑥ to see the actions you can perform, then select an action

GET HELP

Menu Method

☐ Click **Help** on the menu bar, then click **Microsoft Excel Help**
☐ Use Table EX-3 as a reference to select the most appropriate way to search for help using the Microsoft Excel Help task pane

Button Method

☐ Click the **Microsoft Excel Help button** 🔵 on the Standard toolbar
☐ Use Table EX-3 as a reference to select the most appropriate way to search for help using the Microsoft Excel Help task pane

OR

☐ Click the **Type a question for help box** on the menu bar
☐ Type a question or keywords relating to an Excel topic, then press **[Enter]**
☐ View the results of the keyword search in the Microsoft Excel Help task pane, then click a topic title in the task pane to view the topic in a new window

Keyboard Method

☐ Press **[F1]**
☐ Use Table EX-3 as a reference to select the most appropriate way to search for help using the Microsoft Excel Help task pane

Table EX-3 Microsoft Help Task Pane Options

Option	To use
Table of Contents	Click Table of Contents in the task pane, click the Expand indicator next to each topic you want to explore further, then click the topic you want and read the results in the task pane
Search	Type a keyword in the Search for text box, click the Start searching button ➡, then click the blue hyperlinked text to read more in the Microsoft Office Excel Help Window, or click the grayed text to view the topic in the Table of Contents

EXCEL SPECIALIST EXAM REFERENCE

Skill Sets:

1. Creating data and content
2. Analyzing data
3. Formatting data and content
4. Collaborating
5. Managing workbooks

EXCEL SPECIALIST SKILL SET 1: CREATING DATA AND CONTENT

ENTER AND EDIT CELL CONTENT

Enter Text and Numbers

Menu Method

☐ Click the cell where you want to enter text or numbers
☐ Type the appropriate text or number, then press any of the keys shown in Table EX-4 to lock in the entry and move to a new cell

Button Method

☐ Click the cell where you want to enter text or numbers
☐ Type the appropriate text or number, then press the Enter button on the formula bar to lock in the entry, then use Table EX-4 to move to the next cell

Table EX-4 Navigating a Worksheet

Pressing this key	Moves the active cell here
[Enter]	To the cell below
[↑], [↓], [←], [→]	To the cell above, below, left, or right
[Tab]	One cell to the right
[Shift][Tab]	One cell to the left

Enter Symbols

Menu Method

☐ Click the cell where you want to enter a symbol
☐ Click **Insert** on the menu bar, then click **Symbol**
☐ In the Insert Symbol dialog box, click the appropriate symbol, then click **Insert**

Excel

Edit Cell Content

Keyboard Method

- ☐ Click the cell to edit
- ☐ Click the formula bar, then edit the contents in the formula bar, or press **[F2]**, then edit the cell contents directly in the cell
- ☐ Press **[Backspace]** to delete a character to the left of the insertion point, or press **[Delete]** to delete a character to the right of the insertion point

Mouse Method

- ☐ Double-click the cell to edit
- ☐ Edit the cell contents directly in the cell
- ☐ Press **[Backspace]** to delete a character to the left of the insertion point, or press **[Delete]** to delete a character to the right of the insertion point

Use the Fill Handle to Fill Series Content

Keyboard Method

- ☐ Click the cell where the series starts
- ☐ Position the pointer over the **fill handle** in the lower-right corner of the cell until the pointer changes to $+$
- ☐ Drag the fill handle horizontally or vertically to automatically fill in the appropriate values in the cells across which you drag

NAVIGATE TO SPECIFIC CELL CONTENT

Find Text

Menu Method

- ☐ Click **Edit** on the menu bar, then click **Find** to open the Find and Replace dialog box with the Find tab displayed
- ☐ Type the text you want to find or replace in the Find what text box, then click **Find Next** repeatedly to view all instances

Keyboard Method

- ☐ Press **[Ctrl][F]**
- ☐ Follow the steps in the second bullet in the Find Text Menu Method above

Replace Text

Menu Method

- ☐ Click **Edit** on the menu bar, then click **Replace** to open the Find and Replace dialog box with the Replace tab displayed
- ☐ Type the text you want to find or replace in the Find what text box
- ☐ Type the replacement text you want in the Replace with text box, then click Replace to replace current instance, **Replace All** to replace every instance, or **Find Next** to select the next instance
- ☐ Click **Close** in the Find and Replace dialog box

Excel

Keyboard Method

☐ Press **[Ctrl][H]** to open the Replace tab in the Find and Replace dialog box
☐ Follow the steps in the second through fourth bullets in the Replace Text Menu Method

Use Find and Replace to Change Cell Formats

Menu Method

☐ Click **Edit** on the menu bar, then click **Replace**
☐ In the Find and Replace dialog box, click **Options**
☐ Enter the text, formula, or value you wish to locate in the Find what text box, then click **Format**
☐ In the Find Format dialog box, select the appropriate options, then click **OK**
☐ Enter the replacement text, formula, or value you want in the Replace with text box, then click **Format**
☐ In the Replace Format dialog box, select the appropriate options, then click **OK**
☐ In the Find and Replace dialog box, click **Find Next** and **Replace** to locate and replace each instance, or click **Find All** and **Replace All** to replace all instances, then click **Close**

Keyboard Method

☐ Press **[Ctrl][H]**
☐ Follow the second through seventh bullets in the Use Find and Replace to Change Cell Formats Menu Method above

Go to a Specific Cell

Menu Method

☐ Click **Edit** on the menu bar, then click **Go To**
☐ In the Go To dialog box, select any text in the Reference text box, then type the appropriate cell reference
☐ Click **OK**

Keyboard Method

☐ Press **[Ctrl][G]**
☐ Follow the second and third bullet in the Go to a Specific Cell Menu Method above

---

LOCATE, SELECT, AND INSERT SUPPORTING INFORMATION

Use the Research Tool

Menu Method

☐ Click **Tools** on the menu bar, then click **Research**
☐ Type keywords about your chosen topic in the Search for text box, click the **Reference Books list arrow**, click a reference, then click the **Start searching button** →
☐ View the research results in the Research task pane

Button Method

☐ Click the **Research button** 🔍 on the Standard toolbar

☐ Follow the second and third bullets in the Use the Research Tool Menu Method

Keyboard Method

☐ Press and hold **[Alt]**, then click a cell in the open worksheet that contains information you want to research

☐ View the research results in the Research task pane

INSERT, POSITION, AND SIZE GRAPHICS

Create Graphics

Button Method

☐ Click the appropriate button on the Drawing toolbar, using Table EX-5 below as a reference, then draw the graphic using ✛.

Table EX-5 Drawing Toolbar Buttons

Button	Button Name	Use to
AutoShapes ▾	AutoShapes	Insert ready-made shapes such as stars, hearts, and callouts
＼	Line	Draw straight lines
↘	Arrow	Create arrows
▭	Rectangle	Create rectangles; can also use to create squares by pressing and holding [Shift] while dragging
◯	Oval	Create ovals; can also use to create circles by pressing and holding [Shift] while dragging
▣	Text Box	Create a box outside of a worksheet cell where you can insert a text memo
◈	Insert WordArt	Create a text object using the WordArt Gallery that you can resize and format like a graphic

Insert Graphics

Menu Method

☐ Click **Insert** on the menu bar, point to **Picture**, then click an appropriate option, using table EX-6 as a reference

Button Method

☐ Click the appropriate button on the Drawing toolbar, using Table EX-6 as a reference

Table EX-6 Inserting Graphics Using Toolbar Buttons and Insert Menu
Commands

Toolbar button	Toolbar button name	Picture submenu option	Next step
🖼	Insert Clip Art	Clip Art	Use the Clip Art task pane to search for graphics using key-words and specifying media, then click a graphic to insert it
🖼	Insert Picture From File	From File	In the Insert Picture dialog box, navigate to the drive and folder where the graphic is located, click the graphic, then click Insert
		From Scanner or Camera	Follow the steps in the Wizard
AutoShapes ▾	AutoShapes	AutoShapes	Point to a category, then click a shape
🔺	Insert WordArt	WordArt	Click a style, click OK, specify the text you want, specify the font and font size, then click OK
🔳	Insert Diagram or Organization Chart	Organization Chart	Choose a diagram type in the Diagram Gallery if necessary, then use the Organization Chart toolbar to modify the organization chart

Modify Graphics

Menu Method

□ Select the graphic (in the following steps, [Object] refers to the object you are formatting, such as Picture, Diagram, or AutoShape)
□ Click **Format** on the menu bar, then click **[Object]**, or right-click, then click **Format [Object]** on the shortcut menu
□ In the Format [Object] dialog box, select the appropriate options, then click **OK**

Mouse Method

□ Double-click the graphic
□ In the Format [Object] dialog box, select the appropriate options, then click **OK**

Position Graphics

Mouse Method

☐ Select the graphic
☐ Move the pointer over the graphic until it changes to ⁺↖
☐ Press and hold the left mouse button, drag the graphic to a new location, then release the mouse button

Resize a Graphic

Mouse Method

☐ Select the graphic
☐ Move the pointer over any sizing handle on the graphic until it changes to the appropriate pointer, using Table EX-7 below as a reference
☐ Drag the sizing handle until the graphic is the size you want, then release the mouse button

Table EX-7 Resize Pointers

Pointer	Appears over	Used to
↗ or ↘	Corner sizing handles	Resize proportionally
↔	Side sizing handles	Resize horizontally
↕	Top or bottom sizing handles	Resize vertically

Excel

EXCEL SPECIALIST SKILL SET 2: ANALYZING DATA

FILTER LISTS USING AUTOFILTER

Menu Method
☐ Select a range of cells to define as a list, click **Data** on the menu bar, point to **List**, then click **Create List**
☐ In the Create List dialog box, specify the cell range for your list, then click **OK**
☐ Click the **AutoFilter list arrow** of any column, then click a filter on the list to display only the list items containing the filter value you specified

Keyboard Method
☐ Select a range of cells to define as a list, then press **[Ctrl][L]**
☐ Follow the second and third bullets in the Filter Lists Using AutoFilter Menu Method above

SORT LISTS

Menu Method
☐ Select a range of cells to define as a list, click **Data** on the menu bar, point to **List**, then click **Create List**
☐ In the Create List dialog box, specify the cell range for your list, then click **OK**
☐ Click the **AutoFilter list arrow** in the column heading of the column by which you want to sort the list, then click **Sort Ascending** or **Sort Descending** as appropriate

OR

☐ Click any cell in a range that is defined as a list
☐ Click **Data** on the menu bar, then click **Sort**
☐ In the Sort dialog box, click the **Sort by list arrow**, click the column by which you want to sort, click the **Ascending** or **Descending option button** as appropriate, then click **OK**

Button Method
☐ Follow the first and second bullets in the Sort Lists Menu Method above to define a range as a list
☐ Click a cell in the column by which you want to sort
☐ Click the **Sort Ascending** 🔼 or **Sort Descending** 🔽 button on the Standard toolbar

Excel

INSERT AND MODIFY FORMULAS

Create Formulas

Button Method

☐ Click the cell where you want the formula to appear

☐ Type **=** (equals sign) to indicate the beginning of a formula, then type the rest of the formula using values, operators, and cell references and using Table EX-8 as a reference

☐ Click the **Enter button** ☑ on the Formula bar to lock in the completed formula in the cell

Keyboard Method

☐ Follow the first and second bullets in the Create Formulas Button Method above

☐ Press **[Enter]** or **[Tab]**

Table EX-8 Arithmetic Formula Operators

Operation	Operator	Example
Addition	+	=A3+5 (the contents of cell A3, plus 5)
Subtraction or Negation	–	=C2-C5 (the contents of cell C2, minus the contents of cell C5)
Multiplication	*	=B10*25 (25 times the contents of cell B10)
Division	/	=B7/4 (the contents of cell B7, divided by 4)

Edit Formulas Using the Formula Bar

Button Method

☐ Click the cell containing the formula you want to edit, then click the **formula bar**

☐ Modify the formula in the formula bar

☐ Click the **Enter button** ☑ on the formula bar

Keyboard Method

☐ Follow the first and second bullets in the Edit Formulas Using the Formula Bar Button Method above

☐ Press **[Enter]** or **[Tab]**

Enter a Range in a Formula by Dragging

Keyboard Method

☐ Click the appropriate cell

☐ Type **=**, then start to type the formula

☐ To enter a range, type **(**, click the first cell in the range, press and hold the mouse button, drag to select the range, then release the mouse button

☐ Type **)**

☐ Press **[Enter]** or **[Tab]**

Excel

Use Relative References

Use Figure EX-2 as a reference for using relative and absolute references in formulas.

Keyboard Method

☐ Click the appropriate cell, click the **formula bar** then type **=**, or type **=** directly in the cell

☐ To insert a cell reference in the formula, type the cell address you want to reference in the formula bar or in the cell that contains the formula, or click the cell you want to reference

☐ To make the reference absolute, select the cell reference in the formula bar, then press **[F4]**

☐ Complete the formula using appropriate operators, values, and additional cell references, then click the **Enter button** ✓ on the formula bar

Figure EX-2

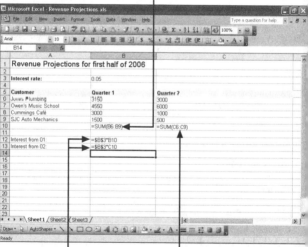

Relative cell reference

Absolute cell references

Formula copied from cell B10 to cell C10; relative cell reference has changed to reflect column C

Use Absolute References in Formulas

Keyboard Method

☐ Click the cell where you want to enter a formula, then enter the formula in the formula bar or type the formula directly in the cell

☐ Select the cell reference in the formula bar for the cell for which you want to make an absolute reference

☐ Press **[F4]**, then verify that the cell reference now reads **A1** (where A1 is the cell address)

☐ Press **[Enter]** or **[Tab]**

USE STATISTICAL, DATE AND TIME, FINANCIAL, AND LOGICAL FUNCTIONS

Add Functions to Formulas

Menu Method

☐ Click the cell where you want the formula to appear

☐ Type = (equals sign) to indicate the beginning of a formula, then start to type the formula

☐ At the appropriate point in the formula, click **Insert** on the menu bar, then click **Function**

☐ In the Insert Function dialog box, click the appropriate option(s), then click **OK**

☐ In the Function Arguments dialog box, specify the appropriate option(s)

☐ If arguments are required for the function, select the cell range in the worksheet to which to apply the function

☐ Click **OK**

Button Method

☐ Follow the first and second bullets in the Add Functions to Formulas Menu Method above

☐ At the appropriate point in the formula, click the **Insert Function button** f_x on the formula bar

☐ Follow the fourth through seventh bullets in the Add Functions to Formulas Menu Method above

Create a Formula Using a Function

Menu Method

☐ Click the appropriate cell

☐ Click **Insert** on the menu bar, then click **Function**

☐ In the Insert Function dialog box, select the appropriate function using Table EX-9 as a reference, then click **OK**

☐ In the Function Argument dialog box, specify the appropriate settings or the appropriate cells if necessary, then click **OK**

Button Method

☐ Click the appropriate cell

☐ Click the **Insert Function button** f_x on the formula bar

☐ Follow the third and fourth bullets in the Create a Formula Using a Function Menu Method above

Excel

Table EX-9 Examples of Commonly Used Excel Functions

Function	Example	Results
SUM	=SUM(A4:C4)	The total of the values in cells A4, B4, and C4
MIN	=MIN(B10,B13,B15)	The lowest value in the cells B10, B13, and B15
MAX	=MAX(C14,C18:C20)	The highest value in the cells C14, C18, C19, and C20
DATE	=DATE(A2,A3,A4)	The date as a sequential serial number (as in 2008, 4, 2), where cells A2, A3, and A4 have the year (2008), month (4), and day (2), respectively
NOW	=NOW()	The current date and time
PMT	=PMT(rate,nper,pv,fv,type)	Payment for a loan where **rate** is the interest rate, **Nper** is the number of payments, **Pv** is the principal on the loan, **Fv** is the cash balance after the last payment (if omitted, is assumed to be zero), **Type** is the number 0 (zero) or 1 and indicates when payments are due
IF	=IF(logical_test, value_if_true, value_if_false)	Performs the logical test, then returns a value if it is true or false, such as whether a budget is within its limits
AVERAGE	=AVERAGE(D2:D10)	The average of the values for the cell range D2 through D10

CREATE, MODIFY, AND POSITION DIAGRAMS AND CHARTS BASED ON WORKSHEET DATA

Create a Chart

Menu Method

☐ Select the cell range you want to use to create a chart
☐ Click **Insert** on the menu bar, then click **Chart**
☐ Navigate through the Chart Wizard, using Table EX-10 as a reference to select the chart type, make changes or accept the defaults as appropriate to create the chart, then click **Finish**

Button Method

☐ Select the range you want to use to create a chart
☐ Click the **Chart Wizard button** 📊 on the Standard toolbar
☐ Follow the third bullet in the Create a Chart Menu Method above

Table EX-10 Common Chart Types

Chart type	Looks like	Could be used to
Column		Show relative amounts for one or multiple values at different points in time (displays vertically)
Bar		Show relative amounts for one or multiple values at different points in time (displays horizontally)
Line		Show growth trends over time
Pie		Show proportions or percentages of parts to a whole

Change a Chart Type

Menu Method

☐ Select the chart
☐ Click **Chart** on the menu bar, then click **Chart Type**, or right-click, then click **Chart Type** on the shortcut menu
☐ In the Chart Type dialog box, make the appropriate selections, then click **OK**

Create a Diagram

Menu Method

☐ Click **Insert** on the menu bar, then click **Diagram**
☐ In the Insert Diagram dialog box, choose a diagram type using Table EX-11 as a reference, then click **OK**

Button Method

☐ Click the **Insert Diagram or Organizational Chart button** on the Drawing toolbar
☐ In the Insert Diagram dialog box, choose a diagram type using Table EX-11 as a reference, then click **OK**

Table EX-11 Common Diagram Types

Diagram type	Could be used to
Venn	Show overlapping areas between and among its parts
Cycle	Show a continuous process
Pyramid	Show a foundation-based relationship
Target	Show the steps that must be achieved in order to reach a goal
Radial	Show the correlations between elements in the diagram and a core element

Excel

Resize a Chart or Diagram

Mouse Method

☐ Select the chart or diagram
☐ Move the pointer over any sizing handle on the chart until it changes to the appropriate pointer, using Table EX-7 on page 101 as a reference
☐ Press and hold the left mouse button while you drag to resize the chart, then release the mouse button

Format Chart and Diagram Objects

Menu Method

☐ Click the appropriate object to select it (in the following steps, [Object] refers to the object you are formatting)
☐ Click **Format** on the menu bar, then click **[Object]**, or right-click the object, then click **Format [Object]** on the shortcut menu
☐ In the Format [Object] dialog box, select the appropriate options, then click **OK**

Button Method

Note: This method works only for chart objects.

☐ Click the appropriate chart object to select it (in the following steps, [Object] refers to the object you are formatting)
☐ Click the **Format [Object] button** 🖼 on the Chart toolbar
☐ In the Format [Object] dialog box, select the appropriate options, then click **OK**

Mouse Method

☐ Double-click the chart object you want to format
☐ In the Format [Object] dialog box, select the appropriate options, then click **OK**

Move a Chart or Diagram

Menu Method

Note: This method only works for charts.

☐ Click the chart area to select the chart
☐ Click **Chart** on the menu bar, then click **Location**
☐ In the Chart Location dialog box, select the appropriate options, then click **OK**

Mouse Method

☐ Select the chart or diagram
☐ Move the pointer over the Chart Area or Diagram Area section
☐ Press and hold the left mouse button, drag the chart to the appropriate location using ⁺↕⁺, then release the mouse button

Excel Specialist Skill Set 3: Formatting Data and Content

Apply and Modify Cell Formats

Apply Formats

Menu Method

☐ Select the cell(s) to format
☐ Click **Format** on the menu bar, then click **Cells**, or right-click, then click **Format Cells** on the shortcut menu
☐ In the Format Cells dialog box, select the appropriate tab, then make the appropriate formatting selections, using Table EX-12 as a reference

Table EX-12 Applying Formats Using the Format Cells Dialog Box

Tab	Options
Number	Change to Currency, Date, or other common number formats
Alignment	**Text alignment** (select vertical or horizontal alignment options between cell borders) **Text control** (text wrapping, shrink text to fit cell size, or merge cells) **Right-to-left** and **Orientation** (select text direction)
Font	**Font** (change font type) **Font style** (change to Regular, Bold, Italic, or Bold/Italic) **Size** (change font size) **Underline** (select text underlining options) **Color** (change font color) **Effects** (change to strikethrough, superscript, or subscript)
Border	Add borders to selected cell edges
Patterns	Fill cell(s) with color or patterns

Excel

Button Method

☐ Select the cell(s) to format
☐ Use the buttons on the Formatting toolbar to apply the appropriate format using Table EX-13 as a reference

Keyboard Method

☐ Select the cell(s) to format
☐ Press **[Ctrl][B]** to apply bold, press **[Ctrl][I]** to apply italics, or press **[Ctrl][U]** to apply underline format

Table EX-13 Applying Formats Using the Formatting toolbar

Button	Formatting	Effect
Arial ▾	Font	Changes font style
12 ▾	Font Size	Changes font size
B	Bold	**Bold**
I	Italic	*Italic*
<u>U</u>	Underline	<u>Underline</u>
≣	Align Left	Aligns to left cell edge
≣	Center	Aligns between left and right cell edges
≣	Align Right	Aligns to right cell edge
⊞	Merge and Center	Merges selected cells and centers text in merged cell
$	Currency Style	$1234.56
%	Percent Style	123456%
,	Comma Style	1,234.56
.0→.00	Increase Decimal	1234.560
.00→.0	Decrease Decimal	1234.6
⇥	Decrease Indent	Decreases indentation from left cell edge
⇤	Increase Indent	Indents from left cell edge
⊞ ▾	Borders	Adds borders to selected cell edges
◇ ▾	Fill Color	Fills cell(s) with color
A ▾	Font Color	Changes font color

Apply AutoFormats

Menu Method
☐ Select the cell(s) to format
☐ Click **Format** on the menu bar, then click **AutoFormat**
☐ In the AutoFormat dialog box, click the appropriate format, then click **O**

APPLY AND MODIFY CELL STYLES

Apply Cell Styles

Menu Method

☐ Select the cell(s) to format
☐ Click **Format** on the menu bar, then click **Style**
☐ In the Style dialog box, click the appropriate options, then click **OK**

Modify Cell Styles

Menu Method

☐ Click **Format** on the menu bar, then click **Style**
☐ In the Style dialog box click the **Style name list arrow**, select the style to modify, then click **Modify**
☐ Make the appropriate changes in the Format Cells dialog box, then click **OK**
☐ Click **OK** in the Style dialog box

MODIFY ROW AND COLUMN FORMATS

Modify Row Height

Menu Method

☐ Click the row heading to select the row or click any cell in the row
☐ Click **Format** on the menu bar, point to **Row**, then click **Height**
☐ In the Row Height dialog box, type the height you want, then click **OK**

Mouse Method

☐ Position the mouse pointer over the bottom edge of the **row heading**, until the pointer changes to ⁺
☐ Use ⁺ to drag downward to increase the row height to the desired size, or drag upward to decrease the row height

OR

☐ Position the mouse pointer over the bottom edge of the **row heading**, until the pointer changes to ⁺
☐ Double-click to automatically adjust the row height to the size of the cell contents

Modify Column Width

Menu Method

☐ Click the column heading to select the column or click any cell in the column
☐ Click **Format** on the menu bar, point to **Column**, then click **Width**
☐ In the Column Width dialog box, type the column width you want, then click **OK**

Mouse Method

☐ Move the mouse pointer over the right edge of the column heading until the pointer changes to ┿

☐ Drag the column heading divider to the right to increase the column width or to the left to decrease the column width

OR

☐ Move the mouse pointer over the divider on the right edge of the colum heading until the pointer changes to ┿

☐ Double-click the divider to automatically adjust the column width to the size of the text

Insert Rows and Columns

Menu Method

☐ Select the column to the right of where you want the new column to appear, or select the row below where you want the new row to appea

☐ Click **Insert** on the menu bar, then click **Rows** or **Columns**

OR

☐ Select the column to the right of where you want the new column to appear, or select the row below where you want the new row to appea

☐ Right-click, then click **Insert** on the shortcut menu

Keyboard Method

☐ Select the column to the right of where you want the new column to appear, or select the row below where you want the new row to appea

☐ Press **[Ctrl][Shift][+]**

☐ In the Insert dialog box click **Entire row** or **Entire column**, then click **OK**

Delete Rows and Columns

Menu Method

☐ Select the row(s) or column(s) to delete

☐ Click **Edit** on the menu bar, then click **Delete**

OR

☐ Select the column or row to delete

☐ Right-click, then click **Delete** on the shortcut menu

Hide Rows and Columns

Menu Method

☐ Click any cell in the row or column to hide

☐ Click **Format** on the menu bar, then point to **Column** or **Row**

☐ Click **Hide**

OR

☐ Select the row or column to hide

☐ Right-click, then click **Hide** on the shortcut menu

Mouse Method

☐ Position ↕ on the bottom edge of the row heading or position ↔ on the right edge of the column heading for the row or column you want to hide
☐ Drag ↕ up until the ScreenTip measurement displays Height: 0.00 or drag ↔ to the left until the ScreenTip displays Width: 0.00

edisplay Rows and Columns

Menu Method

☐ Select both of the rows or columns on either side of the hidden row or column, or select any two cells on both sides of the hidden row or column
☐ Click **Format** on the menu bar, point to **Column** or **Row**, then click **Unhide**

OR

☐ Select both of the rows or columns on either side of the hidden row or column, or select any two cells on both sides of the hidden row or column
☐ Right-click, then click **Unhide** on the shortcut menu

Mouse Method

☐ Select both of the rows or columns on either side of the hidden row or column, or select any two cells on both sides of the hidden row or column
☐ Position ↕ on the row heading for the row you want to display or position ↔ on the column heading for the column you want to redisplay
☐ Drag ↕ down to redisplay the row or drag ↔ to the right to redisplay the column

odify Alignment

Menu Method

☐ Click the cell(s) to align
☐ Click **Format** on the menu bar, then click **Cells**, or right-click, then click **Format Cells** on the shortcut menu
☐ In the Format Cells dialog box, click the **Alignment tab**
☐ Under Text alignment, click the **Horizontal list arrow** or the **Vertical list arrow**, click the appropriate alignment, then click **OK**

Button Method

☐ Select the cell(s) to align
☐ Click the appropriate alignment button on the Formatting toolbar using Table EX-14 as a reference

Excel

Table EX-14 Alignment Buttons on the Formatting Toolbar

Button	Button Name
	Align Left
	Center
	Align Right
	Decrease Indent
	Increase Indent

Keyboard Method

☐ Select the cell(s) to align
☐ Press **[Ctrl][1]**
☐ Follow the third and fourth bullets in the Modify Alignment Menu
  Method

FORMAT WORKSHEETS

Shading Worksheet Tabs

Menu Method

☐ Click **Format** on the menu bar, point to **Sheet**, then click **Tab Color**
☐ In the Format Tab Color dialog box, click the color you want, then
  click **OK**

OR

☐ Right-click the **sheet tab**
☐ Click **Tab Color** on the shortcut menu
☐ In the Format Tab Color dialog box, click the color you want, then
  click **OK**

Name Worksheets

Menu Method

☐ Click **Format** on the menu bar, point to **Sheet**, then click **Rename** t
  highlight the name of the active sheet
☐ Type the new name, then press **[Enter]** or click anywhere in the shee

OR

☐ Right-click the sheet tab, then click **Rename** on the shortcut menu to
  highlight the existing sheet name
☐ Type the new name, then press **[Enter]** or click anywhere in the shee

Mouse Method

☐ Double-click the **sheet tab**
☐ Type the new name, then press **[Enter]** or click anywhere in the shee

sert a Graphic as a Worksheet Background

Menu Method

☐ Click **Format** on the menu bar, point to **Sheet**, then click **Background**

☐ In the Sheet Background dialog box, navigate to the drive and folder where the graphic is located, click the file you want to insert as a worksheet background, then click **Insert**

rmat Worksheets with Borders and Fills

Menu Method

☐ Select the cell(s) to format

☐ Click **Format** on the menu bar, then click **Cells**, or right-click, then click **Format Cells**

☐ In the Format Cells dialog box, click the **Border tab** or the **Patterns tab**

☐ Make the appropriate selections, then click **OK**

Button Method

☐ Select the cell(s) to format

☐ Click the **Borders list arrow** [icon] on the Formatting toolbar, then click the appropriate border option

☐ Click the **Fill Color list arrow** [icon] on the Formatting toolbar, click the appropriate color, then click outside the selected cell(s)

Keyboard Method

☐ Select the cell(s) to format

☐ Press **[Ctrl][1]**

☐ Follow the third and fourth bullets in the Format Worksheets with Borders and Fills Menu Method above

de Worksheets

Menu Method

☐ Click any cell in the worksheet to hide

☐ Click **Format** on the menu bar, point to **Sheet**, then click **Hide**

display Hidden Worksheets

Menu Method

☐ Click **Format** on the menu bar, point to **Sheet**, then click **Unhide**

☐ In the Unhide dialog box, click the sheet you want to unhide, then click **OK**

Excel

EXCEL SPECIALIST SKILL SET 4: COLLABORATING

INSERT, VIEW, AND EDIT COMMENTS

Attach Cell Comments

Menu Method

- ☐ Select the cell to which you want to attach a comment
- ☐ Click **Insert** on the menu bar, then click **Comment**, or right-click, then click **Insert Comment** on the shortcut menu
- ☐ Type the appropriate text in the comment box
- ☐ Click outside the comment box

Button Method

- ☐ Click the **New Comment button** 🖼 on the Reviewing toolbar
- ☐ Follow the third and fourth bullets in the Attach Cell Comments Menu Method above

Edit Cell Comments

Menu Method

- ☐ Move the pointer over the cell marked with a comment (a red triangle in the upper-right corner of the cell)
- ☐ Right-click, then click **Edit Comment** on the shortcut menu
- ☐ Make your modifications
- ☐ Click outside the comment box

Button Method

- ☐ Click the cell marked with a comment (a red triangle in the upper-right corner of the cell)
- ☐ Click the **Edit Comment button** 🖼 on the Reviewing toolbar
- ☐ Follow the third and fourth bullets in the Edit Cell Comments Menu Method above

Excel

EXCEL SPECIALIST SKILL SET 5: MANAGING WORKBOOKS

CREATE NEW WORKBOOKS FROM TEMPLATES

Find a Template Online

Menu Method

- [ ] Click **File** on the menu bar, then click **New**
- [ ] In the New Workbook task pane, type a keyword in the Search online for text box, click **Go**, then click a template in the Search Results task pane
- [ ] In the Template Preview dialog box, click Previous and Next to preview the available templates, choose the template you want, then click Download to open a new workbook with the template applied
- [ ] Click **No** if asked for help with the template

Use a Template from Your Computer

Menu Method

- [ ] Click **File** on the menu bar, then click **New**
- [ ] In the New Workbook task pane, click **On my computer**
- [ ] In the Templates dialog box, click the Spreadsheet Solutions tab, click the template you want, then click **OK**

INSERT, DELETE, AND MOVE CELLS

Insert Cells

Menu Method

- [ ] Click where you want to insert cells
- [ ] Click **Insert** on the menu bar, then click **Cells**
- [ ] In the Insert dialog box, select the appropriate option button
- [ ] Click **OK**

OR

- [ ] Right-click where you want to insert cells
- [ ] Click **Insert** on the shortcut menu
- [ ] In the Insert dialog box, select the appropriate option button, then click **OK**

Delete Cells

Menu Method

- [ ] Click the cell(s), row(s), or column(s) to delete
- [ ] Click **Edit** on the menu bar, then click **Delete**, or right-click, then click **Delete** on the shortcut menu
- [ ] If the Delete dialog box opens, select the appropriate option button, then click **OK**

Excel

Cut and Paste Cells

Menu Method

- ☐ Select the cell(s) to cut
- ☐ Click **Edit** on the menu bar, then click **Cut**, or right-click, then click **Cut** on the shortcut menu
- ☐ Click where you want to paste the cell(s)
- ☐ Click **Edit** on the menu bar, then click **Paste**

Button Method

- ☐ Select the cell(s) to cut
- ☐ Click the **Cut button** 🔳 on the Standard toolbar
- ☐ Click where you want to paste the text
- ☐ Click the **Paste button** 🔳 on the Standard toolbar

Keyboard Method

- ☐ Select the cell(s) to cut
- ☐ Press **[Ctrl][X]**
- ☐ Click where you want to paste the cell(s)
- ☐ Press **[Ctrl][V]**

Copy and Paste Cell(s)

Menu Method

- ☐ Select the cell(s) to copy
- ☐ Click **Edit** on the menu bar, click **Copy**, or right-click, then click **Copy** on the shortcut menu
- ☐ Click where you want to paste the cell(s)
- ☐ Click **Edit** on the menu bar, then click **Paste**

Button Method

- ☐ Select the cell(s) to copy
- ☐ Click the **Copy button** 🔳 on the Standard toolbar
- ☐ Click where you want to paste the cell(s)
- ☐ Click the **Paste button** 🔳 on the Standard toolbar

Keyboard Method

- ☐ Select the cell(s) to copy
- ☐ Press **[Ctrl][C]**
- ☐ Click where you want to paste the cell(s)
- ☐ Press **[Ctrl][V]**

Copy Cells Without Using the Clipboard

Mouse Method

- ☐ Select the cell(s) to copy, then press and hold the **[Ctrl] key**
- ☐ Place the mouse pointer over the edge of the selected range until it becomes ⬆
- ☐ Drag the selected range to the appropriate location, then release the mouse button

Move Cells Without Using the Clipboard

Mouse Method

☐ Select the cell(s) to move
☐ Place the mouse pointer over any edge of the selected range until it becomes ↖
☐ Drag the range to the appropriate location, then release the mouse button

Use Paste Special

Menu Method

☐ Select the cell(s) or object you want to copy
☐ Click **Edit** on the menu bar, then click **Copy**
☐ Click the cell where you want to paste the cut or copied cells, click **Edit** on the menu bar, then click **Paste Special**
☐ In the Paste Special dialog box, click the appropriate options, then click **OK**

CREATE AND MODIFY HYPERLINKS

Insert Hyperlinks

Menu Method

☐ Select the appropriate cell, range, chart, or graphic
☐ Click **Insert** on the menu bar, then click **Hyperlink** or right-click, then click **Hyperlink** on the shortcut menu
☐ In the Insert Hyperlink dialog box, specify the appropriate options using Table EX-15 as a reference, then click **OK**

Button Method

☐ Select the appropriate cell, range, chart, or graphic
☐ Click the **Insert Hyperlink button** 🔗 on the Standard toolbar
☐ In the Insert Hyperlink dialog box, specify the appropriate options using Table EX-15 as a reference, then click **OK**

Keyboard Method

☐ Select the appropriate cell, range, chart, or graphic
☐ Press **[Ctrl][K]**
☐ In the Insert Hyperlink dialog box, specify the appropriate options using Table EX-15 as a reference, then click **OK**

Excel

Table EX-15 Inserting Hyperlinks Using the Insert Hyperlink Dialog Box

To link to another place in the document	To link to another document	To link to a new document	To link to a Web page	To add an e-mail link
Click Place in This Document, select a location in the select a place in this document list, then click OK	Click Existing File or Web Page, click the Look in list arrow, navigate to the appropriate drive and folder, click the filename in the list, then click OK	Click Create New Document, name the document and verify the drive and folder, choose to edit it now or later, then click OK	(Note: Make sure you are connected to the Internet.) Click Existing File or Web Page, click the Address text box, type the URL, then click OK	Click E-mail Address, type the address and any other text to display, then click OK

Edit Hyperlinks

Menu Method

☐ Point to the **hyperlink** until the pointer becomes 👆
☐ Right-click the **hyperlink**, then click **Edit Hyperlink** on the shortcut menu
☐ In the Edit Hyperlink dialog box, make the modifications, then click **OK**

ORGANIZE WORKSHEETS

Insert a New Worksheet into a Workbook

Menu Method

☐ Click **Insert** on the menu bar, then click **Worksheet**

OR

☐ Right-click the worksheet tab to the right of where you want the new one to appear
☐ Click **Insert** on the shortcut menu
☐ In the Insert dialog box, click the **General tab** if necessary
☐ Click the **Worksheet icon**, if necessary, then click **OK**

Delete a Worksheet from a Workbook

Menu Method

☐ Click the **sheet tab** of the worksheet to delete
☐ Click **Edit** on the menu bar, then click **Delete Sheet**, or right-click the sheet tab, then click **Delete** on the shortcut menu
☐ Click **Delete** in the message box if necessary

Move Worksheets Within a Workbook or to Another Workbook

Menu Method

☐ Click **Edit** on the menu bar, then click **Move or Copy Sheet**, or right-click the **sheet tab** of the worksheet to move, then click **Move or Copy** on the shortcut menu

☐ In the Move or Copy dialog box, make the appropriate selections, then click **OK**

Mouse Method

☐ Position the pointer over the tab to move

☐ Use ☒ to drag the tab to the appropriate location in the workbook

☐ Release the mouse button

PREVIEW DATA IN OTHER VIEWS

Preview Printed Worksheets

Menu Method

☐ Click **File** on the menu bar, then click **Print Preview**

☐ Click the **Close button** on the Print Preview window

Button Method

☐ Click the **Print Preview button** 🔍 on the Standard toolbar

☐ Click the **Close button** on the Page Preview window

Preview Worksheets as Web Pages

Menu Method

☐ Click **File** on the menu bar, then click **Web Page Preview**

☐ Click the **Close button** ☒ on the Web browser window

Preview Page Breaks

Menu Method

☐ Click **View** on the menu bar, then click **Page Break Preview**

☐ Use the mouse pointer to drag the blue lines to increase or decrease the print area

CUSTOMIZE WINDOW LAYOUT

Split Workbooks

Menu Method

☐ Click **Window** on the menu bar, then click **Split**

Excel

Arrange Workbooks

Menu Method

- ☐ Maximize all of the workbooks you want to view
- ☐ Click **Window** on the menu bar, then click **Arrange**
- ☐ Choose the appropriate options in the Arrange Windows dialog box, then click **OK**

Freeze Workbooks

Menu Method

- ☐ Select the cell below and to the right of where you want to freeze
- ☐ Click **Window** on the menu bar, then click **Freeze Panes**

Unfreeze Workbooks

Menu Method

- ☐ Click **Window** on the menu bar, then click **Unfreeze Panes**

Hide Worksheets

Menu Method

- ☐ Click any cell in the worksheet you want to hide
- ☐ Click **Format** on the menu bar, then point to **Sheet**
- ☐ Click **Hide** on the submenu

Redisplay Hidden Worksheets

Menu Method

- ☐ Click **Format** on the menu bar, point to **Sheet**, then click **Unhide**
- ☐ Click the sheet to unhide in the Unhide dialog box, then click **OK**

SETUP PAGES FOR PRINTING

Set Print Areas

Menu Method

- ☐ Select the cell(s) that make up the print area
- ☐ Click **File** on the menu bar, point to **Print Area**, click **Set Print Area**, then click outside the selected cell(s)

Set Non-Adjacent Print Areas

Menu Method

- ☐ Select the first cell or range to print
- ☐ Click **File** on the menu bar, point to **Print Area**, click **Set Print Area**, then click outside the selected cell(s)
- ☐ Click **View** on the menu bar, then click **Page Break Preview**
- ☐ To specify to print additional ranges, select the new range in the Page Break Preview window, right-click, then click **Add to Print Area** from the shortcut menu

Change Worksheet Orientation

Menu Method

☐ Click **File** on the menu bar, then click **Page Setup**
☐ In the Page Setup dialog box, click the **Page tab**, if necessary
☐ Under Orientation, click the appropriate option button, then click **OK**

Add Headers and Footers to Worksheets

Menu Method

☐ Click **View** on the menu bar, then click **Header and Footer**
☐ In the Page Setup dialog box, click the **Header** or **Footer list arrow** to select predefined headers or footers, or click **Custom Header** or **Custom Footer** to create your own header or footer, make the appropriate selections for the header or footer in the Header or Footer dialog box, then click **OK** to close the Header or Footer dialog box
☐ Click **OK** to close the Page Setup dialog box

Set Page Options for Printing

Menu Method

☐ Click **File** on the menu bar, then click **Page Setup**
☐ In the Page Setup dialog box, make the appropriate selections using Table EX-16 as a reference, then click **OK**

Table EX-16 Page Setup Dialog Box Tabs

Tab	Options
Page	**Page orientation** (landscape or portrait) **Scaling** (adjust to print to a certain percentage or page determination) **Paper size** (select letter, legal, or other size) **Print quality** (select draft, high, medium, or low quality)
Margins	**Margins** (adjust top, bottom, left, right, header, or footer margins) **Center on page** (horizontal or vertical centering)
Header/Footer	Select preset headers or footers or create custom headers and footers
Sheet	**Print area** (select ranges or objects to print) **Print titles** (select rows or columns to repeat on each page) **Print** (select printing options, such as gridlines, column heads, and more) **Page order** (select whether to print multi-page worksheets going from left-to-right or top-to-bottom)

Excel

PRINT DATA

Print Selected Cells

Menu Method

☐ Select the cell(s) to print
☐ Click **File** on the menu bar, point to **Print Area**, click **Set Print Area**, then click outside the selected cell(s)
☐ Click the **Print Preview button** 🔍 on the Standard toolbar, click **Print** in the Print Preview window, then click **OK** in the Print dialog box

Print Non-Adjacent Selections of Worksheets in a Workbook

Menu Method

☐ Select the ranges to print by pressing and holding down **[Ctrl]** while you drag to select
☐ Click **File** on the menu bar, then click **Print**
☐ Under the Print what section, click the **Selection option button** to select it, then click **Preview**
☐ In the Print Preview window, click **Next** on the Print Preview toolbar if necessary to view the next page
☐ Click **Print** on the Print Preview toolbar, then click **OK**

OR

☐ Select the first range to print
☐ Click **File** on the menu bar, point to **Print Area**, click **Set Print Area**, then click outside the selected cell(s)
☐ Click **View** on the menu bar, then click **Page Break Preview**
☐ To specify to print additional ranges, select the new range in the Page Break Preview window, right-click, then click **Add to Print Area** from the shortcut menu
☐ Click **File** on the menu bar, then click **Print**
☐ Click **OK** in the Print dialog box

Print Worksheets, Workbooks, or Selections

Menu Method

☐ Select the cell(s) or worksheet(s) to print if printing a selection
☐ Click **File** on the menu bar, then click **Print**
☐ In the Print dialog box, click the appropriate option button under the Print what section, then click **OK**

Button Method

☐ To print a worksheet using the default settings click the **Print button** 🖨 on the Standard toolbar

Keyboard Method

☐ Select the cell(s) or worksheet(s) to print if printing a selection
☐ Press **[Ctrl][P]**
☐ In the Print dialog box, click the appropriate option button under the Print what section, then click **OK**

ORGANIZE WORKBOOKS USING FILE FOLDERS

Open a Workbook from a Folder Created for Workbook Storage

Menu Method
- ☐ Click **File** on the menu bar, then click **Open**
- ☐ In the Open dialog box, click the **Look in list arrow**
- ☐ Navigate to the appropriate drive and folder
- ☐ Click the file to open, then click **Open**

Button Method
- ☐ Click the **Open button** 📄 on the Standard toolbar
- ☐ Follow the second through fourth bullets in the Open a Workbook from a Folder Created for Workbook Storage Menu Method above

Keyboard Method
- ☐ Press **[Ctrl][O]**
- ☐ Follow the second through fourth bullets in the Open a Workbook from a Folder Created for Workbook Storage Menu Method above

Locate and Open Existing Workbooks

Menu Method
- ☐ Click **File** on the menu bar, then click **Open**
- ☐ In the Open dialog box, click the **Look in list arrow**
- ☐ Navigate to the appropriate drive and folder
- ☐ Click the file to open, then click **Open**

Button Method
- ☐ Click the **Open button** 📄 on the Standard toolbar
- ☐ Follow the second through fourth bullets in the Locate and Open Existing Workbooks Menu Method above

Keyboard Method
- ☐ Press **[Ctrl][O]**
- ☐ Follow the second through fourth bullets in the Locate and Open Existing Workbooks Menu Method above

Create Folders for Saving Workbooks

Menu Method
- ☐ Click **File** on the menu bar, then click **Save As**
- ☐ In the Save As dialog box, click the **Save in list arrow**, then navigate to the drive and folder where you want to create a new folder
- ☐ Click the **Create New Folder button** 📁
- ☐ In the New Folder dialog box, type the name of the new folder, then click **OK**
- ☐ Type the name of the file in the File name text box, then click **Save**

Rename Folders

Menu Method

☐ Click **File** on the menu bar, then click **Save As**
☐ In the Save As dialog box, click the **Save in list arrow**, then navigate to the drive and folder that contains the folder you want to rename
☐ Right-click the folder you wish to rename, then click **Rename**
☐ With the folder name selected, type the new name, then press **[Enter]**

SAVE DATA IN APPROPRIATE FORMATS FOR DIFFERENT USES

Convert Workbooks to Different File Formats

Menu Method

☐ Click **File** on the menu bar, then click **Save As** to open the Save As dialog box
☐ In the File name text box, change the filename, click the **Save as type list arrow**, then select the appropriate file format
☐ Click **Save**
☐ If necessary, click **Yes** in the message box warning that some features may be lost

Create Web Pages

Menu Method

☐ Select the cells, click **File** on the menu bar, then click **Save as Web Page**
☐ In the Save As dialog box, click the appropriate option button using Table EX-17 below as a reference, type the file name, then click **Save**

Table EX-17 Creating Web Pages from Cells, Worksheets, and Workbooks

Selection	Option button
From selected cells	Selection: [range]
From a Worksheet	Selection: Sheet
From a Workbook	Entire Workbook

Microsoft Office Excel 2003
EXPERT Exam Reference

Skill Sets:
1. Organizing and analyzing data
2. Formatting data and content
3. Collaborating
4. Managing data and workbooks
5. Customizing Excel

Excel Expert Skill Set 1: Organizing and Analyzing Data

Use Subtotals

Subtotal a List

Menu Method

- ☐ Sort the list as appropriate so the rows you want to subtotal are grouped together and the columns are labeled
- ☐ Click any cell in the range that you want to subtotal
- ☐ Click **Data** on the menu bar, then click **Subtotals**
- ☐ In the Subtotal dialog box, click the **At each change in list arrow**, then click the **column header** for the grouped records you want to subtotal
- ☐ Click the **Use function list arrow**, then click the appropriate function
- ☐ In the Add subtotal to list box, click the appropriate check box
- ☐ Make any other appropriate selections, then click **OK**

Define and Apply Advanced Filters

Create an Advanced Filter

Menu Method

- ☐ Insert at least three blank rows above the list that can be used as a criteria range
- ☐ In the first blank row, copy the column labels from the list
- ☐ In the second blank row, enter the filter criteria, using Table EX-18 as a reference, then leave at least one blank row above the list
- ☐ Click anywhere in the list range, click **Data** on the menu bar, point to **Filter**, then click **Advanced Filter**
- ☐ In the Advanced Filter dialog box, click the **Filter the list, in-place option button**, to filter the list by hiding rows that don't match your criteria

☐ To filter the list by copying rows that match your criteria to another area of the worksheet, click the **Copy to another location option button**, click the **Copy to text box**, then click the upper-left cell of the area where you want to paste the rows

☐ In the **List range text box**, verify that the range reference is correct

☐ Click the **Criteria range text box**, then select the rows in the worksheet that contain the criteria labels and filter criteria (*Note*: these will be the first and second of the three rows you inserted)

☐ Click **OK**

Table EX-18 Filter Criteria Operands

Use	To find
Text	All items that begin with that text; for instance, Ma finds "Mary" and "Margaret"
="=text"	To find only the specified text
? (question mark)	Any single character; for example, jo?s finds "jons" and "joes"
* (asterisk)	Any number of characters; for example, *ary finds "Canary" and "Sanctuary"
~ (tilde) followed by ?, *, or ~	A question mark, asterisk, or tilde; for example, Guest~? finds "Guest?", and Taxi~* finds "Taxi*"
<*number*	All numbers less than that number; for example, <7 finds all numbers less than 7
<=*number*	All numbers less than or equal to that number; for example, <10 finds all numbers less than 10, and also all instances of 10
>*number*	All numbers greater than that number; for example, <15 finds all numbers greater than 15
>=*number*	All numbers greater than or equal to that number; for example, >=100 finds all numbers greater than 100, and also all instances of 100
<> *number*	All numbers, except for that number

Create a Custom Filter

Menu Method

☐ Click any cell in the range you want to filter

☐ Click **Data** on the menu bar, point to **Filter**, then click **AutoFilter**

☐ Click the **AutoFilter list arrow** for the column to which you want to apply a filter, then click **(Custom)**

☐ In the Custom AutoFilter dialog box, specify the appropriate filter options, then click **OK**

GROUP AND OUTLINE DATA

Add Group and Outline Criteria to Ranges

Menu Method

☐ Sort the range if necessary, then click anywhere in the range
☐ Click **Data** on the menu bar, point to **Group and Outline**, then click **Auto Outline**
☐ To hide the outline levels and details use the **Hide Detail button** 🔳 on the PivotTable toolbar or click **Data** on the menu bar, point to **Group and Outline**, then click **Hide Detail**
☐ To show the outline levels and details use the **Show Detail button** 🔳 on the PivotTable toolbar or click **Data** on the menu bar, point to **Group and Outline**, then click **Show Detail**

USE DATA VALIDATION

Validate Entered Data

Menu Method

☐ Select the range you want to validate
☐ Click **Data** on the menu bar, then click **Validation**
☐ In the Data Validation dialog box, click the appropriate options using Table EX-19 as a reference, then click **OK**

Table EX-19 Data Validation Dialog Box Tabs

Tab	Use to
Settings	Set validation criteria for input data
Input Message	Set a message that will appear when a user selects a cell in the range
Error Alert	Set a message that will appear when a user enters data that does not meet validation criteria

ADD, SHOW, CLOSE, EDIT, MERGE, AND SUMMARIZE SCENARIOS

Managing Scenarios

Menu Method

☐ Click the appropriate cell
☐ Click **Tools** on the menu bar, then click **Scenarios**
☐ In the Scenario Manager dialog box, click **Add**
☐ In the Add Scenario dialog box, click the **Scenario name text box**, then type the scenario name
☐ Click the **Changing cells text box**, select the appropriate cell or range in the worksheet, click other appropriate options, then click **OK**

☐ In the Scenario Values dialog box, enter appropriate values for the cells to change
☐ If necessary, click **Add**, then repeat the fourth through sixth bullets here to add another scenario
☐ Click **OK**
☐ In the Scenario Manager dialog box, click the appropriate scenario, click **Show**, then click **Close**

Editing Scenarios

Menu Method

☐ Click any cell in a worksheet that contains scenarios
☐ Click **Tools** on the menu bar, then click **Scenarios**
☐ In the Scenario Manager dialog box, click the scenario to modify, then click **Edit**
☐ In the Edit Scenario dialog box, make any modifications, then click **OK**
☐ In the Scenario Values dialog box, edit the specified values as appropriate, then click **OK**
☐ If necessary, click **Edit** again, then repeat the fourth through sixth bullets here to edit another scenario
☐ Click **OK**
☐ In the Scenario Manager dialog box, click the appropriate scenario, click **Show**, then click **Close**

Merging Scenarios

Menu Method

☐ Click **Tools** on the menu bar, then click **Scenarios**
☐ In the Scenario Manager dialog box, click **Merge**
☐ In the Merge Scenario dialog box, specify the workbook and worksheet containing the scenarios you want to merge
☐ Click **OK**
☐ In the Scenario Manager dialog box, click **Close**

Summarizing Scenarios

Menu Method

☐ Click **Tools** on the menu bar, then click **Scenarios**
☐ In the Scenario Manager dialog box, click **Summary**
☐ In the Scenario Summary dialog box, click the **Scenario summary option button**, then choose the result cells if necessary
☐ Click **OK**

PERFORM DATA ANALYSIS USING AUTOMATED TOOLS

Project Values Using Analysis ToolPak

Note: In order to use the Analysis ToolPak, you must install the Data Analysis add-in. Click Tools on the menu bar, then click Add-Ins to start the installation.

Menu Method

☐ Click **Tools** on the menu bar, then click **Data Analysis**
☐ In the Data Analysis dialog box, click the appropriate tool, then click **OK**
☐ In the dialog box, specify the appropriate input and output options, then click **OK**

Create a Trendline

Menu Method

☐ Click any the data series for which you want to create a trendline
☐ Click **Chart** on the menu bar, then click **Add Trendline**
☐ In the Add Trendline dialog box, specify the appropriate options, then click **OK**

Use the Solver Add-In

Note: In order to use the Solver, you must install the Solver Add-in. Click Tools on the menu bar, then click Add-Ins to start the installation.

Menu Method

☐ Click **Tools** on the menu bar, then click **Solver**
☐ In the Solver Parameters dialog box, specify an appropriate target cell, click the appropriate equal to option button, specify the cells to change to achieve the desired result, set constraints and other parameters, then click **Solve**
☐ View the results in the Solver Results dialog box, then click **OK**

USE PIVOTTABLE AND PIVOTCHART REPORTS

Create a PivotTable or PivotChart Report

Menu Method

☐ Define a range as a list, then click anywhere in the list
☐ Click **Data** on the menu bar, then click **PivotTable and PivotChart Report**
☐ Navigate through the PivotTable and PivotChart Wizard, making changes or accepting the defaults as appropriate to create the PivotTable, then click **Finish**
☐ Drag each field from the PivotTable Field List to the appropriate area on the PivotTable, or click the field in the PivotTable Field List, click the **Add To list arrow**, click the appropriate area, then click **Add To**

Excel

Modify a PivotTable Report

Use Table EX-20 and Table EX-21 to make changes to a PivotTable Repo

Table EX-20 Modifying a PivotTable Report

Modification type	Steps
Add an item field	Click the Show Field List button 🔲 on the PivotTable toolbar if necessary, drag each field from the PivotTable Field List to the appropriate area on the PivotTable, or click the field in the PivotTable Field List, click the Add To list arrow, click the area, then click Add To
Rename an item	Click the item, type the new name, then press [Enter]
Formatting	See the activity "Format a PivotTable Report" on the next page

Table EX-21 Selected PivotTable Toolbar Buttons

Button	Menu	Use to
Format Report 📄	Click Format on the menu bar, then click Cells or AutoFormat, or right-click, then click Format Cells	Open the AutoFormat or Forma Cells dialog box to apply table and report formats
Chart Wizard 📊	Click Insert on the menu bar, then click Chart, or right-click the PivotTable, then click PivotChart	Create a PivotChart report from your PivotTable
Field Settings 🔲	Right-click the field, then click Field Settings	Change summary function of selected fields
Show Field List 🔲 or Hide Field List 🔲	Right-click the PivotTable, then click Show Field List or Hide Field List	Display or close the Field List window

Update a PivotTable Report

Menu Method

☐ Modify the report as appropriate
☐ Click **Data** on the menu bar, then click **Refresh Data**, or right-click the PivotTable, then click **Refresh Data**

Button Method

☐ Modify the report as appropriate
☐ Click the **Refresh Data button** 🔲 on the PivotTable toolbar

ormat a PivotTable Report

Menu Method

- [ ] Select the cells to format
- [ ] Click **Format** on the menu bar, then click **Cells**, or right-click, then click **Format Cells** on the shortcut menu
- [ ] In the Format Cells dialog box, select the appropriate options, then click **OK**

OR

- [ ] Click any cell in the PivotTable
- [ ] Click **Format** on the menu bar, then click **AutoFormat**
- [ ] In the AutoFormat dialog box, select the appropriate format, then click **OK**

Button Method

- [ ] Click any cell inside the PivotTable
- [ ] Click the **Format Report button** 🔲 on the PivotTable toolbar
- [ ] In the AutoFormat dialog box, select the appropriate format, then click **OK**

Keyboard Method

- [ ] Select the cell or range you want to format
- [ ] Press **[Ctrl] [1]**
- [ ] In the Format Cells dialog box, select the appropriate options, then click **OK**

reate a PivotChart Report from a PivotTable

Menu Method

- [ ] Click any cell in the PivotTable
- [ ] Click the **Chart Wizard button** 🔲 on the Standard toolbar
- [ ] Make any modifications to the chart using the buttons on the Chart toolbar

reate a PivotChart Report

Menu Method

- [ ] Click any cell in a range that is defined as a list
- [ ] Click **Data** on the menu bar, then click **PivotTable and PivotChart Report**
- [ ] In the first PivotTable and PivotChart Wizard dialog box, click the **PivotChart report (with PivotTable report) option button**
- [ ] Navigate through the rest of the PivotTable and PivotChart Wizard, making changes or accepting the defaults as appropriate to create the PivotChart Report, then click **Finish**
- [ ] Drag each field from the PivotTable Field List to the appropriate area, or click the field in the PivotTable Field List, click the **Add To list arrow**, select the area, then click **Add To**

Excel

Modify a PivotChart Report

Menu Method

☐ Click the appropriate chart object to select it (in the following steps, [Object] refers to the object you are formatting)

☐ Click **Format** on the menu bar, then click **Selected [Object]**, or right click the object, then click **Format [Object]**

☐ In the Format [Object] dialog box, select the appropriate options, then click **OK**

Button Method

☐ Click the appropriate chart object to select it (in the following steps, [Object] refers to the object you are formatting)

☐ Click the **Format [Object] button** 🖼 on the Chart toolbar

☐ In the Format [Object] dialog box, select the appropriate options, then click **OK**

Keyboard Method

☐ Click the appropriate chart object to select it, then Press **[Ctrl][1]**

☐ In the Format [Object] dialog box, select the appropriate options, then click **OK**

Mouse Method

☐ Double-click the chart object you want to format

☐ In the Format [Object] dialog box, select the appropriate options, then click **OK**

USE LOOKUP AND REFERENCE FUNCTIONS

Use VLOOKUP or HLOOKUP to Find Values in a List

Menu Method

☐ Click the cell where the formula will appear

☐ Click **Insert** on the menu bar, then click **Function**

☐ In the Insert Function dialog box, click the **Or select a category list arrow**, then click **All**

☐ Double-click **VLOOKUP** or **HLOOKUP** from the Select a function list box

☐ In the Function Arguments dialog box, select the appropriate options using Table EX-22 as a reference, then click **OK**

Menu Method

☐ Click the cell where the formula is to appear

☐ Click the **Insert Function button** 𝑓ₓ on the formula bar

☐ Follow the third through fifth bullets in the Using VLOOKUP or HLOOKUP to Find Values in a List Menu Method above

Table EX-22 VLOOKUP and HLOOKUP Function Arguments

Argument	Definition
Lookup_value	The value in the first column or row of the array; can be a value, a reference, or a text string
Table_array	The table of information in which data is looked up; use a reference to a range or range name. There are sorting requirements depending on the range_lookup value.
Col_index_num (VLOOKUP) OR Row_index_num (HLOOKUP)	The column or row number in table_array from which the matching value must be returned
Range_lookup (optional)	A logical value that specifies whether you want VLOOKUP to find an exact match or an approximate match. If range_lookup is TRUE, or if there is no value in the formula, the match is approximate. If FALSE is entered as the range_lookup, the match returned will be exact, or there will be an error if there is no exact value.

USE DATABASE FUNCTIONS

Create Database Functions

Menu Method

☐ Click **Tools** on the menu bar, point to **Macro**, then click **Visual Basic Editor**

☐ Click **Insert** on the menu bar, click **Module**, then create the function by typing the code

☐ Click **File** on the menu bar, then click **Close and Return to Microsoft Excel**

Edit Database Functions

Menu Method

☐ Click **Tools** on the menu bar, point to **Macro**, then click **Visual Basic Editor**

☐ Double-click the module name in the left pane, then edit the function code

☐ Click **File** on the menu bar, then click **Close and Return to Microsoft Excel**

Excel

TRACE FORMULA PRECEDENTS, DEPENDENTS, AND ERRORS

Trace Precedents

Menu Method

☐ Click the cell that contains the formula
☐ Click **Tools** on the menu bar, point to **Formula Auditing**, then click **Trace Precedents**
☐ Double-click the **blue arrow** to navigate between the cell containing the formula and the precedent cells

Button Method

☐ Click the cell that contains the formula
☐ Click the **Trace Precedents button** 🔛 on the Formula Auditing toolbar
☐ Double-click the **blue arrow** to navigate between the cell containing the formula and the precedent cells

Trace Dependents

Menu Method

☐ Click the cell that that is referenced in a formula
☐ Click **Tools** on the menu bar, point to **Formula Auditing**, then click **Trace Dependents**
☐ Double-click the **blue arrow** to navigate between the cells

Button Method

☐ Click the cell that is referenced in a formula
☐ Click the **Trace Dependents button** 🔛 on the Formula Auditing toolbar
☐ Double-click the **blue arrow** to navigate between the cells

Locate and Resolve Errors

Menu Method

☐ Click the cell that shows an error, using Table EX-23 as a reference
☐ Click **Tools** on the menu bar, point to **Formula Auditing**, then click **Trace Error**
☐ Use the Formula bar to correct the formula

Button Method

☐ Click the cell that shows an error, using Table EX-23 as a reference
☐ Click the **Trace Error button** 🔽 on the Formula Auditing toolbar to display precedents and dependents in the formula
☐ Use the formula bar to correct the formula

Table EX-23 Common Cell Errors

Error	Means
#DIV/0!	Value is divided by zero
#NAME?	Excel does not recognize text
#N/A	Value is not available for the formula
#NULL!	When a formula specifies an intersection of two areas that do not intersect
#NUM!	Invalid formula number(s)
#REF!	Invalid cell reference
#VALUE!	Operand or argument is incorrect

Remove All Tracer Arrows

Menu Method
☐ Click **Tools** on the menu bar, point to **Formula Auditing**, then click **Remove All Arrows**

Button Method
☐ Click the **Remove All Arrows button** 🔏 on the Formula Auditing toolbar

LOCATE INVALID DATA AND FORMULAS

Use Error Checking

Menu Method
☐ Click **Tools** on the menu bar, then click **Error Checking**
☐ In the Error Checking dialog box, click the appropriate button, using Table EX-24 as a reference, fix or view the error as prompted, then click **OK**
☐ Click the **Next** and **Previous buttons** to navigate through the errors

Table EX-24 Error Checking Dialog Box Options

Button	Action
Help on this error	Opens the Microsoft Excel Help Window and displays an article about this type of function or formula
Show Calculation Steps	Opens the Evaluate Formula dialog box
Ignore Error	Move to the next error without modifying the current error
Edit in Formula Bar	Activates the cell containing the error in the formula bar

Circling Invalid Data

Menu Method

- [ ] Click the **Circle Invalid Data button** ⊞ on the Formula Auditing toolbar

WATCH AND EVALUATE FORMULAS

Using Evaluate Formulas

Menu Method

- [ ] Click the cell that contains the formula
- [ ] Click **Tools** on the menu bar, point to **Formula Auditing**, then click **Evaluate Formula**
- [ ] In the Evaluate Formula dialog box, click the appropriate button, using Table EX-25 as a reference

Button Method

- [ ] Click the cell that contains the formula
- [ ] Click the **Evaluate Formula button** @ on the Formula Auditing toolbar
- [ ] In the Evaluate Formula dialog box, click the appropriate button, using Table EX-25 as a reference

Table EX-25 Evaluate Formula Dialog Box Options

Button	Used to
Evaluate	Shows the result of the underlined value; click repeatedly to display additional levels of the formula
Step In	View the formula that supports the highlighted argument; available when there is a formula within the formula you are evaluating
Step Out	Display the previous cell and formula; available after you have clicked Step In
Restart	Return to the highest level of the formula, then restart the evaluation process

Using Cell Watch

Menu Method

- [ ] Select the cells to watch
- [ ] Click **Tools** on the menu bar, point to **Formula Auditing**, then click **Show Watch Window**
- [ ] Click the **Add Watch button** ⌂, select the cells you want to watch, then click **Add**

DEFINE, MODIFY, AND USE NAMED RANGES

Name One or More Cell Ranges

Menu Method

☐ Select the range you want to name
☐ Click the **Name box** to the far left of the formula bar, type the range name using numbers and letters and without using spaces, then press **[Enter]**

OR

☐ Select the range
☐ Click **Insert** on the menu bar, point to **Name**, then click **Define**
☐ In the Define Name dialog box, type the range name in the Names in workbook text box, then click **OK**

Use Labels to Create Range Names

Menu Method

☐ Select the range, including any row or column labels
☐ Click **Insert** on the menu bar, point to **Name**, then click **Create**
☐ In the Create Names dialog box, click the appropriate check box to use as the range name, then click **OK**

Use a Named Range Reference in One or More Formulas

Keyboard Method

☐ Click the cell where the formula will appear
☐ Type the formula in the cell or in the formula bar, inserting the range name whose values are to be used in the formula where appropriate, then press **[Enter]** or **[Tab]**

STRUCTURE WORKBOOKS USING XML

Save a Workbook in XML

Menu Method

☐ Click **File** on the menu bar, then click **Save As**
☐ In the Save As dialog box, navigate to the appropriate drive and folder
☐ Click the **Save as type list arrow**, click **XML Spreadsheet**, then click **Save**
☐ Click **Yes** in the message box if necessary

Use XML to Share Excel Data on the Web

Menu Method

☐ Click **File** on the menu bar, then click **Save As**
☐ In the Save As dialog box, navigate to the appropriate drive and folder
☐ Type a name for the file in the File name text box
☐ Click the **Save as type list arrow**, click **XML Spreadsheet**, then click **Save**

Excel

☐ Click **Yes** in the message box if necessary
☐ Start **Internet Explorer**, click **File** on the menu bar, then click **Open**
☐ In the Open dialog box, click **Browse**, then in the Microsoft Internet Explorer dialog box, navigate to the appropriate drive and folder that contains the .xml file you saved
☐ Click the **Files of type list arrow**, click **All Files**, click the **XML file**, then click **Open**
☐ In the Open dialog box, click **OK** to open the file in Excel

Add XML Data

Menu Method

☐ Click **Data** on the menu bar, point to **XML**, then click **XML Source**
☐ In the XML Source task pane, click **XML Maps** at the bottom of the task pane
☐ In the XML Maps dialog box, click **Add**, navigate to the appropriate drive and folder, select the map, click **Open**, then click **OK**
☐ Select the XML element in the XML Source task pane, then drag it to the appropriate cell

Modify XML Data

Menu Method

☐ To remove an XML element, right-click the element in the task pane, then click **Remove Element** from the shortcut menu
☐ To move an XML element, position the Move pointer 🔘 over the edge of the element, then drag it to a new cell

Delete XML Data

Menu Method

☐ Click the cell, click the **List button** List▾ on the List toolbar, point to **Delete**, then click **Column**

CREATE EXTENSIBLE MARKUP LANGUAGE (XML) WEB QUERIES

Create XML Web Queries

Menu Method

☐ Make sure your computer is connected to the Internet then open a blank worksheet in Excel
☐ Click **Data** on the menu bar, point to **Import External Data**, then click **New Web Query**
☐ In the New Web Query dialog box, click the **Address text box**, type the path to the appropriate drive and folder followed by the XML file-name, click **Go**, then click **Open** in the File Download dialog box
☐ Click 🔲 for each table you want to import, then click **Import**
☐ In the Import Data dialog box, select the appropriate options, then click **OK**

EXCEL EXPERT SKILL SET 2: FORMATTING DATA AND CONTENT

CREATE AND MODIFY CUSTOM DATA FORMATS

Create and Apply a Custom Number Format

Menu Method

- [ ] Click the cell or select the range to format
- [ ] Click **Format** on the menu bar, then click **Cells**, or right-click, then click **Format Cells** on the shortcut menu
- [ ] In the Format Cells dialog box, click the **Number tab**, then click **Custom** in the Category list box
- [ ] In the Type list box, select the format code to use as a basis, then make the modifications to this format code in the Type text box
- [ ] To apply additional formatting, use the Font, Alignment, and other tabs in the Format Cells dialog box, then click **OK**

Keyboard Method

- [ ] Click the cell or select the range to format
- [ ] Press **[Ctrl] [1]**
- [ ] Follow the third through fifth bullets in the Create and Apply a Custom Number Format Menu Method above

Create and Apply a Custom Format with Text

Menu Method

- [ ] Click the cell or select the range to format
- [ ] Click **Format** on the menu bar, then click **Cells**, or right-click, then click **Format Cells** on the shortcut menu
- [ ] In the Format Cells dialog box, click the **Number tab**, then click **Custom** in the Category list box
- [ ] In the Type list box, select the format code to use as a basis, click in the Type text box after the last character, then type the text to appear surrounded by quotation marks
- [ ] To apply additional formatting, use the Font, Alignment, and other tabs in the Format Cells dialog box, then click **OK**

Keyboard Method

- [ ] Click the cell or select the range to format
- [ ] Press **[Ctrl] [1]**
- [ ] Follow the third through fifth bullets in the Create and Apply a Custom Format with Text Menu Method above

USE CONDITIONAL FORMATS

Menu Method

- [ ] Click the cell or select the range to format
- [ ] Click **Format** on the menu bar, then click **Conditional Formatting**

Excel

☐ In the Conditional Formatting dialog box, select the appropriate conditions for the first condition, then click **Format**

☐ In the Format Cells dialog box, click the appropriate options, then click **OK**

☐ In the Conditional Formatting dialog box, click **Add**, repeat the third and fourth bullets here for additional conditional formatting as appropriate, then click **OK**

FORMAT AND RESIZE GRAPHICS

Crop Graphics

Menu Method

☐ Click the graphic to select it, click **Format** on the menu bar, then click **Picture**

☐ In the Format Picture dialog box, click the **Picture tab** if necessary

☐ Specify appropriate values in the Crop from section of the dialog box

☐ Click **OK**

OR

☐ Right-click the graphic, then click **Format Picture** on the shortcut men

☐ Follow the steps in the second through fourth bullets in the Crop Graphics Menu Method above

Mouse Method

☐ Double-click the graphic to open the Format Picture dialog box

☐ Follow the steps in the second through fourth bullets in the Crop Graphics Menu Method above

Button Method

☐ Click the graphic to select it

☐ Click the **Crop button** on the Picture toolbar

☐ Use the **pointer** to drag the crop handles on the edges of the graphic inward to crop unwanted sections of the graphic

☐ Click outside the graphic to deactivate the cropping feature

Rotate Graphics

Menu Method

☐ Click the graphic to select it, click **Format** on the menu bar, then click **Picture**

☐ In the Format Picture dialog box, click the **Size tab**

☐ Enter appropriate values in the **Rotation text box** in the Size and rotate section of the dialog box

☐ Click **OK**

OR

☐ Right-click the graphic, then click **Format Picture** on the shortcut men

☐ Follow the steps in the second through fourth bullets in the Rotate Graphics Menu Method above

Mouse Method

☐ Double-click the graphic to open the Format Picture dialog box
☐ Follow the steps in the second through fourth bullets in the Rotate Graphics Menu Method

Button Method

☐ Click the graphic to select it
☐ Position the pointer over the **green rotate handle** 🔼 at the top of the graphic
☐ Drag the rotation handle using the **Ѿ pointer** to rotate the graphic to the desired angle

Control Image Contrast and Brightness

Menu Method

☐ Click the graphic to select it, click **Format** on the menu bar, then click **Picture**
☐ In the Format Picture dialog box, click the **Picture tab** if necessary
☐ Specify the appropriate settings using the controls in the Image control section of the dialog box
☐ In the Format Picture dialog box, click **OK**

OR

☐ Right-click the graphic, then click **Format Picture** on the shortcut menu
☐ Follow the steps in the second through fourth bullets in the Control Image Contrast and Brightness Menu Method above

Mouse Method

☐ Double-click the graphic to open the Format Picture dialog box
☐ Follow the steps in the second through fourth bullets in the Control Image Contrast and Brightness Menu Method above

Button Method

☐ Click the graphic to select it
☐ Click the appropriate button on the Picture toolbar to achieve the desired effect using Table EX-26 as a reference

Table EX-26 Image Contrast and Brightness Buttons on the Picture Toolbar

Button name	Button
More Contrast	◑
Less Contrast	◑
More Brightness	☀
Less Brightness	☀

Excel

Scale and Resize Graphics

Menu Method

☐ Click the graphic to select it, click **Format** on the menu bar, then click **Picture**

☐ In the Format Picture dialog box, click the **Size tab**

☐ Enter appropriate values in the Size and rotate and Scale sections of the dialog box

☐ Click **OK**

OR

☐ Right-click the graphic, then click **Format Picture** on the shortcut menu

☐ Follow the steps in the second through fourth bullets in the Scale and Resize Graphics Menu Method above

Mouse Method

☐ Double-click the graphic to open the Format Picture dialog box

☐ Follow the steps in the second through fourth bullets in the Scale and Resize Graphics Menu Method above

Button Method

☐ Click the graphic to select it

☐ Position the pointer over a **sizing handle** on the graphic until the pointer changes, using Table EX-7 on page 101 as a reference

☐ Drag the sizing handle to resize the graphic

FORMAT CHARTS AND DIAGRAMS

Apply Formats to Charts and Diagrams

☐ Select the chart object or diagram object you want to format, then open the Format [Object] dialog box using a method from Table EX-27

☐ Make the appropriate formatting changes in the Format [Object] dialog box, then click **OK**

Table EX-27 Opening the Format Object Dialog Box

Method	Steps
Menu	Click **Format** on the menu bar, then click **Selected Chart Area**, or right-click the chart area or object, then click **Format [Object]**
Button	Click the **Format [Object] button** 🔲 on the Chart toolbar
Keyboard	Press **[Ctrl][1]**
Mouse	Double-click the chart area or object you want to format

Excel Expert Skill Set 3: Collaborating

Protect Cells, Worksheets, and Workbooks

Protect Worksheet Cells

Menu Method

☐ Select the range you want to protect
☐ Click **Format** on the menu bar, then click **Cells**, or right-click, then click **Format Cells** on the shortcut menu
☐ In the Format Cells dialog box, click the **Protection tab**, make sure the **Locked check box** is checked, then click **OK**
☐ Click **Tools** on the menu bar, point to **Protection**, then click **Protect Sheet**
☐ In the Protect Sheet dialog box, click to select the **Protect worksheet and contents of locked cells check box** if necessary, then type a password in the Password to unprotect sheet text box
☐ Click **OK**
☐ In the Confirm Password dialog box, retype the password, then click **OK**

Protect Worksheets

Menu Method

☐ Click **Tools** on the menu bar, point to **Protection**, then click **Protect Sheet**
☐ In the Protect Sheet dialog box, click the **Protect worksheet and contents of locked cells check box** to select it, if necessary
☐ In the Password to unprotect sheet text box, type a password if necessary
☐ Click the appropriate features a user can access, then click **OK**
☐ If necessary, in the Confirm Password dialog box, type the password you specified, then click **OK**

Protect Workbooks and Workbook Elements

Menu Method

☐ Click **Tools** on the menu bar, point to **Protection**, then click **Protect Workbook**
☐ In the Protect Workbook dialog box, select the appropriate checkboxes
☐ If necessary, click the Password text box, type a password, then click **OK**
☐ If necessary, type the password to confirm it, then click **OK**

Apply Workbook Security Settings

Use a Digital Signature

Menu Method

☐ Click **Tools** on the menu bar, then click **Options**
☐ In the Options dialog box, click the **Security tab**, then click **Digital Signatures**

☐ In the Digital Signature dialog box, click **Add**
☐ Save the workbook if prompted, select the certificate, then click **OK** in all open dialog boxes

Set a Password

Menu Method

☐ Click **File** on the menu bar, click **Save As**
☐ In the Save As dialog box, click **Tools** on the toolbar, then click **General Options**
☐ In the Save Options dialog box, click the **Password to open text box** then type a password
☐ Click the **Password to modify text box**, type a different password, then click **OK**
☐ For each password dialog box, confirm the password by typing the appropriate password in the password text box, then click **OK**
☐ In the Save As dialog box, click **Save**

Set Macro Settings

Menu Method

☐ Click **Tools** on the menu bar, point to **Macro**, then click **Security**
☐ In the Security dialog box, select the appropriate option button, then click **OK**

SHARE WORKBOOKS

Create a Shared Workbook

Menu Method

☐ Click **Tools** on the menu bar, then click **Share Workbook**
☐ In the Share Workbook dialog box, click the **Editing tab** if necessary, click the **Allow changes by more than one user at the same time check box** if necessary, then click **OK**
☐ Click **OK** if prompted to save the file

Modify a Shared Workbook

Menu Method

☐ Open the workbook from its network location, click **Tools** on the menu bar, click **Options**, then click the **General tab** in the Options dialog box
☐ Type your name in the User name text box, then click **OK**
☐ Make the modifications to the workbook, then save the workbook
☐ If prompted, resolve any conflicts in the Resolve Conflicts dialog box

MERGE WORKBOOKS

Menu Method

- ☐ Open the original shared workbook
- ☐ Click **Tools** on the menu bar, then click **Compare and Merge Workbooks**
- ☐ Click **OK** if prompted to save the file
- ☐ In the Select Files to Merge Into Current Workbook dialog box, click the file, then click **OK**
- ☐ Click **Tools** on the menu bar, point to **Track Changes**, then click **Highlight Changes**
- ☐ In the Highlight Changes dialog box, click the **When list arrow**, then click **All**
- ☐ Click to select the **List changes on a new sheet check box**, then click **OK**

Excel

TRACK, ACCEPT, AND REJECT CHANGES TO WORKBOOKS

Track Worksheet Changes

Menu Method

- ☐ Click **Tools** on the menu bar, point to **Track Changes**, then click **Highlight Changes**
- ☐ In the Highlight Changes dialog box, click to select the **Track changes while editing check box**
- ☐ Make sure the **Highlight changes on screen check box** is selected, then click **OK**
- ☐ In the message box, click **OK** if necessary

Accept and Reject Changes

Menu Method

- ☐ Click **Tools** on the menu bar, point to **Track Changes**, then click **Accept or Reject Changes**
- ☐ If you get a message box to save the workbook, click **OK**
- ☐ In the Select Changes to Accept or Reject dialog box, in the When list box, make sure **Not yet reviewed** is selected, then click **OK**
- ☐ In the Accept or Reject Changes dialog box, click the appropriate options

Review Changes

Menu Method

- ☐ Click **Tools** on the menu bar, point to **Track Changes**, then click **Highlight Changes**
- ☐ In the Highlight Changes dialog box, make sure the **Track changes while editing check box** is selected
- ☐ Make sure the **Highlight changes on screen check box** is selected, then click **OK**
- ☐ Position the insertion point over a cell with a colored triangle in the corner, then read the screen tip to review the change

EXCEL EXPERT SKILL SET 4: MANAGING DATA AND WORKBOOKS

IMPORT DATA TO EXCEL

Import a Text File

Menu Method

☐ Click the upper-left cell in the range where you want Excel to import the file
☐ Click **Data** on the menu bar, point to **Import External Data**, then click **Import Data**
☐ In the Select Data Source dialog box, navigate to the appropriate drive and folder
☐ Click the **Files of type list arrow**, click **Text Files**, click the file, then click **Open**
☐ Navigate through the Text Import Wizard, making changes or accepting the defaults as appropriate to import the text file, then click **Finish**
☐ In the Import Data dialog box, select the appropriate option button specifying where you want the imported data to appear, then click **OK**

Import Access Database Tables

Menu Method

☐ Click the upper-left cell in the range where you want Excel to import the file
☐ Click **Data** on the menu bar, point to **Import External Data**, then click **Import Data**
☐ In the Select Data Source dialog box, navigate to the appropriate drive and folder
☐ Click the **Files of type list arrow**, click **All Data Sources** if necessary, click the **Access file**, then click **Open**
☐ If the Select Table dialog box opens, click the table or query, then click **OK**
☐ In the Import Data dialog box, select the appropriate option button specifying where you want the imported data to appear, then click **OK**

Import Data Using a Query

Menu Method

Note: If prompted, install MS Query after completing the step in the first bullet.

☐ Open a blank worksheet, click **Data** on the menu bar, point to **Import External Data**, then click **New Database Query**
☐ In the Choose Data Source dialog box, click **MS Access Database**, then click **OK**

☐ In the Select Database dialog box, navigate to the appropriate drive and folder, click the database you want to import, then click **OK**
☐ Navigate through the Query Wizard, making changes or accepting the defaults as appropriate to import the database, then click **Finish**
☐ In the Import Data dialog box, select the appropriate option button specifying where you want the imported data to appear, then click **OK**

Import Graphics

Menu Method

☐ Click **Insert** on the menu bar, point to **Picture**, then click **From File**
☐ In the Insert Picture dialog box, navigate to the drive and folder that contains the graphic you want to import
☐ Click the graphic file you want, then click **Insert**

Button Method

☐ Click the **Insert Picture From File button** 🖼 on the Drawing tool-bar or the Picture toolbar
☐ Follow the second and third bullets in the Import Graphics Menu Method above

Import Data from the World Wide Web

Menu Method

☐ Start Internet Explorer, then navigate to the Web page that contains the data to import
☐ Select the data you want to import into Excel, click **Edit** on the Internet Explorer menu bar, then click **Copy**
☐ Click the Microsoft Excel program button on the taskbar, then click the cell where you want to import the data
☐ Click **Edit** on the Excel menu bar, then click **Paste**

Keyboard Method

☐ Start Internet Explorer, then navigate to the Web page that contains the data to import
☐ Select the data you want to import into Excel, then press **[Ctrl] [C]**
☐ Click the Microsoft Excel program button on the taskbar, then click the cell where you want to import the data
☐ Press **[Ctrl] [V]**

Link to Web Page Data

Note: Data on the Web page must be saved as an Excel file rather than an HTML file in order to create a link.

Menu Method

☐ Connect to the Internet, start Internet Explorer, then navigate to the Web page that contains the data to link
☐ Select the data, copy the data, then return to the Microsoft Excel workbook

Excel

☐ Click **Edit** on the menu bar, then click **Paste Special**
☐ In the Paste Special dialog box, click **Paste Link** then click **OK**

EXPORT DATA FROM EXCEL

Embed an Excel Chart in a Word Document

Menu Method

☐ In Microsoft Excel, select the chart, click **Edit** on the menu bar, then click **Copy**
☐ Start Microsoft Word, open the file or create a new document, then click where you want to embed the chart
☐ Click **Edit** on the menu bar, then click **Paste Special**
☐ In the Paste Special dialog box, make sure **Microsoft Office Excel Chart Object** is selected, then click **OK**

Link Excel Charts or Data to a PowerPoint Presentation

Menu Method

☐ Select the cell(s), chart, or object you want to copy
☐ Click **Edit** on the menu bar, then click **Copy**
☐ Start Microsoft PowerPoint, open the presentation in which you want place the linked data or object, or create a new presentation, then click the slide where you want to place the linked data
☐ Click **Edit** on the menu bar, then click **Paste Special**
☐ In the Paste Special dialog box, click the **Paste link option button**, make sure that Microsoft Office Excel Worksheet Object or Microsoft Office Excel Chart Object is selected in the As list box, then click **OK**

Convert a List to an Access Table

Menu Method

☐ Start Microsoft Access, then open the appropriate file or create a new database
☐ Click **File** on the menu bar, point to **Get External Data**, then click **Import**
☐ In the Import dialog box, navigate to the appropriate drive and folder, click the **Files of type list arrow**, click **Microsoft Excel**, click the file you want to import, then click **Import**
☐ Navigate through the Import Spreadsheet Wizard, making changes or accepting the defaults as appropriate to import the spreadsheet, then click **Finish**
☐ Click **OK** in the message box

PUBLISH AND EDIT WEB WORKSHEETS AND WORKBOOKS

Publish Web-Based Worksheets

Menu Method

☐ Click **File** on the menu bar, then click **Save as Web Page**
☐ In the Save As dialog box, click **Publish**
☐ In the Publish as Web Page dialog box, click the **Choose list arrow**, then click the appropriate option
☐ In the Publish as section, click **Browse**
☐ In the Publish As dialog box, navigate to the appropriate drive and folder, type the filename in the File name text box, then click **OK**
☐ In the Publish as Web Page dialog box, select any other appropriate options, then click **Publish**

Publish an Interactive Workbook to the Web

Menu Method

☐ Click **File** on the menu bar, click **Save as Web Page**
☐ In the Save As dialog box, make sure the **Entire Workbook option button** is selected, click to select the **Add interactivity check box**, then click **Publish**
☐ In the Publish as Web Page dialog box, select any other appropriate options, then click **Publish**

Use Interactive Workbooks

Menu Method

☐ Start Internet Explorer
☐ Click **File** on the menu bar, then click **Open**
☐ In the Open dialog box, click **Browse**
☐ In the Microsoft Internet Explorer dialog box, navigate to the appropriate drive and folder, click the file, then click **Open**
☐ In the Open dialog box, click **OK**
☐ Make the modifications to the Excel file, then click the **Export to Microsoft Office Excel button** 💱
☐ To save the changes to your computer, save the file in Excel with a new name

Excel

CREATE AND EDIT TEMPLATES

Create a Workbook Template

Menu Method

☐ Click **File** on the menu bar, then click **Save As**
☐ In the Save As dialog box, click the **Save as type list arrow**, then click **Template**
☐ Type the filename in the File name text box, then click **Save**

Create a New Workbook Based on a Template You Created

Task Pane Method

☐ In the New Workbook task pane, click **From existing workbook**
☐ In the New from Existing Workbook dialog box, navigate to the drive and folder where the template you want is stored
☐ Click the **Files of type list arrow**, click **All Microsoft Office Excel Files** if necessary, click the appropriate template, then click **Create Ne**
☐ Enter the appropriate information in the worksheet
☐ Click **File** on the menu bar, then click **Save As**
☐ In the Save As dialog box, click the **Save as type list arrow**, then click **Microsoft Office Excel Workbook**, if necessary
☐ Navigate to the drive and folder where you want to save the new file, type the filename in the File name text box, then click **Save**

Modify a Workbook Template

Menu Method

☐ Click **File** on the menu bar, then click **Open**
☐ In the Open dialog box, navigate to the drive and folder where the ter plate is stored
☐ Click the **Files of type list arrow**, then click **Templates**
☐ Click the template you want to modify, then click **Open**
☐ Make the appropriate modifications
☐ Click **File** on the menu bar, then click **Save**

Button Method

☐ Click the **Open button** 📄 on the Standard toolbar
☐ Follow the second through fifth bullets in the Modify a Workbook Template Menu Method above
☐ Click the **Save button** 🖫 on the Standard toolbar

Keyboard Method

☐ Press **[Ctrl] [O]**
☐ Follow the second through fifth bullets in the Modify a Workbook Template Menu Method
☐ Press **[Ctrl] [S]**

CONSOLIDATE DATA

Consolidate Data from Multiple Worksheets

Menu Method

☐ Select the range where the consolidated data will appear
☐ Click **Data** on the menu bar, then click **Consolidate**
☐ In the Consolidate dialog box, click the **Function list arrow**, select the appropriate function, then click the **Reference text box**
☐ If the data to consolidate is in the currently open worksheet, click the worksheet, select the range, then click **Add**, or if the data to consolidate is in another worksheet, click **Browse**, select the file, click **Open**, select the worksheet and range, then click **Add**
☐ Repeat for all workbooks, worksheets, and ranges, then click **OK**

DEFINE AND MODIFY WORKBOOK PROPERTIES

Manage Workbook Properties

Menu Method

☐ Click **File** on the menu bar, then click **Properties**
In the [Filename] Properties dialog box, click the **Summary tab**, make the appropriate changes, then click **OK**

Excel

EXCEL EXPERT SKILL SET 5: CUSTOMIZING EXCEL

CUSTOMIZE TOOLBARS AND MENUS

Add Toolbar Buttons

Button Method

☐ Click the **Toolbar Options button** ▓ on the right side of the toolbar you want to customize
☐ Point to **Add or Remove Buttons**, then point to the toolbar name
☐ In the toolbar button list, click the checkbox for the button you want t add, then click anywhere in the worksheet

Remove Toolbars Buttons

Menu Method

☐ Click the **Toolbar Options button** ▓ on the right side of the toolbar you want to customize
☐ Point to **Add or Remove Buttons**, then point to the toolbar name
☐ In the toolbar button list, click the check box for button you want to remove, then click anywhere in the worksheet

Keyboard Method

☐ Press and hold **[Alt]**, then position the ▲ pointer over the button to remove
☐ Drag the button from the toolbar to the worksheet area to remove it

Add a Custom Menu

Menu Method

☐ Click **Tools** on the menu bar, then click **Customize**, or right-click any toolbar, then click **Customize** on the shortcut menu
☐ In the Customize dialog box, click the **Commands tab**, then click **New Menu** in the Categories list box
☐ Drag **New Menu** from the Commands list, until the **position indicato** I and the **menu position pointer** ▓ are over the menu bar to the right of the Help menu, then release the mouse button
☐ Click the appropriate option in the Categories list to display commands for that category in the Commands list box, drag the **commands** you want from the Commands list box on top of the new menu name on the menu bar so that a box appears below the menu name, drag the **command** onto the box, then release the mouse button

☐ With the Customize dialog box still open, right-click **New Menu** on the menu bar, point to **Name**, drag to select **New Menu**, type the menu name, then press **[Enter]**

☐ Click anywhere in the worksheet to close the shortcut menu, then click **Close** in the Customize dialog box

CREATE, EDIT, AND RUN MACROS

Record a Macro

Menu Method

☐ Click **Tools** on the menu bar, point to **Macro**, then click **Record New Macro**

☐ In the Record Macro dialog box, type the macro name in the Macro name text box

☐ Click the **Store macro in list arrow**, then click the appropriate macro storage option

☐ To assign a keyboard shortcut to the macro, click the **Shortcut key text box**, then type the key

☐ Click **OK**

☐ Perform the actions for the macro

☐ Click **Tools** on the menu bar, point to **Macro**, then click **Stop Recording**

Edit a Macro

Menu Method

☐ Click **Tools** on the menu bar, point to **Macro**, then click **Macros**

☐ In the Macro dialog box, select the appropriate macro, then click **Edit**

☐ In the Microsoft Visual Basic window, make the modifications to the macro code

☐ Click **File** on the menu bar, then click **Close and Return to Microsoft Excel**

Keyboard Method

☐ Press **[Alt] [F8]**

☐ In the Macro dialog box, select the appropriate macro, then click **Edit**

☐ In the Microsoft Visual Basic window, make the modifications to the macro code

☐ Press **[Alt] [Q]**

Run a Macro

Menu Method
☐ Click **Tools** on the menu bar, point to **Macro**, then click **Macros**
☐ In the Macro dialog box, click the appropriate macro, then click **Run**

Keyboard Method
☐ Press **[Alt] [F8]**
☐ In the Macro dialog box, click the appropriate macro, then click **Run**
OR
☐ Press the keyboard combination you assigned to the macro if appropria

MODIFY EXCEL DEFAULT SETTINGS

Menu Method
☐ Click **Tools** on the menu bar, then click **Options**
☐ In the Options dialog box, click the **General tab**
☐ Change the default font, number of worksheets, file location, or other options, then click **OK**

Excel

MICROSOFT OFFICE ACCESS 2003
EXAM REFERENCE
Getting Started with Access 2003

The Access Microsoft Office Specialist exam assumes a basic level of proficiency in Access. This section is intended to help you reference these basic skills while you are preparing to take the Access Specialist exam.

- ☐ Starting and exiting Access
- ☐ Viewing the database window
- ☐ Using toolbars
- ☐ Using task panes
- ☐ Opening, saving, and closing databases
- ☐ Getting Help

START AND EXIT ACCESS

Start Access

Button Method
- ☐ Click the Start button ![start] on the Windows taskbar
- ☐ Point to **All Programs**
- ☐ Point to **Microsoft Office**, then click **Microsoft Office Access 2003**

OR

- ☐ Double-click the Microsoft Office Access program icon ![icon] on the desktop

Exit Access

Menu Method
- ☐ Click **File** on the menu bar, then click **Exit**

Button Method
- ☐ Click the **Close button** ![X] on the Access program window title bar

Keyboard Method
- ☐ Press **[Alt][F4]**

VIEW THE DATABASE WINDOW

Figure AC-1   The Access Window

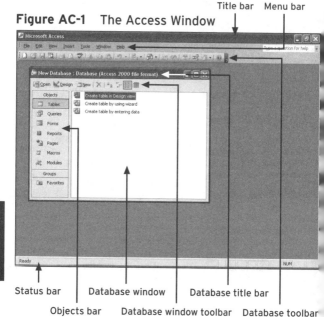

Title bar   Menu bar

Status bar · Database window · Database title bar · Objects bar · Database window toolbar · Database toolbar

USE TOOLBARS

Display Toolbars

Menu Method

☐ Click **View** on the menu bar, point to **Toolbars**, then click the toolbar to display

OR

☐ Right-click any toolbar, then click the toolbar to display on the shortcut menu

Customize Toolbars

Menu Method

☐ Click **Tools** on the menu bar, then click **Customize**, or click **View** on the menu bar, point to **Toolbars**, then click **Customize**, or right-click any toolbar, then click **Customize** on the shortcut menu

☐ In the Customize dialog box, select the appropriate options, then click **Close**

Button Method

☐ Click the **Toolbar Options button** 〓 on the toolbar to customize
☐ Point to Add or Remove Buttons, then click Customize
☐ Follow the steps in the second bullet in the Customize Toolbars Menu Method

Reposition Toolbars

Mouse Method

☐ Position the pointer over the Toolbar Move handle ▌ at the left end of any docked toolbar, or over the title bar of any floating toolbar
☐ When the pointer changes to ✛, press and hold the mouse button
☐ Drag the toolbar to a blank area of the window or to a different location, then release the mouse button

USE TASK PANES

Display Task Panes

Menu Method

☐ If no task pane is open, click **View** on the menu bar, then click **Task Pane** or right-click any toolbar, then click **Task Pane** on the shortcut menu
☐ Click the **Other Task Panes list arrow** ▼ on the task pane title bar, then click the appropriate task pane
☐ Click the **Back button** ⬅ on the task pane title bar to return to the previously displayed task pane

Close Task Panes

Menu Method

☐ Click **View** on the menu bar, then click **Task Pane** or right-click any toolbar, then click **Task Pane** on the shortcut menu

Button Method

☐ Click the **Close button** ✕ on the task pane title bar

OPEN, SAVE, AND CLOSE DATABASES

Open an Existing Database

Menu Method

☐ Click **File** on the menu bar, then click **Open**
☐ In the Open dialog box, navigate to the appropriate drive and folder
☐ Click the file you want, then click **Open**

Button Method

☐ Click the **Open button** 🗐 on the Database toolbar
☐ Follow the second and third bullets in the Open an Existing Database Menu Method

Keyboard Method

☐ Press **[Ctrl][O]**
☐ Follow the second and third bullets in the Open an Existing Database Menu Method

Task Pane Method

☐ Click a database in the Open section of the Getting Started task pane
OR

☐ Click **More** in the Open section of the Getting Started task pane, then follow the second and third bullets in the Open an Existing Database Menu Method

Save a Database

Menu Method

☐ Click **File** on the menu bar, then click **Save**

Button Method

☐ Click the **Save button** 🖫 on the Database toolbar

Keyboard Method

☐ Press **[Ctrl][S]**

Close Databases

Menu Method

☐ Save and close all database objects, and return to the database window
☐ Click **File** on the menu bar, then click **Close**
☐ If prompted to save the database or an object, click Yes or No as appropriate

Button Method

☐ Save and close all database objects, and return to the database window
☐ Click the **Close Window button** ☒ on the menu bar if the database window is maximized, or click the **Close button** ☒ on the database window title bar if the database window is not maximized
☐ If prompted to save the database or an object, click Yes or No as appropriate

Keyboard Method

☐ Close all database objects, and return to the database window
☐ Press **[Ctrl][W]**
☐ If prompted to save the database or an object, click Yes or No as appropriate

GET HELP

Menu Method

☐ Click **Help** on the menu bar, then click **Microsoft Office Access Help**
☐ Use Table AC-1 as a reference to select the most appropriate way to search for help using the Access Help task pane

Button Method

☐ Click the **Microsoft Office Access Help button** 🔞 on the Database toolbar
☐ Use Table AC-1 as a reference to select the most appropriate way to search for help using the Microsoft Office Access Help task pane

OR

☐ Click the **Type a question for help box** on the menu bar
☐ Type a question or keywords relating to an Access topic, then press **[Enter]**
☐ View the results of the keyword search in the Access Help task pane, then click a topic title in the task pane to view the topic in a new window

Keyboard Method

☐ Press **[F1]**
☐ Use Table AC-1 as a reference to select the most appropriate way to search for help using the Microsoft Office Access Help task pane

Table AC-1 Access Help Task Pane Options

Option	To use
Table of Contents	Click the Table of Contents button in the task pane, click the Expand indicator next to each topic you want to explore further, then click the topic you want and read the results in the Help window that opens
Search for text box	Type a keyword in the Search for text box, click the Start Searching button ➡, then click the blue hyper-linked text to read more in the Microsoft Office Access Help window, or click the grayed text to view the topic in the Table of Contents

Access

ACCESS **SPECIALIST** EXAM
REFERENCE

Skill Sets:

1. Structuring databases
2. Entering data
3. Organizing data
4. Managing databases

ACCESS SPECIALIST SKILL SET 1: STRUCTURING DATABASES

CREATE ACCESS DATABASES

Create a New Database Using a Template

Menu Method

☐ Click **File** on the menu bar, then click **New**
☐ In the New File task pane, click **On my computer** in the Templates section
☐ In the Templates dialog box, click the appropriate tab, click the appropriate template, then click **OK**
☐ In the File New Database dialog box, navigate to the appropriate drive and folder, type the filename, then click **Create**
☐ If necessary, navigate through the Database Wizard, making changes or accepting the defaults as appropriate to create the database, then click **Finish**

Button Method

☐ Click the **New button** 🗋 on the Database toolbar
☐ Follow the steps in the second through fifth bullets of the Create a New Database Using a Template Menu Method above

Keyboard Method

☐ Press **[Ctrl][N]**
☐ Follow the steps in the second through fifth bullets of the Create a New Database Using a Template Menu Method above

Create a Blank Database

Menu Method

☐ Click **File** on the menu bar, then click **New**
☐ In the New File task pane, click **Blank database** in the New section
☐ In the File New Database dialog box, navigate to the appropriate drive and folder, type the filename in the File name text box, then click **Create**

Button Method

☐ Click the **New button** 🔲 on the Database toolbar
☐ Follow the steps in the second and third bullets of the Create a Blank Database Menu Method

Keyboard Method

☐ Press **[Ctrl][N]**
☐ Follow the steps in the second and third bullets of the Create a Blank Database Menu Method

---

CREATE AND MODIFY TABLES

Create Tables Using the Table Wizard

Menu Method

☐ Return to the database window, if necessary, click **Insert** on the menu bar, click **Table**, click **Table Wizard** in the New Table dialog box, then click **OK**
☐ Navigate through the Table Wizard, selecting the type of table you want and the fields you want it to contain, specifying a name for your table and other options, then click **Finish**

OR

☐ Click the **Tables button** 🔲 Tables on the Objects bar, right-click **Create table by using wizard**, then click **Open** on the shortcut menu
☐ Navigate through the Table Wizard, selecting the type of table you want and the fields you want it to contain, specifying a name for your table and other options, then click **Finish**

Button Method

☐ In the database window, Click the **Tables button** 🔲 Tables on the Objects bar
☐ Click the **New button** 🔲 on the Database Window toolbar
☐ In the New Table dialog box, click **Table Wizard**, then click **OK**
☐ Follow the steps in the second bullet of the Create Tables Using the Table Wizard Menu Method above

OR

☐ Click the **Tables button** 🔲 Tables on the Objects bar, then double-click **Create table by using wizard**
☐ Follow the steps in the second bullet of the Create Tables Using the Table Wizard Menu Method above

Access

Create and Modify Tables Using Table Design View

Menu Method

- [ ] Click **Insert** on the menu bar, then click **Table**
- [ ] In the New Table dialog box, click **Design View**, then click **OK**
- [ ] For each field you want in the table, type the field name in the Field Name column, then press **[Enter]**
- [ ] To specify the type of data for a field, click the **Data Type list arrow**, then click the appropriate data type for the field, using Table AC-2 as a reference
- [ ] To set properties for data that is entered in a field, click the appropriate property text box in the Field Properties pane, then specify and modify the property for that field using Table AC-3 as a reference
- [ ] Click the field you want to define as the primary key, click **Edit** on the menu bar, then click **Primary Key**

Button Method

- [ ] In the database window, click the **Tables button** ☐ Tables on the Objects bar, then click the **New button** 🔤 on the Database Window toolbar
- [ ] In the New Table dialog box, click **Design View**, then click **OK**
- [ ] Follow the steps in the third through fifth bullets of the Create and Modify Tables Using Table Design View Menu Method above
- [ ] Click the **Primary Key button** 🔑 on the Table Design toolbar

Table AC-2 Descriptions of Data Types

Data type	Description
Text	Text, combinations of text and numbers, or formatted numbers such as phone numbers
Memo	Text longer than 255 characters
Number	Numeric information to be used in calculations
Date/Time	Dates and times
Currency	Monetary values
AutoNumber	Integers assigned by Access to sequentially order each record added to a table
Yes/No	Only two values (Yes/No, On/Off, True/False) can be chosen for this type of field
OLE Object	Files created in other programs (OLE stands for Object Linking and Embedding)
Hyperlink	Links to Web page addresses, files, or objects

Table AC-3 Selected Field Properties

Field property	Can be used to	Used for data type(s)
Field Size	Set the maximum size for data stored in a field set	Text, Number, and AutoNumber
Format	Customize the way numbers, dates, times, and text are displayed and printed, or use special symbols to create custom formats, such as to display information in all uppercase	Text, Memo, Date/Time, AutoNumber, Yes/No, Hyperlink, and Number
Decimal Places	Specify the number of decimal places that are displayed, but not how many decimal places are stored	Number and Currency
Input Mask	Make data entry easier and to control the values users can enter in a text box control, such as (___) ___-____ for a phone number	Text and Date
Caption	Provide helpful information to the user through captions on objects in various views	All fields
Default Value	Specify a value that is entered in a field automatically when a new record is added. For example, in an Addresses table you can set the default value for the State field to Massachusetts. When a new record is added to the table, you can either accept this value or enter a new state	All fields except AutoNumber or OLE object
Validation Rule	Specify requirements for data entered into a record, field, or control	All fields except AutoNumber or OLE object
Validation Text	Specify a message to be displayed when the user enters data that violates the Validation Rule property	All fields where a Validation Rule is specified
Required	Specify whether a value is required in a field	All fields except AutoNumber
Indexed	Set a single-field index that will speed up queries on the indexed fields as well as sorting and grouping operations	Text, Number, Date/Time, Currency, AutoNumber, and Yes/No, Hyperlink, and Memo
Smart Tags	Specify that certain data be marked as a smart tag	Text, Currency, Number, Date/Time, AutoNumber, and Hyperlink

Access

Modify Table Properties

Button Method

☐ Click the table in the database window whose properties you want to modify
☐ Click the **Design button** 🖾 on the Database Window toolbar
☐ In Design view, use the Field Properties pane to make the appropriate modifications to the table properties, click the **Save button** 🖫 on the Table Design toolbar, then close the table

Modify Table Structure

Menu Method

☐ Open the table in Design view
☐ To rename a field, double-click the **field name**, then type the new field name
☐ To add a new field, click a **blank Field Name cell**, type the new field name, then select the data type
☐ To move a field, click the **row selector button** to the left of the field to move to select the entire field, then drag the **row selector button** to the new location
☐ To delete a field, click the **row selector button** to the left of the field to select the entire field, then press **[Delete]**
☐ Save your changes

Change the Height and Width of Rows and Columns in Datasheet View

Menu Method

☐ Open the table in Datasheet view
☐ Make the appropriate structural changes using Table AC-4 as a reference

Table AC-4 Working in Datasheet View

Change	Menu method
Increase or decrease row height	Select the row(s) whose height you wish to change, right-click, then click Row Height, OR click Format on the menu bar, then click Row Height. In the Row Height dialog box, make the appropriate modifications, then click OK.
Increase or decrease column width	Select the column(s) whose width you wish to change, right-click, then click Column Width, OR click Format on the menu bar, then click Column Width. In the Column Width dialog box, make the appropriate modifications, then click OK.
Insert a new column	Place the insertion point or select the column to the right of where you want the new column to appear, click Insert on the menu bar, then click Column or right-click, then click Insert Column.
Delete a column	Select the column you want to delete, right-click, then click Delete Column.

Access

Mouse Method

☐ Open the table in Datasheet view
☐ To increase or decrease column width, position the pointer over one of the column dividers until the pointer changes to **↔**, then drag **↔** to the left or right as desired
☐ To increase or decrease row height, position the pointer over one of the row dividers until the pointer changes to **↕**, then drag **↕** up or down as desired

---

DEFINE AND MODIFY FIELD TYPES

Create Lookup Fields

Menu Method

☐ Open the table in Design view, then click a blank field
☐ Click **Insert** on the menu bar, then click **Lookup Field**
☐ Navigate through the Lookup Wizard, making selections or accepting the defaults as appropriate to create the Lookup field, then click **Finish**

Button Method

☐ Open the table in Design view, then click a blank field
☐ Click the cell in the Data Type column for the selected field, click the **list arrow** that appears, then click **Lookup Wizard**
☐ Navigate through the Lookup Wizard, making selections or accepting the defaults as appropriate to create the Lookup field, then click **Finish**

Modify Lookup Properties

Menu Method

☐ Open the table in Design view
☐ Click the Lookup field to modify, then click the **Lookup tab** in the Field Properties pane
☐ Click the **Row Source property text box**, then modify the entry

Button Method

☐ Follow the first and second bullets in the Modify Lookup Properties Menu Method above
☐ Click the **Row Source property text box**, then click the **Build button**
☐ In the Query Builder window, modify the query, save your changes, then click the **Close button** ✕

Change Field Types

Button Method

☐ Open the table in Design view
☐ To modify the data type for a particular field, click the Data Type field, click the **Data Type list arrow**, then click the appropriate data type for the field, using Table AC-2 on page 164 as a reference

MODIFY FIELD PROPERTIES

Note: Make sure Input Mask feature is installed before performing these steps

Change Field Properties to Display an Input Mask

Wizard Method

☐ Open the table in Design view
☐ Select the appropriate field, then click the **Input Mask property text box** in the Field Properties pane
☐ Click the **Build button** ..., then click **Yes** if prompted to save the table
☐ Navigate through the Input Mask Wizard, making selections or accepting the defaults as appropriate to create the Input Mask, then click **Finish**

Modify Input Masks

Menu Method

☐ Open the table in Table Design view
☐ Click the field to modify, click the **General tab** in the Field Properties pane if necessary, then click the **Input Mask property text box**
☐ Modify the Input Mask as appropriate using Table AC-5 as a reference

Table AC-5 The Parts of the Input Mask Entry

Part	Description	Options	Examples (parts appear in bold)	How a sample entry appears in Datasheet view or Form view
First	Controls display of data and data type that can be entered	9: an optional number 0: a required number ?: an optional letter L: a required letter \: the next character will display as entered	Telephone Number **\(999\)\\-000\\-0000**;1;*	(978)-555-7000 OR ( ) 555-7000
Second	Establishes whether all displayed characters (such as slashes in the Date field) are stored in the field, or just the part you type	0: stores all characters 1: stores only typed characters	Zip Code 00000\\-9999;**0**;	56178- OR 56178-7157

Table AC-5 The Parts of the Input Mask Entry (continued)

Part	Description	Options	Examples (parts appear in bold)	How a sample entry appears in Datasheet view or Form view
Third	Establishes the placeholder characters that will display to represent characters that will be typed in a field	* (asterisk) _ (underscore) # (pound sign)	Social Security Number 000\-00\-0000;0;**#**	Before typing, appears as: ###-##-#### After typing, appears as: 444-33-1111

Modify Field Properties for Tables Using Table Design View

Menu Method

☐ Open the table in Design view
☐ To specify how the data should be formatted, click the appropriate property box in the Field Properties pane, then make the modifications using Table AC-3 on page 165 as a reference

CREATE AND MODIFY RELATIONSHIPS

Create One-to-Many Relationships

Menu Method

☐ Switch to the database window if necessary, click **Tools** on the menu bar, then click **Relationships**, or right-click the database window, then click **Relationships** on the shortcut menu
☐ In the Relationships window, click **Relationships** on the menu bar, then click **Show Table** to display the Show Table dialog box if necessary
☐ In the Show Table dialog box, click the object(s) to include, clicking **Add** after each, then click **Close**
☐ Drag the field you want to relate from its field list to the field to which you want it to relate in the appropriate object field list
☐ In the Edit Relationships dialog box, click **Create**
☐ Click **File** on the menu bar, then click **Save**

Button Method

☐ Switch to the database window, if necessary, then click the **Relationships button** 🔢 on the Database toolbar
☐ In the Relationships window, click the **Show Table button** 🔓 to display the Show Table dialog box if necessary
☐ Follow the steps in the third through fifth bullets in the Create One-to-Many Relationships Menu Method above
☐ Click the **Save button** 🔲 on the Relationships toolbar

Access

Modify One-to-Many Relationships

Menu Method

☐ Switch to the database window if necessary, click **Tools** on the menu bar, then click **Relationships**, or right-click the database window, then click **Relationships** on the shortcut menu

☐ In the Relationships window, Click **Relationships** on the menu bar, then click **Edit Relationship**, or right-click the relationship arrow, then click **Edit Relationship** on the shortcut menu

☐ In the Edit Relationships dialog box, make the appropriate modifications, then click **OK**

Create Many-to-Many Relationships

Menu Method

☐ Open a database that contains two unrelated tables for which you want to establish a many-to-many relationship

☐ Create a new table in Table Design view that will be a junction table to join the two tables

☐ In the new table, designate foreign key fields to serve as the "many" side of a "one-to-many" link for each of the original tables

☐ Click the field to be the primary key, click **Edit** on the menu bar, then click **Primary Key**

☐ Click **File** on the menu bar, then click **Save**

☐ In the Save As dialog box, type the table name in the Table Name text box, click **OK**, then close Table Design view

☐ Click **Tools** on the menu bar, then click **Relationships**

☐ If necessary, in the Relationships window, click **Relationships** on the menu bar, then click **Show Table** to display the Show Table dialog box

☐ In the Show Table dialog box, click the two original tables and the new junction table, clicking **Add** after each, then click **Close** in the Show Table dialog box

☐ Create one-to-many relationships between the two original tables and the junction table by dragging the primary key field from the original table to the foreign key field of the junction table

☐ In the Edit Relationship dialog box, make the appropriate selections, then click **Create**

Button Method

☐ Follow the first through third bullets in Create Many-to-Many Relationships Menu Method above

☐ Click the field to be the primary key, then click the **Primary Key button** 🔑 on the Table Design toolbar

☐ Click the **Save button** 🖫 on the Table Design toolbar

☐ In the Save As dialog box, type the table name in the Table Name text box, click **OK**, then close Table Design view

☐ Click the **Relationships button** 🔲 on the Database toolbar

☐ If necessary, in the Relationships window, click the **Show Table button** 🔲 on the Relationship toolbar to display the Show Table dialog box

☐ Follow the ninth through eleventh bullets in the Create Many-to-Many Relationships Menu Method above

ENFORCE REFERENTIAL INTEGRITY

Menu Method

☐ Switch to the database window if necessary, click **Tools** on the menu bar, then click **Relationships**, or right-click the database window, then click **Relationships** on the shortcut menu

☐ In the Relationships window, double-click the relationship to which you want to enforce referential integrity

☐ In the Edit Relationships dialog box, click the **Enforce Referential Integrity check box** to select it, then click **OK**

Button Method

☐ Switch to the database window, if necessary, then click the **Relationships button** 🔳 on the Database toolbar to open the Relationships window

☐ Follow the steps in the second and third bullets of the Enforce Referential Integrity Menu Method above

---

CREATE AND MODIFY QUERIES

Create Queries Using Design View

Menu Method

☐ Switch to the database window, if necessary, click **Insert** on the menu bar, then click **Query**

☐ In the New Query dialog box, click **Design View**, then click **OK**

☐ In the Show Table dialog box, click each object you want to query, clicking **Add** after each, then click **Close**

☐ Move the fields into the query design grid by dragging the fields from the field list to the appropriate column in the query design grid

☐ To specify a sort order for a field, click the **Sort cell list arrow**, then click the sort order

☐ Click **Query** on the menu bar, then click **Run**

☐ Click **File** on the menu bar, click **Save** to open the Save As dialog box, type an appropriate name in the Query Name text box, then click **OK**

Create Queries Using the Query Wizard

Menu Method

☐ Switch to the database window, if necessary, click **Insert** on the menu bar, then click **Query**

☐ In the New Query dialog box, click the query wizard option you want, using Table AC-6 as a reference, then click **OK**

☐ Navigate through the Query Wizard, making changes or accepting the defaults as appropriate to create the query, then click **Finish**

Access

Button Method

☐ Switch to the database window, if necessary, click the **Queries button** on the Objects bar, then double-click **Create query by using wizard**

☐ Navigate through the Query Wizard, making changes or accepting the defaults as appropriate to create the form, then click **Finish**

Table AC-6 New Query Dialog Box Options

Option	Description
Design View	Create a new query in Design view
Simple Query Wizard	Wizard that helps you create a query by choosing fields
Crosstab Query Wizard	Wizard that helps you create a crosstab query in a format similar to a spreadsheet
Find Duplicates Query Wizard	Wizard that helps you create a query to locate records that contain duplicate values in a table or query
Find Unmatched Query Wizard	Wizard that helps you create a query to find records in a table that have no related records in another specified table

SPECIFY MULTIPLE QUERY CRITERIA

Use AND Conditions in a Query

Menu Method

☐ Create a new query in Design view

☐ Click **Query** on the menu bar, then click **Show Table** to open the Show Table dialog box if necessary

☐ In the Show Table dialog box, click the appropriate table(s) and/or query(ies), clicking **Add** after each, then click **Close**

☐ Drag at least two fields from the appropriate field list to the appropriate column of the query design grid

☐ Click the **Criteria cell** for each field, then type the criteria

☐ Click the **Datasheet View button** on the Query Design toolbar to view the query results

Use OR Conditions

Menu Method

☐ Create a new query in Design view
☐ Click **Query** on the menu bar, then click **Show Table** to open the Show Table dialog box if necessary
☐ In the Show Table dialog box, click the appropriate table(s) and/or query(ies), clicking **Add** after each, then click **Close**
☐ Drag at least two fields from the appropriate field list to the appropriate column of the query design grid
☐ Click the **Criteria cell** for the first field, then type the criteria
☐ Click the **Or cell** (the Criteria cell in the second row) for the next field, then type the criteria
☐ Click the **Datasheet View button** 🔳 on the Query Design toolbar to view the query results

Modify Queries Using Query Design View

☐ Open the query in Design view, then make the modifications using Table AC-7 as a reference

Table AC-7 Query Design Modifications

Option	Method
Add a table or query	Click Query on the menu bar, click Show Table, choose the table or query in the Show Table dialog box, then click Close.
Remove a table or query	In the database window, right-click the table or query, then click Remove Table or Remove Query.
Add a field	Drag the field in the field list to the query grid.
Perform calculations	Type an expression in an empty field cell, using brackets around any field names. If your expression includes a function (such as SUM), display the Totals row, then change Group By in the calculated field to Expression.
Specify AND criteria	Enter multiple parameters separated by "And" in the Criteria field cell.
Specify OR criteria	Enter the first parameter in the Criteria cell, then enter the second parameter in the Or cell.
Sort records	Click a field's Sort list arrow, then choose Ascending, Descending, or (not sorted).

Access

CREATE FORMS

Create Forms Using the Form Wizard

Menu Method

☐ Switch to the database window if necessary, click **Insert** on the menu bar, then click **Form**

☐ In the New Form dialog box, click **Form Wizard**, then click **OK**

☐ Click the **Tables/Queries list arrow**, click the appropriate object, specify the fields you want in the form, then click **Next**

☐ Navigate through the rest of the Form Wizard, making appropriate selections and specifying a title as appropriate to create the form, then click **Finish**

Button Method

☐ Switch to the database window if necessary

☐ Click the **Forms button** 🔳 on the Objects bar, then double-click **Create form by using wizard**, or click the **Forms button** 🔳, click the **New button** 🔲 on the Database Window toolbar, click **Form Wizard** in the New Form dialog box, then click **OK**

☐ Follow the steps in the second through fourth bullets in the Create Forms Using the Form Wizard Menu Method above

Create Forms Using AutoForms

Menu Method

☐ Switch to the database window, if necessary, click **Insert** on the menu bar, then click **Form**

☐ In the New Form dialog box, click an appropriate **AutoForm**

☐ Click the **Choose the table or query where the object's data come from list arrow**, click the appropriate object, then click **OK**

Button Method

☐ In the database window, click the object from which you want to create a form

☐ Click the **New Object list arrow** 🔳▾ on the Database toolbar, then click **AutoForm**

Create a Form in Design View

Menu Method

☐ Switch to the database window, if necessary, click the **Forms button** on the Objects bar, then double-click **Create form in Design view**

☐ Click **View** on the menu bar, then click **Properties** or right-click the form, then click **Properties** on the shortcut menu

☐ In the property sheet, click the **Data tab** if necessary, then make sure that Form appears in the text box above the Data tab (if it does not appear, click the **text box list arrow**, then click **Form**)

☐ Click the **Record Source list arrow**, then click the source object on which you want to base the form

☐ Click **View** on the menu bar, then click **Properties** to close the property sheet

☐ Drag each field from the field list to the appropriate location on the form

☐ Click **File** on the menu bar, click **Save**, type an appropriate name for the form in the Save As dialog box, then click **OK**

Button Method

☐ In the database window, click the **Forms button** 🖼 on the Objects bar, then click the **New button** 🖼 on the Database Window toolbar

☐ In the New Form dialog box, click **Design View**, specify the object on which you want to base the form, then click **OK**

☐ If the field list is not open, click the **Field List button** on the Forms toolbar

☐ Drag each field from the source object window to the appropriate location on the form

☐ Click the **Save button** 🖫 on the Form Design toolbar

ADD AND MODIFY FORM CONTROLS AND PROPERTIES

Apply an AutoFormat to a Form

Button Method

☐ Open the form you want to format in Design view

☐ Click the **AutoFormat button** 🔯 on the Form Design toolbar

☐ In the AutoFormat dialog box, click the AutoFormat you want, then click **OK**

Modify a Control on a Form

☐ Open the form you want to modify in Design view
☐ Click the control you want to modify to select it
☐ Use Table AC-8 as a reference to modify the control appropriately
☐ Use the pointers described in Table AC-9 to move or resize a control

Table AC-8 Common Formatting Toolbar Buttons

Formatting (Form/Report) toolbar buttons	Button name	Used to
	Font list box	Change the font
11	Font Size list box	Change font size
B	Bold	Apply bold formatting
I	Italic	Apply italic formatting
U	Underline	Apply underline formatting
	Fill/Back Color	Change background color
A	Font/Fore Color	Change font color
	Line/Border Color	Change border color
	Line/Border Width	Change border widths
	Special Effect	Apply shadowed, etched, and other special effects

Table AC-9 Form Design View Pointer Shapes

Shape	When does this shape appear?	Action
▷	By default when you point to any control on the form that is not selected	Single-click to select a control
🖐	When you point to a selected control's edge (not to a sizing handle or the move handle)	Drag to move the selected control(s)
☝	When you point to a selected control's larger sizing handle in the upper-left corner of the control	Drag to move only the single control where pointer is currently positioned and not any other selected controls
↔,↕, ↘,↗	When you point to a sizing handle	Drag to resize a control; double-click to resize the control to fit the text

CREATE REPORTS

Create Reports Using the Report Wizard

Menu Method

- [ ] Switch to the database window, click **Insert** on the menu bar, then click **Report**
- [ ] In the New Report dialog box, click **Report Wizard**, specify the table or query on which you want to base the report, then click **OK**
- [ ] Navigate through the Report Wizard, specifying the fields, grouping levels, sort order, layout, style, and title to create the report, then click **Finish**

Button Method

- [ ] Click the **Reports button** 🔲 on the Objects bar, click the **New button** 🔲 on the Database Window toolbar, click **Report Wizard** in the New Report dialog box, then click **OK**
- [ ] Follow the steps in the third bullet of the Create Reports Using the Report Wizard Menu Method above

Create and Modify a Report in Report Design View

Menu Method

- [ ] Switch to the database window if necessary, click **Insert** on the menu bar, click **Report**
- [ ] In the New Report dialog box, click **Design View**, specify the table or query from which you want the report's data to come, then click **OK**
- [ ] If the field list is not open, click the **Field List button** 🔲 on the Report Design toolbar
- [ ] Drag the field(s) you want to include in the report from the field list to the appropriate section(s) of the report using Table AC-10 as a reference
- [ ] Add other objects as necessary to complete the report, then make any modifications you want by moving, resizing, or formatting the report controls

Button Method

- [ ] Switch to the database window, click the **Reports button** 🔲 on the Objects bar, then click the **New button** 🔲 on the Database Window toolbar
- [ ] Follow the steps in the second through fifth bullets in the Create and Modify a Report in Report Design View Menu Method above

Access

Table AC-10 Report Sections

Section	Information that can appear here	Location in printed report
Report Header	Report title, company graphics, graphic line to separate the title	Only on the first page of the report at the top of the page
Page Header	Page numbers, author information, a date field	On the top of every page; on the first page, it appears below the report header
Group Header	Text boxes for the grouped records	Before each record group
Detail	Text boxes for the fields in the table or query that the report is based on	For each record
Group Footer	Any calculations for a group of records	After each group of records
Page Footer	Page numbers, author information, a date field	On the bottom of each page
Report Footer	Summary information or calculations for all of the records and groups in the report	Only on the last page of the report, at the bottom of the page

Sort and Group Data in Reports

Menu Method

☐ Open the report in Design view
☐ Click **View** on the menu bar, then click **Sorting and Grouping**
☐ Select the appropriate options in the Sorting and Grouping dialog box, then click the **Close button** ☒

Button Method

☐ Open the report in Design view
☐ Click the **Sorting and Grouping button** ▦ on the Report Design toolba
☐ Select the appropriate options in the Sorting and Grouping dialog box, then click the **Close button** ☒

ADD AND MODIFY REPORT CONTROL PROPERTIES

Format Reports Using Report Design View

Button Method

☐ Open the report in Report Design view
☐ Click the control you want to modify to select it
☐ Modify the control, using Table AC-8 on page 176 as a reference

Add Calculated Controls to Reports

Button Method

☐ Open the report in Report Design view
☐ Click the **Text Box button** ▣ on the Toolbox, then click the location in the report where you want add the calculated control to insert a text box control
☐ Type = in the new field value text box, type the formula or function you want, then press **[Enter]**
☐ Click the label for the new text box control to select it, select the placeholder label text, type appropriate text for the new label, then press **[Enter]**

Add Subtotals for Groups of Records

Button Method

☐ Open the report in Report Design view
☐ Click the **Text Box button** ▣ on the Toolbox, then click the location on the report where you want to place a text box to hold the subtotal for the record group (such as in the Group Footer section)
☐ Click the **Properties button** ▣ on the Report Design toolbar to open the property sheet for the new text box
☐ In the property sheet, click in the **Control Source property box** if necessary, type **=SUM ([Fieldname])**, where "Fieldname" is the name of the field you want to subtotal
☐ Close the property sheet, click the field label text box for the new text box control, select the placeholder label text, type an appropriate label, then press **[Enter]**

Add Date and Time Controls

Menu Method

☐ Open the report in Design view
☐ Click **Insert** on the menu bar, then click **Date and Time**
☐ Select the appropriate options in the Date and Time dialog box, then click **OK**
☐ If necessary, move the Date and Time controls from the Report Header section to appropriate locations in the report

Button Method

☐ Open the report in Design view
☐ Click the **Text Box button** ▣ on the Toolbox toolbar, then click the report where you want the date or time to appear
☐ Click **Unbound** in the new field value text box, type either **=Date()** or **=Time()**, then press **[Enter]**
☐ Replace the placeholder label text in the field name text box with appropriate text, or delete the field name text box for the label

Add SubReport Controls to Access Reports

Button Method

☐ Open the report in Design view

☐ Click the **Subform/Subreport button** 🖩 on the Toolbox, then click the report where you want to add the subreport controls

☐ Navigate through the SubReport Wizard, making changes or accepting the defaults to create the SubReport as appropriate, then click **Finish**

CREATE A DATA ACCESS PAGE

Menu Method

☐ Switch to the database window, if necessary, click **Insert** on the menu bar, then click **Page**

☐ In the New Data Access Page dialog box, click **Page Wizard**, then click **OK**

☐ Navigate through the Page Wizard, specifying the table or query on which you want to base the page, selecting fields, specifying grouping levels and a sort order, and entering an appropriate title to create the data access page, then click **Finish**

Wizard Method

☐ Switch to the database window, if necessary, click the **Pages button** 🖩 on the Objects bar, then double-click **Create data access page by using wizard**

☐ Follow the steps in the third bullet in the Create a Data Access Page Menu Method above

Access Specialist Skill Set 2: Entering Data

Enter, Edit, and Delete Records

Enter Records in Datasheet View or Form View

Menu Method

☐ Open the table in Datasheet view or Form view
☐ To enter a new record, click in the first blank cell in the table or form, type the data for the first field, then press **[Tab]** to go to the next field in the record

Add Records in Datasheet View or Form View

Menu Method

☐ Open the table in Datasheet view or Form view
☐ Click **Insert** on the menu bar, then click **New Record** or in Datasheet view, right-click any record selector button, then click **New Record** on the shortcut menu

Button Method

☐ Open the table in Datasheet view or Form view
☐ In Datasheet view, click the **New Record button** ▸ on the Table Datasheet toolbar, or in Form View, click the **New Record button** ▸✳ on the Record Navigation bar

Delete Records in Datasheet View or Form View

Menu Method

☐ Open the table in Datasheet view or Form view
☐ In Datasheet view, click anywhere in the record you want to delete, or in Form View, navigate to the record you want to delete
☐ Click **Edit** on the menu bar, then click **Delete Record**
☐ Click **Yes** in the alert box to confirm the deletion

Button Method

☐ Open the table in Datasheet view or Form view
☐ In Datasheet view, click the **Delete Record button** ▨ on the Table Datasheet toolbar, or in Form View, click the **Delete Record button** ▨ on the Form View toolbar
☐ Click **Yes** in the alert box to confirm the deletion

Edit Records in Datasheet View or Form View

Button and Keyboard Methods

☐ Open the table in Datasheet view or Form view, then use Table AC-11 as a reference to edit the records

Access

Table AC-11 Methods for Editing Records in Form View or Datasheet View

Action	Keyboard	Button
Deletes one character to the left of the insertion point	[Backspace]	
Deletes one character to the right of the insertion point	[Delete]	
Toggles between Edit and Navigation mode	[F2]	
Undoes the change to the current field	[Esc]	Undo button 🔄
Undoes all changes to the current record	[Esc][Esc]	
Starts the Spell Check feature	[F7]	Spelling button ✓
Inserts the value from the same field in the previous record into the current field	[Ctrl][']	
Inserts the current date in a date field	[Ctrl][;]	

NAVIGATE AMONG RECORDS

Button Method

☐ Open the table in Datasheet view or Form view, then use Table AC-12 as a reference to navigate among the records

Table AC-12 Navigation Buttons on the Record Navigation Bar

Button	Name
⏮	First Record button
◀	Previous Record button
▶	Next Record button
⏭	Last Record button

Keyboard Method

☐ Open the table in Table Datasheet or Form view, then use Table AC-13 as a reference to navigate among the records. (*Note*: In Form view, you need to press [F2] so that you are in Edit mode before using these methods.)

Table AC-13 Common Keyboard Navigation Techniques

Keyboard key or key combination	Moves to the following location
↑	Same field in the previous record (Datasheet view)
↓	Same field in the next record (Datasheet view)
→, [Enter] or [Tab]	Next field in same record

Table AC-13 Common Keyboard Navigation Techniques (continued)

Keyboard key or key combination	Moves to the following location
←, or [Shift][Tab]	Previous field in same record
↑, or [Shift][Tab]	Previous field (Form view)
↓, or [Tab]	Next field (Form view)
[Ctrl][Home]	First field of the first record
[Home]	First field of the current record
[Ctrl][End]	Last field of the last record
[End]	Last field of the current record
[Page Down] or [Page Up]	Down or up one screen at a time

IMPORT DATA TO ACCESS

Import Data from an Excel Workbook

Menu Method

- ☐ Click **File** on the menu bar, point to **Get External Data**, then click **Import**
- ☐ In the Import dialog box, navigate to the appropriate drive and folder, click the **Files of type list arrow**, click **Microsoft Excel**, click the filename of the file you want to import, then click **Import**
- ☐ Navigate through the Import Spreadsheet Wizard, making the appropriate selection or specifying appropriate settings to create the database, then click **Finish**
- ☐ Click **OK** in the message box

Button Method

- ☐ Switch to the database window, if necessary, click the **Tables button** ▦ Tables on the Objects bar, then click the **New button** ▦ on the Database Window toolbar
- ☐ In the New Table dialog box, click **Import Table**, then click **OK**
- ☐ Follow the steps in the second through fourth bullets in the Import Data from an Excel Workbook Menu Method above

Import Objects from Another Access Database

Menu Method

- ☐ Click **File** on the menu bar, point to **Get External Data**, then click **Import**
- ☐ In the Import dialog box, navigate to the appropriate drive and folder, click the **Files of type list arrow**, click **Microsoft Office Access** if necessary, click the filename of the file you want to import, then click **Import**
- ☐ In the Import Objects dialog box, click the appropriate tab(s), then click the object(s) you want to import
- ☐ Click **OK** to import the object(s) to the open database

Access

ACCESS SPECIALIST SKILL SET 3: ORGANIZING DATA

CREATE AND MODIFY CALCULATED FIELDS AND AGGREGATE FUNCTIONS

Add a Calculated Field to a Query

Keyboard Method

- ☐ Open the query in Design view
- ☐ Click the first blank field cell in the query design grid
- ☐ Type the heading for the calculated field, type **:** [colon], type an appropria[] expression using brackets around any field names, then press **[Enter]**

OR

- ☐ Open the query in Design view
- ☐ Right-click the first blank field cell in the query design grid, then click **Zoom** on the shortcut menu
- ☐ In the Zoom dialog box, type the expression using square brackets around any field names, then click **OK**

USE AGGREGATE FUNCTIONS IN QUERIES

Button Method

- ☐ Open the query in Design view
- ☐ Click the **Totals button** Σ on the Query Design toolbar to display th[] Total row in the query design grid
- ☐ Click **Group By** in the Total row for the field, click the **Group By list arrow**, then click the appropriate aggregate function, using Table AC-[] as a reference

Table AC-14 Aggregate Functions

Function	Used to calculate the	Used for field types
Sum	Total value	Number, Date/Time, Currency, and AutoNumber
Avg	Average value	Number, Date/Time, Currency, and AutoNumber
Min	Lowest value in a field	Text, Number, Date/Time, Currency, and AutoNumber

Table AC-14 Aggregate Functions (continued)

Function	Used to calculate the	Used for field types
Max	Highest value in a field	Text, Number, Date/Time, Currency, and AutoNumber
Count	Number of values in a field (not counting null values)	Text, Memo, Number, Date/Time, Currency, AutoNumber, Yes/No, and OLE Object
StDev	Standard deviation of values	Number, Date/Time, Currency, and AutoNumber
Var	Variance of values	Number, Date/Time, Currency, and AutoNumber

MODIFY FORM LAYOUT

Align and Space Form Controls

☐ Open the form in Design view, then select the control(s) you want to modify

☐ Make the desired alignment changes using Table AC-15 as a reference

☐ To change the spacing of a form control, drag it to the location you want using the 🖐 pointer

Table AC-15 Alignment Controls

Button	Button name
🔲	Align Left
🔲	Align Right
🔲	Center

Show Form Headers and Footers

Menu Method

☐ Open the form in Design view

☐ Click **View** on the menu bar or right-click a section title bar on the form, then click **Form Header/Footer**

Access

Hide Form Headers and Footers

Menu Method

☐ Open the form in Design view
☐ Move any controls that contain information you want to keep from the header and footer to another section of the report before turning the header and footer off
☐ Click **View** on the menu bar or right-click a section title bar on the form, then click **Form Header/Footer** to toggle the header and footer on and off
☐ Click **Yes** in the message box to delete the controls in the header and footer if necessary

MODIFY REPORT LAYOUT AND PAGE SETUP

Align and Space Report Controls

☐ Open the report in Design view, then select the control(s) to modify
☐ Make the desired alignment changes using Table AC-15 as a reference
☐ To change the position of a report control, drag the control to the location you want using the 🖑 pointer

Resize Report Controls

Mouse method

☐ Open the report in Design view, then select the control(s) you want to resize
☐ Position the pointer over a sizing handle until it changes to one of the resize pointers (↔, ↕, ↙, ↘), drag to resize it appropriately, then release the mouse pointer

Change Page Orientation

☐ Open the report in either Design view or Print Preview
☐ Click **File** on the menu bar, then click **Page Setup**
☐ In the Page Setup dialog box, click the **Page tab**
☐ Click either the **Portrait** or **Landscape option button** to change the page orientation, then click **OK**

FORMAT DATASHEETS

Menu Method

☐ Open the table or query in Datasheet view
☐ Click **Format** on the menu bar, click **Font**, then select the appropriate options in the Font dialog box
☐ Click **OK**

Button Method

☐ Open the table or query in Datasheet view
☐ Apply appropriate formatting to the datasheet using the buttons on the Formatting toolbar and using Table AC-16 as a reference

Keyboard Method

☐ Open the table or query in Datasheet view
☐ Apply appropriate formatting to the datasheet by pressing the appropriate keyboard combinations using Table AC-16 as a reference

Table AC-16 Button and Keyboard Methods for Applying Formatting Effects

Formatting toolbar button	Keyboard shortcut	Used to
Font		Change font type
Font Size 11		Change font size
Bold **B**	[Ctrl][B]	Turn bold font style on and off
Italic _I_	[Ctrl][I]	Turn italic font style on and off
Underline U	[Ctrl][U]	Turn underline font style on and off
Fill/Back Color		Change the datasheet background color
Font/Fore Color **A**		Change the datasheet text color
Line/Border Color		Change the datasheet gridline color
Gridlines		Determine which gridlines appear on the datasheet
Special Effect		Change the effect (flat, raised, or sunken) of the datasheet cells

SORT RECORDS

Sort Records in Datasheet View

Menu Method

☐ Open the table or query in Datasheet view
☐ Click any value in the field by which to sort
☐ Click **Records** on the menu bar, point to **Sort**, then click the appropriate sort option

Button Method

☐ Open the table or query in Datasheet view
☐ Click any value in the field by which you want to sort
☐ Click the **Sort Descending button** 📊 or the **Sort Ascending button** 📊 on the Datasheet toolbar

Sort Records in Query Design View

Button Method

☐ Open the query in Design view
☐ Click the **Sort cell** for the field by which to sort, click the **list arrow**, then click **Ascending** or **Descending**

FILTER RECORDS

Filter Records Using Filter by Selection

Menu Method

☐ Open the table or query in Datasheet view
☐ Click the cell in the datasheet that contains criteria that you want to apply as a filter to the rest of the data in the table or query
☐ Click **Records** on the menu bar, point to **Filter**, then click **Filter by Selection**

Button Method

☐ Open the table or query in Datasheet view
☐ Click the cell in the datasheet that contains criteria that you want to apply as a filter to the rest of the data in the table or query
☐ Click the **Filter By Selection button** 🔀 on the Datasheet toolbar

Filter Records Using Filter by Form

Menu Method

☐ Open the table or query in Datasheet view
☐ Click **Records** on the menu bar, point to **Filter**, then click **Filter by Form**
☐ Click the cell that contains the value that you want all records in the filter results to contain, then type the criteria using Table AC-17 as a reference, or click the cell by which to filter, click the **list arrow**, then click the value by which to filter
☐ To filter by additional criteria, click the **Or tab**, then enter additional criteria
☐ Click **Filter** on the menu bar, then click **Apply Filter/Sort**

Button Method

☐ Open the table or query in Datasheet view
☐ Click the **Filter By Form button** 🔀 on the Filter/Sort toolbar
☐ Click the cell that contains the value by which to filter, type the filter criteria using Table AC-17 as a reference, or click the cell by which to sort, click the **list arrow**, then click the value by which to filter
☐ To filter by additional criteria, click the **Or tab**, then enter additional criteria
☐ Click the **Apply Filter button** 🔀 on the Filter/Sort toolbar

Table AC-17 Comparison Operators

Operator	Description	Expression	Meaning
<	Less than	<"Cassidy"	Names from A through Cassidy, but not Cassidy
<=	Less than or equal to	<="Delaney"	Names from A through, and including, Delaney
>	Greater than	>450	Numbers greater than 450
>=	Greater than or equal to	>=450	Numbers greater than or equal to 450
<>	Not equal to	<>"Malone"	Any name except for Malone
OR	Needs to meet 1 of 2 criteria	"Murphy" OR "Malone"	Only names Murphy and Malone
AND	Needs to meet both of 2 criteria	>="Cassidy" AND <="Murphy"	All names between and including Cassidy and Murphy

Create and Apply Advanced Filters

Menu Method

☐ Open the table in Datasheet view, click **Records** on the menu bar, point to **Filter**, then click **Advanced Filter/Sort**

☐ Double-click each field you want in the filter to add it to the filter design grid

☐ Click the **Criteria cell** for each field, then type the criteria you want each record in the filter results to meet using Table AC-17 as a reference

☐ Click the **Sort cell** for each field, click the **list arrow**, then click **Ascending** or **Descending** as appropriate

☐ Click **Filter** on the menu bar, then click **Apply Filter/Sort**

Button Method

☐ Follow the first through fourth bullets in the Create and Apply Advanced Filters Menu Method above

☐ Click the **Apply Filter button** 🔽 on the Table Datasheet toolbar

Access

ACCESS SPECIALIST SKILL SET 4: MANAGING DATABASES

IDENTIFY OBJECT DEPENDENCIES

Task Pane Method

☐ Open the object for which you want to view dependencies
☐ Click **View** on the menu bar, click **Object Dependencies**, then click the control or field for which you want to view dependencies
☐ Click the **Objects that I depend on** or the **Objects that depend on me option button** in the Object Dependencies task pane to toggle to different dependency views
☐ Click the **Expand** or **Collapse indicators** next to objects and categories in the Object Dependencies task pane to display or hide objects
☐ Click **OK** in the message box, if necessary
☐ View the information in the task pane

VIEW OBJECTS AND OBJECT DATA IN OTHER VIEWS

Preview a Report for Printing

Menu Method

☐ In the database window, click the **Reports button** 🖭 on the Objects bar, then click the report you want to preview
☐ Click **File** on the menu bar, then click **Print Preview**

OR

☐ In the database window, click the Reports button 🖭 on the Objects bar, then right-click the report you want to preview
☐ Click **Print Preview** on the shortcut menu

Button Method

☐ In the database window, click the **Reports button** 🖭 on the Objects bar, then click the report you want to preview
☐ Click the **Preview button** 🔍 Preview on the Database Window toolbar

OR

☐ Open the report you want to preview in Design view, then click the **Print Preview button** 🔍 on the Report Design toolbar

OR

☐ In the database window, click the **Reports button** 🖭 on the Objects bar, then double-click the report

View Database Objects

Menu Method

☐ On the Objects bar, click the button for the object type you want to view
☐ Right-click the object you want to view
☐ On the shortcut menu, click **Open** to edit the object, or **Design View** to modify the object's design, using Table AC-18 as a reference

Button Method

☐ In the database window, click the button for the object type you want to view on the Objects bar

☐ Click the **Open button** 📷 on the Database Window toolbar to open the object in a view used for editing data, or the **Design button** 🔍 on the Database Window toolbar to open the object in Design view, using Table AC-18 as a reference

Keyboard Method

☐ In the database window, click the button for the object type you want to view on the Objects bar

☐ Click the object you want to view, then press **[Enter]** to open it in the view used to edit data

Mouse Method

☐ In the database window, click the button for the object type you want to view on the Objects bar

☐ Double-click the object you want to view to open it in the view used to edit data

Table AC-18   Access Views

Object	View	Used to
Form	Form view	Edit and enter data
Form	Form Design view	Modify the design and structure of the form
Form	PivotTable/PivotChart	Change the layout of a form to analyze and recalculate data
Report	Print Preview	View a report on screen before you print it
Report	Report Design view	Change the layout and format of a report
Report	Layout Preview	View the layout of a report without viewing the actual data
Table played	Datasheet view	View data for many records dis- in row and column format
Table	Table Design view	Add or delete fields, set field properties
Table	Datasheet view	Find, edit, and enter records
Table/Chart	PivotTable/PivotChart	Change the layout of a table to

Access

Table AC-18 Access Views (continued)

Object	View	Used to
Query	Query Design view	Modify the query
Query	Query Datasheet view	Find, edit, and enter records
Query	PivotTable/PivotChart	Change the layout of a query to analyze and recalculate data
Query	SQL view	View and modify the SQL statement
Data Access Page	Web Page Preview	Preview the data access page in your browser

PRINT DATABASE OBJECTS AND DATA

Print a Database Object

Menu Method

☐ Open the object you want to print
☐ Click **File** on the menu bar, click **Print**, then click **OK** in the Print dialog box

OR

☐ Right-click the object in the database window
☐ Click **Print** on the shortcut menu

Button Method

☐ Open the object to print
☐ Click the **Print button** 🔲 on the toolbar

Print Selected Records

Menu Method

☐ Open the object that contains the data you want to print, then select the record(s) you want to print
☐ Click **File** on the menu bar, then click **Print**
☐ In the Print dialog box, click the **Selected Record(s) option button**, then click **OK**

EXPORT DATA FROM ACCESS

Export Data to an Excel Workbook

Menu Method

☐ In the database window, click the **Tables button** or the **Queries button** on the Objects bar as appropriate, then click the object you want to export
☐ Click **File** on the menu bar, then click **Export**
☐ In the Export dialog box, navigate to the appropriate drive and folder, click the **Save as type list arrow**, click **Microsoft Excel 97-2003**, then click **Export**

Button Method

☐ In the database window, click the **Tables button** or the **Queries button** on the Objects bar as appropriate, then click the object you want to export
☐ Click the **OfficeLinks list arrow** 🖳▾ on the Database toolbar, then click **Analyze It with Microsoft Office Excel**

Export Data to a Web Page

Menu Method

☐ Open the report you want to export
☐ Click **File** on the menu bar, then click **Export**
☐ In the Export Report dialog box, navigate to the appropriate drive and folder, click the **Save as type list arrow**, click **HTML Documents**, then click **Export**
☐ Click **OK** in the HTML Output Options dialog box

BACK UP A DATABASE

Menu Method

☐ Switch to the database window, if necessary, click **Tools** on the menu bar, point to **Replication**, then click **Create Replica**
☐ Click **Yes** in the message box to close the database
☐ Click **Yes** in the message box to make a backup of the database and convert the database to a Design Master
☐ In the **Location of New Replica** dialog box, select the location, select any other appropriate options, then click **OK**
☐ Click **OK** in the message box

COMPACT AND REPAIR DATABASES

Menu Method

☐ Make sure no database is open
☐ Click **Tools** on the menu bar, point to **Database Utilities**, then click **Compact and Repair Database**
☐ In the Database to Compact From dialog box, click the **Look in list arrow**, navigate to the appropriate drive and folder, click the database, then click **Compact**
☐ In the Compact Database Into dialog box, click the **Save in list arrow**, navigate to the appropriate drive and folder, type the filename, then click **Save**

MICROSOFT OFFICE POWERPOINT
2003 EXAM REFERENCE

Getting Started with PowerPoint 2003

The PowerPoint Microsoft Office Specialist exam assumes a basic level of proficiency in PowerPoint. This section is intended to help you reference these basic skills while you are preparing to take the PowerPoint Specialist exam.

> □ Starting and exiting PowerPoint
> □ Viewing the PowerPoint window
> □ Using toolbars
> □ Using task panes
> □ Creating, opening, and closing presentations
> □ Navigating in the PowerPoint window
> □ Saving presentations
> □ Getting Help

START AND EXIT POWERPOINT

Start PowerPoint

Button Method
□ Click the **Start button** ![start] on the Windows taskbar
□ Point to **All Programs**
□ Point to **Microsoft Office**
□ Click **Microsoft Office PowerPoint 2003**

OR
□ Double-click the **Microsoft PowerPoint program icon** ![icon] on the desktop

Exit PowerPoint

Menu Method
□ Click **File** on the menu bar, then click **Exit**

Button Method
□ Click the **Close button** ![X] on the program window title bar

Keyboard Method
□ Press **[Alt][F4]**

VIEW THE POWERPOINT WINDOW

Figure PPT-1   PowerPoint Window

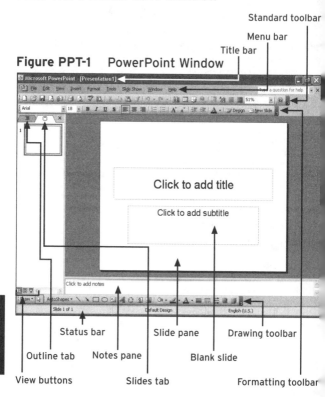

USE TOOLBARS

Display Toolbars

Menu Method

☐ Click **View** on the menu bar, point to **Toolbars**, then click the toolbar you want to display

OR

☐ Right-click any toolbar, then click the toolbar you want to display on the shortcut menu

Customize Toolbars

Menu Method

☐ Click **Tools** on the menu bar, then click **Customize**, or click **View** on the menu bar, point to **Toolbars**, then click **Customize**, or right-click any toolbar, then click **Customize** on the shortcut menu

☐ In the Customize dialog box, select the appropriate options, then click **Close**

Button Method

☐ Click the **Toolbar Options button** 🔹 or 🔹 on the right end of the toolbar you want to customize

☐ Point to **Add or Remove Buttons**, then click **Customize**

☐ In the Customize dialog box, select the appropriate options, then click **Close**

Reposition Toolbars

Mouse Method

☐ Position the pointer over the **Toolbar Move handle** ⋮ at the left end of any docked toolbar, or over the title bar of any floating toolbar

☐ When the pointer changes to ↔, press and hold the mouse button

☐ Drag the toolbar to a different location, then release the mouse button

USE TASK PANES

Display Task Panes

Menu Method

☐ If no task pane is open, click **View** on the menu bar, point to **Toolbars**, then click **Task Pane**, or right click the **Standard toolbar**, then click **Task Pane** on the shortcut menu

☐ Click the **Other Task Panes list arrow** ▼ on the task pane title bar, then click the appropriate task pane

☐ Click the **Back button** 🔙 on the task pane title bar to navigate to previously displayed task panes

Display Task Panes

Menu Method

☐ Click **View** on the menu bar, then click **Task Pane** or right-click any toolbar, then click **Task Pane** on the shortcut menu

Menu Method

☐ Click the **Close button** ✕ on the task pane title bar to close the task pane

PowerPoint

CREATE, OPEN, AND CLOSE PRESENTATIONS

Create a New Presentation

Menu Method
☐ Click **File** on the menu bar, then click **New**
☐ Choose the appropriate options in the New Presentation task pane

Button Method
☐ Click the **New button** 🔲 on the Standard toolbar
☐ Choose the appropriate options in the New Presentation task pane

Keyboard Method
☐ Press **[Ctrl][N]**
☐ Choose the appropriate options in the New Presentation task pane

Open an Existing Presentation

Menu Method
☐ Click **File** on the menu bar, then click **Open**
☐ In the Open dialog box, navigate to the appropriate drive and folder
☐ Click the file you want, then click **Open**

Task Pane Method
☐ Click a presentation under the Open section in the Getting Started task pane or click **More** under the Open section
☐ Follow the second and third bullets in the Open an Existing Presentation Menu Method above

Button Method
☐ Click the **Open button** 📄 on the Standard toolbar
☐ Follow the second and third bullets in the Open an Existing Presentation Menu Method above

Keyboard Method
☐ Press **[Ctrl][O]**
☐ Follow the second and third bullets in the Open an Existing Presentation Menu Method above

Close a Presentation

Menu Method
☐ Click **File** on the menu bar, then click **Close**
☐ If prompted to save the presentation, click **Yes** or **No** as appropriate

Button Method
☐ Click the **Close Window button** ☒ on the menu bar
☐ If prompted to save the presentation, click **Yes** or **No** as appropriate

Keyboard Method
☐ Press **[Ctrl][W]** or **[Alt][F4]**
☐ If prompted to save the presentation, click **Yes** or **No** as appropriate

NAVIGATE IN THE POWERPOINT WINDOW

Use Table PPT-1 as a reference to navigate in the PowerPoint window.

Table PPT-1 Keyboard Navigation Techniques

Key	Moves the insertion point
[Ctrl][Home] or [Ctrl][End]	To the beginning or end of the currently selected text box, or to the first or last slide on the Outline or Slides tab (if no slide object is selected)
[Home] or [End] box	To the beginning or end of the line of text in a selected text
[Page Down], [Page Up]	Down or up one slide at a time
[Tab] or	Between objects on a slide

SAVE A PRESENTATION

Save an Existing Presentation

Menu Method
☐ Click **File** on the menu bar, then click **Save**

Button Method
☐ Click the **Save button** 🖫 on the Standard toolbar

Keyboard Method
☐ Press **[Ctrl][S]**

Use Save As

Menu Method
☐ Click **File** on the menu bar, then click **Save As**
☐ In the Save As dialog box, click the **Save in list arrow** then navigate to the drive and folder where you want to store the presentation
☐ Type an appropriate presentation name in the File name text box, then click **Save**

Keyboard Method
☐ Press **[F12]**
☐ Follow the steps in the second and third bullets of the Use Save As Menu Method above

GET HELP

Menu Method
☐ Click **Help** on the menu bar, then click **Microsoft Office PowerPoint Help**
☐ Use Table PPT-2 as a reference to select the most appropriate way to search for help using the Microsoft PowerPoint Help task pane

PowerPoint

Button Method

☐ Click the **Microsoft PowerPoint Help button** 🔲 on the Standard toolbar
☐ Use Table PPT-2 as a reference to select the most appropriate way to search for help using the Microsoft PowerPoint Help task pane

OR

☐ Click the **Type a question for help box** on the menu bar
☐ Type a question or keywords relating to a PowerPoint topic, then press **[Enter]**
☐ View the results of the keyword search in the Search Results task pane, click an appropriate topic title, then read about the topic you clicked in the Microsoft Office PowerPoint Help window

Keyboard Method

☐ Press **[F1]**
☐ Use Table PPT-2 as a reference to select the most appropriate way to search for help using the Microsoft PowerPoint Help task pane

Table PPT-2 PowerPoint Help Task Pane Options

Option	To use
Table of Contents	Click the Table of Contents button in the task pane, click the **Expand indicator** next to each topic you want to explore further, then click the topic you want and read the results in the task pane
Search	Type a keyword in the Search for text box, click the **Start Searching button** ➡, then click the blue hyperlinked text to read more in the Microsoft Office Word Help Window, or click the grayed text to view the topic in the Table of Contents

POWERPOINT SPECIALIST EXAM REFERENCE

Skill Sets:

1. Creating content
2. Formatting content
3. Collaborating
4. Managing and delivering presentations

POWERPOINT SPECIALIST SKILL SET 1: CREATING CONTENT

CREATE NEW PRESENTATIONS FROM TEMPLATES

Create a Presentation Using the AutoContent Wizard

Menu Method

☐ Click **File** on the menu bar, then click **New**
☐ In the New Presentation task pane, click **From AutoContent wizard** under New
☐ Navigate through the AutoContent Wizard, making appropriate selections and specifying appropriate text to create the presentation, then click **Finish**

Create a Presentation Using a Design Template

Menu Method

☐ Click **File** on the menu bar, then click **New**
☐ In the New Presentation task pane, click **From design template** under New
☐ In the Slide Design task pane, click the appropriate template in the Apply a design template section

INSERT AND EDIT TEXT-BASED CONTENT

Add Text Boxes to Slides

Menu Method

☐ On the Slides or Outline tab, select the slide to which you want to add a text box
☐ Click **Insert** on the menu bar, then click **Text Box**
☐ Click the slide where you want to place the text box, then type the text

Button Method

☐ On the Slides or Outline tab, select the slide to which you want to add a text box

PowerPoint

□ Click the **Text Box button** 🔲 on the Drawing toolbar
□ Click the slide where you want to place the text box, then type the text

Add Text to a Text Placeholder

Menu Method

□ On the Slides or Outline tab, select the appropriate slide
□ Click the text placeholder in the Slide pane
□ Type the appropriate text

Delete Text from Slides

Keyboard Method

□ On the Slides or Outline tab, select the appropriate slide
□ Select the text in its text placeholder or text box on the slide
□ Edit the text appropriately, using Table PPT-3 as a reference

Table PPT-3 Keyboard Editing Techniques

Keyboard	Effect
[Backspace]	Deletes one character to the left of the insertion point
[Ctrl][Backspace]	Deletes one word to the left of the insertion point
[Delete]	Deletes one character to the right of the insertion point
[Ctrl][Delete]	Deletes one word to the right of the insertion point

Correct Spelling and Grammar Errors

Menu Method

□ Click **Tools** on the menu bar, then click **Spelling**
□ In the Spelling and Grammar dialog box, choose to ignore or change misspelled words, add words to the dictionary, and accept or ignore grammar suggestion as appropriate
□ When the spelling and grammar check is complete, click **OK** in the message box

Button Method

□ Click the **Spelling and Grammar button** 🔲 on the Standard toolbar
□ Follow the steps in the second and third bullets in the Correct Spelling and Grammar Errors Menu Method above

Keyboard Method

□ Press **[F7]**
□ Follow the steps in the second and third bullets in the Correct Spelling and Grammar Errors Menu Method above

Use the Thesaurus

Menu Method

☐ Select the word for which you want to find a synonym
☐ Click **Tools** on the menu bar, then click **Thesaurus**
☐ In the Research task pane, point to the appropriate synonym, click the down arrow that appears, then click **Insert**

OR

☐ Right-click the word for which you want to find a synonym
☐ Point to **Synonyms** on the shortcut menu, then click the appropriate synonym, or click **Thesaurus**, then in the Research task pane, point to the appropriate synonym, click the down arrow that appears, then click **Insert**

Keyboard Method

☐ Select the word for which you want to find a synonym
☐ Press **[Shift][F7]**
☐ In the Research task pane, point to the appropriate synonym, click the down arrow that appears, then click **Insert**

Import Text from an Outline

Menu Method

☐ Click **Insert** on the menu bar, then click **Slides from Outline**
☐ In the Insert Outline dialog box, click the **Look in list arrow**, then navigate to the drive and folder where the Word document you want to import is stored
☐ Click the filename of the Word document, then click **Insert**

Import Slides from Another File

Menu Method

☐ Click **Insert** on the menu bar, then click **Slides from Files**
☐ In the Slide Finder dialog box, click **Browse**
☐ In the Browse dialog box, navigate to the appropriate drive and folder, click the file that contains the slides you want, then click **Open**
☐ In the Slide Finder dialog box, select the slides you want to insert, then click **Insert** or click **Insert All**
☐ Click **Close**

INSERT TABLES, CHARTS, AND DIAGRAMS

Create Tables on Slides

Menu Method

☐ On the Slides or Outline tab, select the appropriate slide or click the **New Slide button** [New Slide] on the Formatting toolbar to insert a new slide
☐ Click **Insert** on the menu bar, then click **Table**

☐ In the Insert Table dialog box, specify the number of rows and columns, then click **OK**

☐ Type text and insert graphics in the table as appropriate, using Table PPT-4 as a reference to navigate between cells

Button Method

☐ On the Slides or Outline tab, select the appropriate slide or click the **New Slide button** [New Slide] on the Formatting toolbar to insert a new slide

☐ Click the **Insert Table button** 🔳 on the Standard toolbar

☐ On the palette that opens, drag to select the number of columns and rows, then release the **mouse button**

☐ Type text and insert graphics in the table as appropriate, using Table PPT-4 as a reference to navigate between cells

OR

☐ On the Slides or Outline tab, select the appropriate slide

☐ Click the **Draw Table button** 🔳 on the Tables and Borders toolbar

☐ Draw columns and rows by dragging ⌀ on the slide in the Slide pane

☐ Type text and insert graphics in the table as appropriate, using Table PPT-4 as a reference to navigate between cells

Task Pane Method

☐ On the Slides or Outline tab, select the appropriate slide, then open the Slide Layout task pane

☐ Click the appropriate Content Layout option in the Content Layouts section of the Slide Layout task pane (*Note*: Do not use the Blank layout option)

☐ Click the **Insert Table button** 🔳 on the content layout placeholder

☐ Follow the third and fourth bullets in the Create Tables on Slides Menu Method

Table PPT-4 Table Navigation Techniques

Keyboard	Effect
[Tab]	Moves to the next cell; at the end of a table, inserts a new row
[Shift][Tab]	Moves to the previous cell
[↓]	Moves to the cell directly below in the next row down
[↑]	Moves to the cell directly above in the previous row above

Add Charts to Slides

Menu Method

☐ On the Slides or Outline tab, select the appropriate slide

☐ Click **Insert** on the menu bar, then click **Chart**

☐ Type the data for the chart in the datasheet, press **[Tab]** to navigate between cells

☐ Click the **datasheet close button**

Button Method

☐ On the Slides or Outline tab, select the appropriate slide
☐ Click the **Insert Chart button** 📊 on the Standard toolbar
☐ Follow the third and fourth bullets in the Add Charts to Slides Menu Method

Task Pane Method

☐ On the Slides or Outline tab, select the appropriate slide
☐ Click the appropriate Content Layout option in the Content Layouts section of the Slide Layout task pane (*Note*: Do not use the Blank layout option)
☐ Click the **Insert Chart button** 📊 on the content layout placeholder
☐ Follow the third and fourth bullets in the Add Charts to Slides Menu Method

Add an Organization Chart or Diagram to a Slide

Menu Method

☐ On the Slides or Outline tab, select the appropriate slide
☐ Click **Insert** on the menu bar, then click **Diagram**
☐ In the Diagram Gallery, click the appropriate diagram or organization chart option, then click **OK**

Button Method

☐ On the Slides or Outline tab, select the appropriate slide
☐ Click the **Insert Diagram or Organization Chart button** 🔲 on the Drawing toolbar
☐ In the Diagram Gallery, click the appropriate diagram type or organization chart option, then click **OK**

INSERT PICTURES, SHAPES, AND GRAPHICS ON SLIDES

Add Clip Art Images to Slides

Menu Method

☐ On the Slides or Outline tab, select the appropriate slide
☐ Click **Insert** on the menu bar, point to **Picture**, then click **Clip Art**
☐ In the Clip Art task pane, type appropriate keywords in the Search for text box, then click **Go**
☐ Point to the image you want in the Clip Art task pane until a list arrow appears, click the **list arrow**, then click **Insert**
☐ Use the Move pointer ⁺🔾 to drag the image where you want it on the slide

Button Method

☐ On the Slides or Outline tab, select the appropriate slide
☐ Click the **Insert Clip Art button** 🖼 on the Drawing toolbar
☐ Follow the third through fifth bullets in the Add Clip Art Images to Slides Menu Method above

PowerPoint

Task Pane Method

☐ On the Slides or Outline tab, select the appropriate slide
☐ Click the appropriate content layout option in the Content Layouts section of the Slide Layout task pane (*Note:* Do not use the Blank layout option)
☐ Click the **Insert Clip Art button** 🖼 on the content layout placeholder
☐ In the Select Picture dialog box, type appropriate keywords in the Search text text box, then click **Go**
☐ Click the image you want to insert in the search results area, then click **OK**
☐ Use ⁺⁺ to drag the image to where you want it on the slide

Add Text to an AutoShape

Menu Method

☐ On the Slides or Outline tab, select the appropriate slide
☐ Click **Insert** on the menu bar, point to **Picture**, then click **AutoShapes**
☐ Click the appropriate AutoShape button on the AutoShapes toolbar to open a palette of AutoShapes for that button using Table PPT-5 as a reference, then click the AutoShape you want on the palette
☐ Click the appropriate location on the slide, type the text you want to appear in the AutoShape, then resize the AutoShape to fit the text, if necessary

Button Method

☐ On the Slides or Outline tab, select the appropriate slide
☐ Click the **AutoShapes button** AutoShapes ▾ on the Drawing toolbar, point to an AutoShape category to open the palette for that category using Table PPT-5 as a reference, then click the AutoShape you want on the palette
☐ Click the appropriate location on the slide, type the AutoShape text, then resize the AutoShape to fit the text if necessary

Table PPT-5 AutoShapes Toolbar and Palette Buttons

Button	Allows you to select a variety of	Examples
🖉	Lines	Straight, curly, freeform
🖾	Connectors	Straight, arrow, curved arrow
🖺	Basic Shapes	Rectangle, smiley face, donut, heart
🖻	Block Arrows	Left, right, curved, quad
🖳	Flowchart	Merge, extract, document
🖉	Stars and Banners	Scrolls, ribbons, 16-point star
🖵	Callouts	Line, cloud, oval
🖷	Action Buttons	Forward or Next, Back or Previous
🖸	More AutoShapes	CD drive, household items, and other clip art images

Add WordArt

Menu Method

☐ On the Slides or Outline tab, select the appropriate slide
☐ Click **Insert** on the menu bar, point to **Picture**, then click **WordArt**
☐ In the WordArt Gallery, click the appropriate style, then click **OK**
☐ In the Edit WordArt Text dialog box, type the text you want to create as WordArt, apply appropriate formatting to it, then click **OK**
☐ Use ↖ to drag the WordArt object to the appropriate location on the slide

Button Method

☐ On the Slides or Outline tab, select the appropriate slide
☐ Click the **Insert WordArt button** ◢ on the Drawing toolbar
☐ Follow the third through fifth bullets in the Add WordArt Menu Method above

---

INSERT OBJECTS

Add Images to Slides

Menu Method

☐ On the Slides or Outline tab, select the appropriate slide
☐ Click **Insert** on the menu bar, point to **Picture**, then click **From File**
☐ In the Insert Picture dialog box, navigate to the drive and folder that contains the image file you want
☐ Click the appropriate image file, then click **Insert**

Button Method

☐ On the Slides or Outline tab, select the appropriate slide
☐ Click the **Insert Picture button** 🖾 on the Drawing toolbar
☐ Follow the third and fourth bullets in the Add Images to Slides Menu Method above

Task Pane Method

☐ On the Slides or Outline tab, select the appropriate slide, then open the Slide Layout task pane
☐ Click the appropriate content layout option in the Content Layouts section of the Slide Layout task pane (*Note*: Do not use the Blank layout option)
☐ Click the **Insert Picture button** 🖾 on the content layout placeholder
☐ Follow the third and fourth bullets in the Add Images to Slides Menu Method above

Add Freeform Objects to Slides

Button Method

☐ On the Slides or Outline tab, select the appropriate slide
☐ Click the appropriate button on the Drawing toolbar, using Table PPT-6 as a reference
☐ Position ✛ where you want the upper-left portion of the shape to appear, drag to create the shape, then release the mouse button

PowerPoint

Table PPT-6 Drawing Toolbar Buttons

Button	Used to draw
Line button	Straight lines
Arrow button	Arrows
Oval button	Ovals or circles (Press and hold [Shift] while dragging to draw a circle)
Rectangle button	Rectangles or squares (Press and hold [Shift] while dragging to draw a square)

Add Sound Effects to Slides

Menu Method

☐ On the Slides or Outline tab, select the appropriate slide
☐ Click **Insert** on the menu bar, point to **Movies and Sounds**, then click **Sound from File**
☐ In the Insert Sound dialog box, navigate to the appropriate drive and folder, click the sound file you want, then click **OK**
☐ In the message box, specify whether the sound will play automatically or when clicked
☐ Use ⤢ to drag the sound icon to the appropriate location on the slide

Add Video Effects to Slides

Menu Method

☐ On the Slides or Outline tab, select the appropriate slide
☐ Click **Insert** on the menu bar, point to **Movies and Sounds**, then click **Movie from File**
☐ In the Insert Movie dialog box, navigate to the appropriate drive and folder, click the movie file you want, then click **OK**
☐ In the message box, specify whether the movie will play automatically or when clicked
☐ Use ⤢ to drag the movie icon to the appropriate location on the slide

Embed Word Tables or Excel Charts on Slides

Menu Method

☐ On the Slides or Outline tab, select the appropriate slide
☐ Click **Insert** on the menu bar, then click **Object**
☐ In the Insert Object dialog box, click the **Create from file option button**, then click **Browse**
☐ In the Browse dialog box, navigate to the appropriate drive and folder, click the Word or Excel file you want to embed, then click **OK**
☐ In the Insert Object dialog box, click **OK**

Link Word Tables on Slides

Menu Method

☐ On the Slides or Outline tab, select the appropriate slide
☐ Click **Insert** on the menu bar, then click **Object**
☐ In the Insert Object dialog box, click the **Create from file option button**, then click **Browse**
☐ In the Browse dialog box, navigate to the appropriate drive and folder that contains the Word file you want to link, click the file, then click **OK**
☐ In the Insert Object dialog box, click the **Link check box**, then click **OK**

Link Excel Charts to Slides

Menu Method

☐ Start Microsoft Excel, open the file that contains the chart to which you want to link, then select the chart
☐ Click **Edit** on the menu bar, then click **Copy**
☐ Click the **Microsoft PowerPoint button** on the task bar
☐ On the Slides or Outline tab, select the appropriate slide
☐ Click **Edit** on the menu bar, then click **Paste Special**
☐ In the Paste Special dialog box, click **Microsoft Office Excel Chart Object** in the As: text box, click the **Paste link option button**, then click **OK**

PowerPoint

POWERPOINT SPECIALIST SKILL SET 2: FORMATTING CONTENT

Format Text-Based Content

Menu Method
- ☐ On the Slides or Outline tab, select the appropriate slide
- ☐ Select the text to format
- ☐ Click **Format** on the menu bar, then click **Font**
- ☐ In the Font dialog box, make the appropriate selections, then click **OK**

Button Method
- ☐ On the Slides or Outline tab, select the appropriate slide
- ☐ Select the text to format
- ☐ Format the text by clicking the appropriate button on the Formatting toolbar, using Table PPT-7 as a reference

Keyboard Method
- ☐ On the Slides or Outline tab, select the appropriate slide
- ☐ Select the text to format
- ☐ Format the text by pressing the appropriate keyboard combination, using Table PPT-7 as a reference

Table PPT-7 Formatting Effects

Formatting effect	Button	Keyboard
Change font color	A ⋅	
Change font type	Arial	[Ctrl][T]
Increase font size	A˙	[Ctrl][ ]] (right bracket)
Decrease font size	A˙	[Ctrl][[ ] (left bracket)
Bold face	B	[Ctrl][B]
Italic	I	[Ctrl][I]
Underline	U	[Ctrl][U]
Shadow	S	
Left align	≣	[Ctrl][L]
Center align	≣	[Ctrl][E]
Right align	≣	[Ctrl][R]

FORMAT PICTURES, SHAPES, AND GRAPHICS

Resize Objects

Menu Method

☐ On the Slides or Outline tab, select the appropriate slide
☐ Select the object, click **Format** on the menu bar, then click **[Object]** (where [Object] is the element you are formatting), or right-click the object, then click **Format [Object]** on the shortcut menu
☐ In the Format [Object] dialog box, click the **Size tab**, make the appropriate selections, then click **OK**

Mouse Method

☐ On the Slides or Outline tab, select the appropriate slide
☐ Select the object to resize, move the pointer over any sizing handle on the object until it changes to the appropriate pointer, using Table PPT-8 as a reference
☐ Drag the sizing handle until the graphic is the size you want, then release the mouse button

Table PPT-8 Resize Pointers

Pointer	Used to
↗ or ↖	Resize proportionally
↔	Resize horizontally
↕	Resize vertically

Change Colors of Graphics

Note: You cannot recolor .bmp or .tif files.

Menu Method

☐ On the Slides or Outline tab, select the appropriate slide
☐ Select the graphic you want to recolor, click **Format** on the menu bar, then click **Picture**
☐ In the Format Picture dialog box, click the **Picture tab**, then click **Recolor**
☐ In the Recolor Picture dialog box, change the New colors as appropriate, then click **OK**
☐ Click **OK i**n the Format Picture dialog box

PowerPoint

Change Colors of Shapes, AutoShapes, and WordArt

Menu Method

- ☐ On the Slides or Outline tab, select the appropriate slide
- ☐ Select the shape, AutoShape, or WordArt object you want to recolor, click **Format** on the menu bar, then click **[Object]** (where [Object] is the element you want to recolor)
- ☐ In the Format [Object] dialog box, click the **Colors and Lines tab**, click the **Color list arrow** in the Fill section, then choose a color
- ☐ Click **OK** to close the Format [Object] dialog box

Button Method

- ☐ On the Slides or Outline tab, select the appropriate slide
- ☐ Select the shape, AutoShape, or WordArt object you want to recolor, click the **Fill Color list arrow** 🎨 ▾ on the Drawing toolbar, then click a color

Align Objects

Button Method

- ☐ On the Slides or Outline tab, select the appropriate slide
- ☐ Select the object you want to align, then click the **Draw button** Draw ▾ on the Drawing toolbar
- ☐ Point to **Align or Distribute**, then click the appropriate option

Group Objects

Button Method

- ☐ On the Slides or Outline tab, select the appropriate slide
- ☐ Select the first object, press and hold **[Shift]**, click additional object(s), then release **[Shift]**
- ☐ Click the **Draw button** Draw ▾ on the Drawing toolbar, then click **Group**

Rotate Objects

Menu Method

- ☐ On the Slides or Outline tab, select the appropriate slide
- ☐ Select the object you want to rotate, click **Format** on the menu bar, then click [Object] (where [Object] is the element you are rotating), or right-click the object, then click **Format [Object]**
- ☐ In the Format [Object] dialog box, click the **Size tab**, then type the rotation value in the Rotation text box
- ☐ Click **OK** in the Format [Object] dialog box

Button Method

- ☐ On the Slides or Outline tab, select the appropriate slide
- ☐ Select the object you want to rotate, then click the **Rotate Left 90°** **button** 🔄 on the Picture toolbar repeatedly until the object is rotated as desired

Mouse Method

☐ On the Slides or Outline tab, select the appropriate slide
☐ Click the object you want to rotate, position the pointer over the green rotate handle ↥ so that the pointer changes to ↻, then drag the handle to rotate the object as desired

dd Effects to Objects

Menu Method

☐ On the Slides or Outline tab, select the appropriate slide
☐ Select the object, click **Slide Show** on the menu bar, then click **Custom Animation**, or right-click the object, then click **Custom Animation** on the shortcut menu
☐ In the Custom Animation task pane, click **Add Effect**, point to an option on the drop-down menu, then click the effect you want
☐ Modify the effect settings in the Modify:[Effect] section of the task pane by changing the Start, Direction, and Speed settings as appropriate

---

ORMAT SLIDES

dd Fill Effects to Slide Backgrounds

Menu Method

☐ On the Slides or Outline tab, select the appropriate slide
☐ Click **Format** on the menu bar, then click **Background**
☐ In the Background dialog box, click the **Background fill list arrow**, then click **Fill Effects**
☐ In the Fill Effects dialog box, click the appropriate options, then click **OK**
☐ In the Background dialog box, click **Apply** or **Apply to all** as appropriate

dd Graphics to Slide Backgrounds

Menu Method

☐ On the Slides or Outline tab, select the appropriate slide
☐ Click **Format** on the menu bar, then click **Background**
☐ In the Background dialog box, click the **Background fill list arrow**, then click **Fill Effects**
☐ In the Fill Effects dialog box, click the **Picture tab**, then click **Select Picture**
☐ In the Select Picture dialog box, navigate to the appropriate drive and folder, click the image you want, then click **Insert**
☐ In the Fill Effects dialog box, click **OK**
☐ In the Background dialog box, click **Apply** or **Apply to all** as appropriate

pply Slide Layouts to Slides

Menu Method

☐ On the Slides or Outline tab, select the appropriate slide(s)
☐ Click **Format** on the menu bar, then click **Slide Layout**
☐ Click the appropriate layout option in the Slide Layout task pane

PowerPoint

Apply More than One Design Template to Presentations

Button Method
☐ On the Slides or Outline tab, select the appropriate slide(s)
☐ Click the **Slide Design button** ⬚Design on the Formatting toolbar
☐ In the Slide Design task pane, click **Design Templates** if necessary
☐ Scroll down the list of templates, click the **list arrow** for the template you want, then click **Apply to Selected Slides**
☐ Repeat the first through fourth bullets to apply a different design template to other slides

Change Page Setup
☐ Click **File** on the menu bar, then click **Page Setup**
☐ In the Page Setup dialog box, change the settings as appropriate, then click **OK**

APPLY ANIMATION SCHEMES

Apply an Animation Scheme to a Single Slide

Menu Method
☐ On the Slides or Outline tab, select the appropriate slide
☐ Click **Slide Show** on the menu bar, then click **Animation Schemes**
☐ In the Slide Design task pane, click the appropriate scheme

Button Method
☐ On the Slides or Outline tab, select the appropriate slide
☐ Click the **Slide Design button** ⬚Design on the Formatting toolbar
☐ In the Slide Design task pane, click **Animation Schemes**
☐ In the Slide Design task pane, click the appropriate scheme

Apply an Animation Scheme to a Group of Slides

Menu Method
☐ On the Slides or Outline tab, select the appropriate slides
☐ Click **Slide Show** on the menu bar, then click **Animation Schemes**
☐ In the Slide Design task pane, click the appropriate scheme

Button Method
☐ On the Slides or Outline tab, select the appropriate slides
☐ Click the **Slide Design button** ⬚Design on the Formatting toolbar
☐ In the Slide Design task pane, click **Animation Schemes**
☐ In the Slide Design task pane, click the appropriate scheme

Apply an Animation Scheme to an Entire Presentatio

Menu Method
☐ Click **Slide Show** on the menu bar, then click **Animation Schemes**
☐ In the Slide Design task pane, click the appropriate scheme
☐ In the Slide Design task pane, click **Apply to All Slides**

Button Method

☐ Click the **Slide Design button** [🗇 Design] on the Formatting toolbar
☐ In the Slide Design task pane, click **Animation Schemes**
☐ Follow the second and third bullets in the Apply an Animation Scheme to an Entire Presentation Menu Method

---

APPLY SLIDE TRANSITIONS

Apply Transition Effects to a Single Slide

Menu Method

☐ On the Slides or Outline tab, select the appropriate slide
☐ Click **Slide Show** on the menu bar, then click **Slide Transition**
☐ In the Slide Transition task pane, scroll down the list of transitions, click the transition you want, then specify the settings in the Modify transition and Advance slide sections of the task pane as appropriate

Apply Transition Effects to a Group of Slides in a Presentation

Menu Method

☐ On the Slides or Outline tab, select the appropriate slides
☐ Click **Slide Show** on the menu bar, then click **Slide Transition**
☐ In the Slide Transition task pane, scroll down the list of transitions, click the transition you want, then specify the settings in the Modify transition and Advance slide sections of the task pane as appropriate

Apply Transition Effects to an Entire Presentation

Menu Method

☐ Click **Slide Show** on the menu bar, then click **Slide Transition**
☐ In the Slide Transition task pane, scroll down the list of transitions, click the transition you want, then specify the settings in the Modify transition and Advance slide sections of the task pane as appropriate
☐ In the Slide Transition task pane, click **Apply to All Slides**

CUSTOMIZE SLIDE TEMPLATES

Customize Templates

Menu Method

☐ Click **View** on the menu bar, point to **Master**, then click **Slide Master**
☐ Click the appropriate slide element
☐ Make the appropriate formatting modifications using Table PPT-7 on page 210 and Table PPT-9 on page 216 as references
☐ Repeat the third bullet to make formatting changes to other slide elements as appropriate
☐ Click **File** on the menu bar, then click **Save As**
☐ In the Save As dialog box, click the **Save as type list arrow**, then click **Design Template**
☐ Type the filename in the File name text box, then click **Save**

PowerPoint

Table PPT-9 Outlining Toolbar Buttons

Button	Button name	Used to
⬆	Promote	Promote text to the next level up in the outline hierarchy
➡	Demote	Demote text to the next level down in the outline hierarchy
⬆	Move Up	Move selected element up a level in the text box
⬇	Move Down	Move selected element down a level in the text box

WORK WITH MASTERS

Add Information to the Slide Master

Menu Method

□ Click **View** on the menu bar, point to **Master**, then click **Slide Master**
□ Add a text box and type the content you want to appear on every slide or add a new object to appear on every slide
□ Click **Close Master View** on the Slide Master View toolbar

Add Information to the Footer Area of the Slide Master

Menu Method

□ Click **View** on the menu bar, then click **Header and Footer**
□ In the Header and Footer dialog box, verify that the **Footer check box** is selected
□ Click the **Footer text box**, then add the appropriate information to the footer
□ Click **Apply** or **Apply to All** as appropriate

OR

□ Click **View** on the menu bar, point to **Master**, then click **Slide Master**
□ Click the **Footer Area text box**, then type the appropriate footer text
□ Click **Close Master View** on the Slide Master View toolbar

Modify Headers and Footers in Handouts and Notes Pages

Menu Method

□ Click **View** on the menu bar, then click **Header and Footer**
□ In the Header and Footer dialog box, click the **Notes and Handouts tab**
□ Verify that the **Header check box** is selected, then edit the text in the Header text box as appropriate
□ Verify that the **Footer check box** is selected, then edit the text in the Footer text box as appropriate
□ Click **Apply to All**

OR

- [ ] Click **View** on the menu bar, point to **Master**, then click **Handout Master** or **Notes Master**
- [ ] Edit the text in the Header Area text box or Footer Area text box as appropriate
- [ ] Click **Close Master View** on the Handout Master View or Notes Master View toolbar

reate and Manage Slide Masters

Menu Method

- [ ] Click **View** on the menu bar, point to **Master**, then click **Slide Master**
- [ ] Click **Insert** on the menu bar, then click **New Slide Master**
- [ ] Make the appropriate formatting modifications, using Table PPT-7 on page 210 and Table PPT-9 on page 216 as references
- [ ] Click **Edit** on the menu bar, then click **Rename Master**
- [ ] In the Rename Master dialog box, enter a name for the new master, then click **Rename**
- [ ] Click **View** on the menu bar, then click **Normal**
- [ ] On the Slides or Outline tab, select the slides to which you want to apply the new slide master
- [ ] Position the pointer over the new slide master in the Slide Design task pane, click the **list arrow**, then click **Apply to Selected Slides**

Button Method

- [ ] Click **View** on the menu bar, point to **Master**, then click **Slide Master**
- [ ] Click the **Insert New Slide Master button** 🔲 on the Slide Master View toolbar
- [ ] Make the appropriate formatting modifications, using Tables PPT-7 and PPT-9 as references
- [ ] Click the **Rename Master button** 🔲 on the Slide Master View toolbar
- [ ] In the Rename Master dialog box, enter a name for the new master, then click **Rename**
- [ ] Click **Close Master View** on the Slide Master View toolbar
- [ ] On the Slides or Outline tab, select the slides to which you want to apply the new slide master
- [ ] Position the pointer over the new slide master in the Slide Design task pane, click the **list arrow**, then click **Apply to Selected Slides**

elete Placeholders on a Slide Master

Keyboard Method

- [ ] Click **View** on the menu bar, point to **Master**, then click **Slide Master**
- [ ] Select the placeholder to remove, then press **[Ctrl][X]** or **[Delete]**
- [ ] Return to Normal view

lodify Placeholders on a Slide Master

- [ ] Click **View** on the menu bar, point to **Master**, then click **Slide Master**
- [ ] Select the placeholder to modify, then make the appropriate text or paragraph formatting changes, or reposition and resize the placeholder as appropriate
- [ ] Click **Close Master View** on the Slide Master View toolbar

PowerPoint

PowerPoint Specialist Skill Set 3: Collaborating

Merge, Track, and Review Presentation Comments and Edits

Menu Method

☐ Open the PowerPoint file with which you want to merge a reviewer's comments

☐ Click **Tools** on the menu bar, then click **Compare and Merge Presentations**

☐ In the Choose Files to Merge with Current Presentation dialog box, click the appropriate PowerPoint file that contains the reviewer's comments, click **Merge**, then click **Continue** in the message box

☐ Use the Revisions task pane to view the comments and changes for a slide, then click **Next** at the bottom of the task pane to move to the next slide

☐ Click the appropriate button on the Reviewing toolbar to view and respond to changes, using Table PPT-10 as a reference

Table PPT-10 Reviewing Toolbar Buttons

Button	Button name	Effect
	Show/Hide Markup	Shows or hides comments and editing changes
Reviewers...	Reviewers	Displays comments and editing changes for certain reviewers
	Previous Item	Returns to the previous comment or editing change
	Next Item	Advances to the next comment or editing change
	Apply	Applies editing changes to the current slide or to the entire presentation
	Unapply	Rejects editing changes to the current slide or to the entire presentation
	Insert Comment	Inserts a new comment
	Edit Comment	Allows a comment to be edited
	Delete Comment	Deletes selected comment
	Revisions Pane	Opens the Revisions task pane

SET UP A REVIEW CYCLE

Menu Method

☐ Click **File** on the menu bar, point to **Send To**, then click **Mail Recipient (for Review)**

☐ If the Choose Profile dialog box opens, select your **profile name**, then click **OK**

☐ If a message box opens about accessing e-mail addresses stored in Outlook, click **Yes**

☐ If a dialog box opens asking if you want to save the document, click **Yes**

☐ In the Outlook message window, type the e-mail address of the recipient in the To text box, then click the **Send button** [≡ Send] on the Message Window toolbar

PowerPoint

POWERPOINT SPECIALIST SKILL SET 4: MANAGING AND DELIVERING PRESENTATIONS

ORGANIZE A PRESENTATION

Add Slides to Presentations

Menu Method

☐ On the Slides or Outline tab, click the slide you want to appear before the new slide

☐ Click **Insert** on the menu bar, then click **New Slide**, or right-click, the click **New Slide** on the shortcut menu

Button Method

☐ On the Slides or Outline tab, click the slide you want to appear before the new slide

☐ Click the **New Slide button** [⬛ New Slide] on the Formatting toolbar

Keyboard Method

☐ On the Slides or Outline tab, click the slide you want to appear before the new slide

☐ Press **[Ctrl][M]**, or press **[Enter]**

Delete Slides from Presentations

Menu Method

☐ On the Slides or Outline tab, click the slides you want to delete

☐ Click **Edit** on the menu bar, then click **Delete Slide**, or right-click, then click **Delete Slide** on the shortcut menu

Keyboard Method

☐ On the Slides or Outline tab, click the slide you want to delete

☐ Press **[Delete]**, or press **[Ctrl][X]**

Rearrange Slides

Button Method

☐ On the Outline tab, click the slide icon ▦ for the slide you want to reposition

☐ Click the **Move Up button** 🔼 or the **Move Down button** 🔽 on the Outlining toolbar

Mouse Method

☐ Click the slide on the Slides tab, then drag it to the new location using ▦

OR

☐ In Slide Sorter view, drag the slide you want to move to the new location using ▦

Change Views

Menu Method

☐ Click **View** on the menu bar, then click the view you want, using Table PPT-11 as a reference

Button Method

☐ Click the appropriate View button using Table PPT-11 as a reference

Table PPT-11 PowerPoint Views

Button	View	Description
⊡	Normal	Consists of four work areas: **Outline tab** (used to edit slide text) **Slides tab** (used to view slide thumbnails and navigate) **Slide pane** (used to edit text and graphics) **Notes pane** (used to enter speaker notes)
⊞	Slide Sorter	Used to rearrange slide order and to view all slides in the presentation at once
⧉	Slide Show	Each slide fills the screen; used for delivering a presentation to an audience

Add Hyperlinks to Slides

☐ On the Slides or Outline tab, select the appropriate slide
☐ Select the object or text to which you want to apply the hyperlink
☐ Open the Insert Hyperlink dialog box using Table PPT-12 as a reference
☐ Make the appropriate selections using Table PPT-13 as a reference, then click **OK**

Table PPT-12 Methods for Opening the Insert Hyperlink Dialog Box

Menu	Button	Keyboard
Click Insert on the menu bar, then click Hyperlink, or right-click the object, then click Hyperlink	Click the Insert Hyperlink button 🔘 on the Standard toolbar	Press [Ctrl][K]

Table PPT-13 Inserting Hyperlinks Using the Insert Hyperlink Dialog Box

To Link to another place in the document	To link to another document	To link to a new document	To link to a Web page	To add an e-mail link
Click Place in This Document, select a location in the Select a place in this document list, then click OK	Click Existing File or Web Page, click the Look in list arrow, navigate to the appropriate drive and folder, click the filename in the list, then click OK	Click Create New Document, name the document and verify the drive and folder, choose to edit it now or later, then click OK	(*Note*: Make sure you are connected to the Internet) Click Existing File or Web Page, click the Address text box, then type the URL, then click OK	Click E-mail Address, type the address and any other text to display, then click OK

Setting Grids and Guides

☐ Click **View** on the menu bar, then click **Grid and Guides**
☐ In the Grid and Guides dialog box, specify the appropriate settings, then click **OK**

SET UP SLIDE SHOWS FOR DELIVERY

Prepare Slide Shows for Delivery

Menu Method

☐ Click **Slide Show** on the menu bar, then click **Set Up Show**
☐ Click the appropriate options in the Set Up Show dialog box, using Tabl PPT-14 as an example
☐ Click **OK**

Table PPT-14 Set Up Show Dialog Box Options

Dialog box section	Options
Show type	Choose whether show will be delivered by a speaker, or browsed by an individual in a window or at a kiosk
Show options	Select whether to loop, or show with or without narration or animation
Performance	Set resolution options and graphics accelerator options
Show slides	Specify whether to show all or selected slides
Advance slides	Choose to proceed through slides manually or using timings
Multiple monitors	Set show to run on one or multiple monitors

PowerPoint

Setup a Custom Show

Menu Method

- [ ] Click **Slide Show** on the menu bar, then click **Custom Shows**
- [ ] In the Custom Shows dialog box, click **New**
- [ ] In the Define Custom Show dialog box, click the **Slide show name text box**, then type the name of the slide show
- [ ] Select each slide you want to include in the slide show, then click **Add** after each
- [ ] Change the slide order of selected slides by using the **Move Up button** 🔼 or the **Move Down button** 🔽
- [ ] Click **OK**, then click **Close** in the Custom Shows dialog box

Edit a Custom Show

- [ ] Click **Slide Show** on the menu bar, then click **Custom Shows**
- [ ] In the Custom Shows dialog box, click the appropriate slide show, then click **Edit**
- [ ] In the Define Custom Show dialog box, make the appropriate modifications, then click **OK**
- [ ] Click **Close** in the Custom Shows dialog box

Add and Modify an Action button

- [ ] Click **Slide Show** on the menu bar, then click **Action Buttons**
- [ ] Click the button you want to add on the Action Buttons submenu
- [ ] Draw the button using ╂, specify the appropriate options in the Action Settings dialog box, then click **OK**
- [ ] To modify an action button, double-click it, make the appropriate modifications in the Action Settings dialog box, then click **OK**

Hide Slides

- [ ] On the Slides or Outline tab, select the appropriate slide(s)
- [ ] Click **Slide Show** on the menu bar, then click **Hide Slide**

REHEARSE TIMING

Menu Method

- [ ] Click **Slide Show** on the menu bar, then click **Rehearse Timings**
- [ ] Advance through the presentation, clicking the **Next button** 🔼 when finished rehearsing each slide
- [ ] When a message box appears, click **Yes** to keep the new slide timings

PowerPoint

DELIVER PRESENTATIONS

Run Slide Shows

Menu Method

☐ Click **Slide Show** on the menu bar, then click **View Show**

Button Method

☐ Click the first slide in the presentation
☐ Click the **Slide Show from current slide button** 🖵

Keyboard Method

☐ Press **[F5]**

Use Onscreen Navigation Tools

Menu Method

☐ Click **Slide Show** on the menu bar, then click **View Show**
☐ Right-click the slide, then click the appropriate navigation option on the shortcut menu

Keyboard Method

☐ View the presentation in Slide Show view
☐ Navigate through the presentation, using Table PPT-15 as a reference

Table PPT-15 Slide Show Navigation Keyboard Shortcuts

Press	Effect
[N]; [Enter]; [PgDn]; or [Spacebar]	Trigger the next animation or advance to the next slide
[P]; [PgUp]; or [Backspace]	Trigger the previous animation or return to the previous slide
[*Number*][Enter]	Go to specified slide number
[Esc]; [Ctrl][Break]; or [-] (hyphen)	End slide show
[Home] or [1][Enter]	Return to first slide
[End]	Go to last slide
[Tab]	Go to first or next hyperlink on a slide
[Shift][Tab]	Go to last or previous hyperlink on a slide

Mouse Method

☐ Click to trigger the next animation or advance to the next slide

Use Pens, Highlighters, Arrows, and Pointers

Menu Method

□ View the presentation in Slide Show view, then right-click the slide you wish to annotate

□ Point to **Pointer Options** on the shortcut menu, then click the appropriate arrow, pen, or highlighter option on the submenu

□ Drag to create the annotation you want, then release the mouse button

□ Advance through all the slides in the presentation making appropriate annotations, then click **Keep** or **Discard** in the message box that appears asking if you want to keep your annotations

PREPARE PRESENTATIONS FOR REMOTE DELIVERY

Use Package for CD

Menu Method

□ Insert a blank CD onto which to save your presentation in the appropriate drive on your computer

□ Click **File** on the menu bar, then click **Package for CD**

□ In the Package for CD dialog box, type an appropriate name in the Name the CD text box

□ Click **Copy to Folder** or **Copy to CD**

□ In the Copy to Folder or Copy to CD dialog box, make the appropriate selections, then click **Close**

Work with Embedded Fonts

Menu Method

□ Click **Tools** on the menu bar, click **Options**

□ In the Options dialog box, click the **Save tab**

□ Click the **Embed TrueType fonts check box**, then click **OK**

Schedule and Define Settings for Online Broadcasts

Note: In order to schedule an online broadcast, you will need an add-in from the Microsoft Web site. Click **Tools** on the menu bar, click **Add-Ins**, click **Online Broadcast** in the Add-Ins dialog box, then click **OK**.

Menu Method

□ Click **Slide Show** on the menu bar, point to **Online Broadcast**, then click **Schedule a Live Broadcast**

□ Click **Save**, if necessary, in the warning box

□ Type the appropriate information in the Schedule Presentation Broadcast dialog box, then click **Settings**

□ In the Broadcast Settings dialog box, click the **Presenter tab**, then click **Browse**

PowerPoint

- ☐ In the Choose Directory dialog box, navigate to the appropriate drive and shared folder, then click **Select**
- ☐ If you were able to specify a shared folder on a network, click **OK** in the Schedule Presentation Broadcast dialog box, then click **Schedule** in the Broadcast dialog box, otherwise, close all open dialog boxes
- ☐ To broadcast the show at the scheduled time, click **Slide Show** on the menu bar, point to **Online Broadcast**, then click **Start Live broadcast now**

SAVE AND PUBLISH PRESENTATIONS

Save a Presentation in a New Folder

Menu Method

- ☐ Click **File** on the menu bar, then click **Save As**
- ☐ In the Save As dialog box, navigate to the drive and folder where you want to create a new folder, then click the **Create New Folder button** 🗀
- ☐ In the New Folder dialog box, type the folder name in the Name text box, then click **OK**
- ☐ In the Save As dialog box, type the filename in the File name text box, then click **Save**

Save a Presentation as a Web Page

Menu Method

- ☐ Click **File** on the menu bar, then click **Save as Web Page**
- ☐ In the Save As dialog box, navigate to the drive and folder where you want to save the Web page
- ☐ Type the filename in the File name text box, then click **Save**

Publish Slides and Presentations as Web Pages and Set Publishing Options

- ☐ Click **File** on the menu bar, then click **Save as Web Page**
- ☐ In the Save As dialog box, click **Publish**
- ☐ In the Publish as Web Page dialog box, make the appropriate selections, then click **Publish**

PRINT SLIDES, OUTLINES, HANDOUTS, AND SPEAKER NOTES

Print Slides

Menu Method

- ☐ Click **File** on the menu bar, then click **Print**
- ☐ In the Print dialog box, click the **Print what list arrow**, click **Slides**, then specify other appropriate options
- ☐ Click **OK**

Button Method

☐ Click the **Print button** 🖨 on the Standard toolbar

Keyboard Method

☐ Press **[Ctrl][P]**
☐ Follow the second and third bullets in the Print Slides Menu Method

Preview and Print Outlines

Menu Method

☐ Click **File** on the menu bar, then click **Print**
☐ In the Print dialog box, click the **Print what list arrow**, then click **Outline View**
☐ Click **Preview**
☐ Click the **Print button** 🖨 Print... on the Print Preview toolbar, then click **OK** in the Print dialog box

Keyboard Method

☐ Press **[Ctrl][P]**
☐ Follow the second through fourth bullets in the Preview and Print Outlines Menu Method above

Print Handouts

Menu Method

☐ Click **File** on the menu bar, then click **Print**
☐ In the Print dialog box, click the **Print what list arrow**, then click **Handouts**
☐ Click the **Slides per page list arrow** in the Handouts area then click the appropriate handouts option if necessary
☐ Click **Preview**
☐ Click the **Print button** 🖨 Print... on the Print Preview toolbar, then click **OK** in the Print dialog box

Keyboard Method

☐ Press **[Ctrl][P]**
☐ Follow the second through fifth bullets in the Print Handouts Menu Method

Print Speaker Notes

Menu Method

☐ Click **File** on the menu bar, then click **Print**
☐ In the Print dialog box, click the **Print what list arrow**, then click **Notes Pages**
☐ Click **Preview**
☐ Click the **Print button** 🖨 Print... on the Print Preview toolbar, then click **OK** in the Print dialog box

PowerPoint

Keyboard Method

- □ Press **[Ctrl][P]**
- □ Follow the second through fourth bullets in the Print Speaker Notes Menu Method

Print Comments Pages

Menu Method

- □ Click **File** on the menu bar, then click **Print**
- □ In the Print dialog box, click the **Print what list arrow**, then click **Slides**
- □ Click the **Print comments and ink markup check box** to select it
- □ Click **OK**

Keyboard Method

- □ Press **[Ctrl][P]**
- □ Follow the second through fourth bullets in the Print Comments Pages Menu Method above

Preview Slides for Printing

Menu Method

- □ Click **File** on the menu bar, then click **Print Preview**
- □ Use the **Zoom list arrow** `100%` to change the magnification level of the slides on your screen

Button Method

- □ Click the **Print Preview button** on the Standard toolbar

Change Preview Options

Menu Method

- □ Click **File** on the menu bar, then click **Print Preview**
- □ Click the **Options button** on the toolbar, then choose an appropriate option

Button Method

- □ Click the **Print Preview button** on the Standard toolbar
- □ Click the **Options button** on the toolbar, then choose an appropriate option

Change Print Options

Menu Method

- □ Click **File** on the menu bar, then click **Print**
- □ In the Print dialog box, specify the print settings you want
- □ Click **Properties** in the Print dialog box, specify additional settings on the Layout and Paper/Quality tabs, then click **OK**
- □ Click **OK** in the Print dialog box

Keyboard Method
☐ Press **[Ctrl][P]**
☐ Follow the second through fourth bullets in the Change Print Options Menu Method

---

EXPORT A PRESENTATION TO ANOTHER MICROSOFT OFFICE PROGRAM

Export a Presentation as an RTF File

Menu Method
☐ Click **File** on the menu bar, then click **Save As**
☐ In the Save As dialog box, click the **Save as type list arrow**, then click **Outline/RTF**
☐ Navigate to the drive and folder where you want to save the outline, then type the filename in the File name text box
☐ Click **Save**

Export a Presentation as a Word file

Menu Method
☐ Click **File** on the menu bar, point to **Send To**, then click **Microsoft Word**
☐ In the Send to Microsoft Office Word dialog box, click the layout you want, then click **OK**

MICROSOFT OFFICE OUTLOOK 2003
EXAM REFERENCE
Getting Started with Outlook 2003

The Microsoft Outlook Office Specialist exam assumes a basic level of proficiency in Outlook. This section is intended to help you reference these basic skills while you are preparing to take the Outlook Specialist exam.

> ☐ Starting and exiting Outlook
> ☐ Setting up an Outlook profile
> ☐ Using toolbars
> ☐ Opening Outlook tools
> ☐ ViewingOutlook Tools
> ☐ Getting Help

START AND EXIT OUTLOOK

Start Outlook

Button Method
☐ Click the **Start button** *start* on the Windows taskbar
☐ Point to **All Programs**
☐ Point to **Microsoft Office**, then click **Microsoft Office Outlook 2003**
OR
☐ Double-click the **Microsoft Outlook program icon** on the desktop

Exit Outlook

Menu Method
☐ Click **File** on the menu bar, then click **Exit**

Button Method
☐ Click the **Close button** ☒ on the program window title bar

Keyboard Method
☐ Press **[Alt][F4]**

Refreshing the Inbox

Menu Method
☐ Click **Tools** on the menu bar, point to **Send/Receive**, then click the appropriate option

Button Method
☐ In the Inbox folder, click the **Send/Receive button** Send/Receive on the Standard toolbar

Keyboard Method

☐ Press **[F9]** to send and receive all messages in Outlook

SET UP AN OUTLOOK PROFILE

Button Method

☐ Click the **Start button** `start` on the Windows taskbar, then click **Control Panel**
☐ In the Control Panel window, make sure you are in Category view, click **User Accounts**, then double-click the **Mail icon**
☐ In the Mail Setup – Outlook dialog box, click **Show Profiles**
☐ In the Mail dialog box, click **Add**
☐ In the New Profile dialog box, type a name for the profile in the Profile name text box, then click **OK**
☐ Navigate through the E-mail Accounts Wizard, making selections. and specifying settings as appropriate to create the profile, then click **Finish**
☐ Click **OK** in the Mail dialog box

USE TOOLBARS

Display Toolbars

Menu Method

☐ Click **View** on the menu bar, point to **Toolbars**, then click the toolbar you want to display

OR

☐ Right-click any toolbar, then click the toolbar you want to display on the shortcut menu

Customize Toolbars

Menu Method

☐ Click **Tools** on the menu bar, then click **Customize**, or click **View** on the menu bar, point to **Toolbars**, then click **Customize**, or right-click any toolbar, then click **Customize** on the shortcut menu
☐ In the Customize dialog box, select the appropriate options, then click **Close**

Button Method

☐ Click the **Toolbar Options button** ▪ on the toolbar you want to customize
☐ Point to **Add or Remove Buttons**, then click **Customize**
☐ Follow the steps in the second bullet in the Customize Toolbars Menu Method above

Reposition Toolbars

Mouse Method

☐ Position the pointer over the **Toolbar Move handle** ▌ at the left end of any docked toolbar, or over the title bar of any floating toolbar
☐ When the pointer changes to ↔, press and hold the mouse button
☐ Drag the toolbar to a blank area of the window or to a different location, then release the mouse button

---

OPEN OUTLOOK TOOLS

Menu Method

☐ Click **Go** on the menu bar, then click the appropriate item, using Table OL-1 as a reference

Button Method

☐ Click the appropriate button on the Navigation Pane, using Table OL-1 as a reference

Keyboard Method

☐ Press the appropriate keyboard combination, using Table OL-1 as a reference

Table OL-1 Common Outlook Navigation Options

Command on the Go menu	Navigation Pane button	Keyboard combination	Description
Mail		[Ctrl][1]	View new e-mail messages, create new e-mail messages, and move messages to folders
Calendar		[Ctrl][2]	View, create, and manage appointments
Contacts		[Ctrl][3]	Create, view, and edit contacts
Tasks		[Ctrl][4]	Schedule and assign tasks
Notes		[Ctrl][5]	Create and edit electronic notes
Folder List		[Ctrl][6]	View the contents of a folder or create a new folder
Shortcuts		[Ctrl][7]	View and manage shortcuts to folders in Outlook
Journal		[Ctrl][8]	View and manage actions related to your contacts in an outline form

Outlook

VIEW OUTLOOK TOOLS

View the Inbox Folder

Using the Inbox folder you can send, receive, and read mail, as well as read and respond to any tasks or meeting requests. See Figure OL-1.

Figure OL-1 The Inbox Folder

Title bar   Standard toolbar

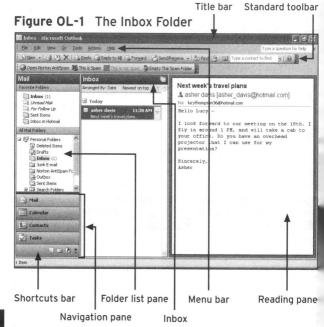

Shortcuts bar   Folder list pane   Menu bar   Reading pane

Navigation pane   Inbox

Outlook

View the Calendar Window

You can use the Calendar to create appointments and events, organize meetings, view group schedules, and manage another user's Calendar. You can view the Calendar by day, week, or month. See Figure OL-2.

Figure OL-2 The Calendar

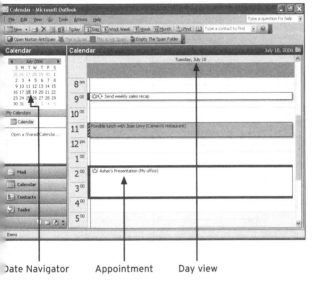

Date Navigator   Appointment   Day view

View the Contacts Window

You use the Contacts window to store e-mail addresses, addresses, phone numbers, and any other information that relates to your contacts, such as birthdays or spouse's names. See Figure OL-3.

Figure OL-3   The Contacts Window

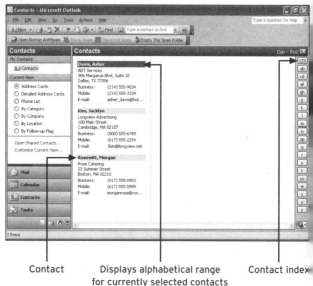

Contact   Displays alphabetical range   Contact index
                 for currently selected contacts

View the Tasks Window

The Tasks window contains a list of all tasks you have created for yourself or others, or that others have assigned for you to do. You can use the tasks list to update the status of your projects, set a task as recurring, delegate tasks, and mark tasks as completed. See Figure OL-4.

Figure OL-4   The Tasks Window

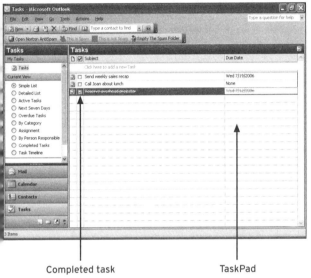

Completed task   TaskPad

View the Notes Window

You use the Notes window to create electronic notes to remind yourself of questions, directions, or any other important items to help you create a document or complete a task. You can leave notes open on the screen as you work. See Figure OL-5.

Figure OL-5   The Notes Window

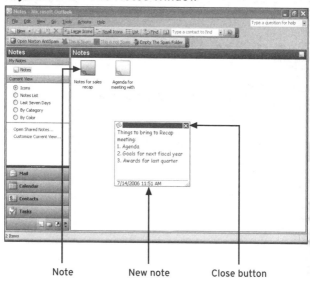

          Note   New note   Close button

GET HELP

Menu Method

☐ Click **Help** on the menu bar, then click **Microsoft Office Outlook Help**
☐ Use Table OL-2 as a reference to select the most appropriate way to search for help using the Outlook Help task pane

Button Method

☐ Click the **Microsoft Office Outlook Help button** 🗊 on the Standard toolbar

☐ Use Table OL-2 as a reference to select the most appropriate way to search for help using the Outlook Help task pane

OR

☐ Click the **Type a question for help box** on the menu bar

☐ Type a question or keywords relating to an Outlook topic, then press **[Enter]**

☐ View the results of the keyword search in the Search Results task pane, then click a topic title in the task pane to view the topic in a new window

Keyboard Method

☐ Press **[F1]**

☐ Use Table OL-2 as a reference to select the most appropriate way to search for help using the Outlook Help task pane

Table OL-2 Outlook Help Task Pane Options

Option	To use
Table of Contents	Click Table of Contents in the task pane, click the Expand indicator next to each topic you want to explore further, then click the topic you want and read the results in the task pane
Search	Type a keyword in the Search for text box, click the Start Searching button →, then click the blue hyperlinked text to read more in the Microsoft Office Outlook Help Window, or click the grayed text to view the topic in the Table of Contents

OUTLOOK SPECIALIST EXAM
REFERENCE

Skill Sets:

1. Messaging
2. Scheduling
3. Organizing

OUTLOOK SPECIALIST SKILL SET 1: MESSAGING

ORIGINATE AND RESPOND TO E-MAIL AND INSTANT MESSAGES

Sending and Addressing E-mail Messages

Menu Method

☐ Click **File** on the menu bar, point to **New**, then click **Mail Message**
☐ In the Untitled Message window, type the e-mail address(es) for the recipient(s) in the To and Cc boxes, separating each e-mail address with a semicolon (;), or to select recipient names from the Address Book, click the **To button** 〖🔲To...〗 or the **Cc button** 〖🔲Cc...〗 to open the Select Names dialog box, select the appropriate names, then click **OK**
☐ In the Subject text box, type an appropriate subject for the message
☐ In the message body, type the message
☐ Click the **Send button** 〖📧Send〗 on the Standard toolbar

Button Method

☐ Click the **New list arrow** 〖🖊New ▾〗 on the Standard toolbar, then click **Mail Message** (*Note*: button may differ based on current view)
☐ Follow the steps in the second through fifth bullets in the Sending and Addressing E-mail Messages Menu Method above

Keyboard Method

☐ Press **[Ctrl][Shift][M]**
☐ Follow the steps in the second through fifth bullets in the Sending and Addressing E-mail Messages Menu Method above

Open E-mail Messages

Menu Method

☐ Click the message you want to open in the Inbox folder to view it in the reading pane
☐ To open the message, click **File** on the menu bar, point to **Open**, then click **Selected Items**

Keyboard Method

☐ Click the message you want to open in the Inbox folder to view it in the reading pane
☐ To open the message, press **[Ctrl][O]**

Mouse Method

☐ Click the message you want to open in the Inbox folder to view it in the reading pane
☐ To open the message, double-click it

Respond to E-mail Messages

Menu Method

☐ Open and maximize the mail message to which you want to respond
☐ Click **Actions** on the menu bar, then click one of the menu options described in Table OL-3, as appropriate
☐ Type the message in the message body, then add any additional recipients as appropriate
☐ Click the **Send button** 🖃 Send on the Standard toolbar

Button Method

☐ Open and maximize the mail message to which you want to respond
☐ Click the appropriate button on the Standard toolbar, using Table OL-3 as a reference
☐ Follow the steps in the third and fourth bullets in the Respond to E-mail Messages Menu Method above

Keyboard Method

☐ Open and maximize the mail message to which you want to respond
☐ Press one of the keyboard combinations listed in Table OL-3 as appropriate
☐ Follow the steps in the third and fourth bullets in the Respond to E-mail Messages Menu Method above

Outlook

Table OL-3 E-mail Message Response Options

Command on the Action menu	Button	Keyboard combination	Action
Reply		[Ctrl][R]	To send a message that includes the original text and your comments directly to the original sender
Reply to All		[Ctrl][Shift][R]	To send a message that includes the original message and your comments directly to the sender and all recipients of the original message
Forward		[Ctrl][F]	To send a message that includes the original message and your comments directly to the recipient(s) of your choosing, but not to the sender

Sending and Addressing Instant Messages

Note: In order to use the Instant Message features you must have Windows Messenger installed and activated, the IM address for a contact entered in your contact list, and the contact must be online.

Button Method

☐ Position the pointer over the e-mail address of the person to whom you want to send a message in a new Message window, a new Meeting Request or, in a Contact window, until the **Person Names Smart tag** 🔲 appears

☐ Click 🔲, then click **Send Instant Message**

☐ In the message text box, type the message, then click the **Send button**

Respond to Instant Messages

Menu Method

☐ When an instant message is sent to you, a Windows Messenger window pops up on the status bar, indicating the sender and the message

☐ To respond, click the Windows Messenger window

☐ In the message text box, type the message, then click the **Send button** 🔲

ATTACH FILES TO ITEMS

Insert E-mail Message Attachments

Menu Method

- □ Open a new e-mail message, then maximize the Untitled Message window if necessary
- □ Click **Insert** on the menu bar, then click **File**
- □ In the Insert File dialog box, navigate to the appropriate drive and folder, click the file you want to attach, then click **Insert**

Button Method

- □ Open a new e-mail message, then maximize the Untitled Message window if necessary
- □ Click the **Insert File button** 📄 on the E-mail toolbar
- □ In the Insert File dialog box, navigate to the appropriate drive and folder, click the file you want to attach, then click **Insert**

Insert Instant Message Attachments

Menu Method

- □ Open a new instant message window
- □ Click **File** on the menu bar, then click **Send a File or Photo**
- □ In the Send a File to [contact] dialog box, navigate to the appropriate drive and folder, click the file, then click **Open**

Button Method

- □ Open a new instant message window
- □ Click the **Send a File or Photo button** 📄 in the right pane
- □ In the Send a File to [contact] dialog box, navigate to the appropriate drive and folder, click the file, then click **Open**

CREATE AND MODIFY A PERSONAL SIGNATURE FOR MESSAGES

Create an E-mail Signature

Menu Method

- □ Click **Tools** on the menu bar, then click **Options**
- □ In the Options dialog box, click the **Mail Format tab**
- □ Under Signatures, click **Signatures**
- □ In the Create Signature dialog box, click **New**
- □ In the Create New Signature dialog box, type the signature name, select the appropriate option under Choose how to create your signature, then click **Next**
- □ In the Edit Signature [signature name] dialog box, type the signature text, select any other appropriate options, then click **Finish**
- □ In the Create Signature dialog box, click **OK**
- □ Click **Apply** in the Options dialog box, then click **OK**

Modify an E-mail Signature

Menu Method

☐ Click **Tools** on the menu bar, then click **Options**

☐ In the Options dialog box, click the **Mail Format tab**, then click **Signatures**

☐ Select a signature, then click **Edit**

☐ In the Edit Signature [signature name] dialog box, make the appropriate changes, click **OK**, click **OK** in the Create Signature dialog box, then click **OK** in the Options dialog box

Create E-mail Signatures for Multiple Accounts

Menu Method

☐ Click **Tools** on the menu bar, then click **Options**

☐ In the Options dialog box, click the **Mail Format tab**

☐ Click the **Select signatures for account list arrow**, choose an account, select a signature, then click **Apply**

☐ Repeat for additional signatures, then click **OK**

MODIFY E-MAIL MESSAGE SETTINGS AND DELIVERY OPTIONS

Flag an E-mail Message

Menu Method

☐ In the Inbox folder, open and maximize the message window for the message you want to flag

☐ Click **Actions** on the menu bar, point to **Follow Up**, then click the appropriate flag color

OR

☐ In the Inbox folder, open and maximize the message window for the message you want to flag

☐ Click **Actions** on the menu bar, point to **Follow Up**, then click **Add Reminder**

☐ In the Flag for Follow Up dialog box, select the appropriate action, due date, and flag color, then click **OK**

Button Method

☐ In the Inbox folder, open and maximize the message window for the message you want to flag
☐ Click the **Flag button** 🏳 on the Standard toolbar
☐ In the Flag for Follow Up dialog box, select the appropriate action, due date, and flag color, then click **OK**

hange the Format of an E-mail Message

☐ In the Inbox folder, open and maximize a new message window
☐ If Microsoft Word is your e-mail editor, click the **Message format list arrow** ⌷HTML⌷ on the Standard toolbar, then click **HTML**, **Rich Text**, or **Plain Text**
☐ If Microsoft Word is not your e-mail editor, click **Format** on the menu bar, then click **HTML**, **Rich Text**, or **Plain Text**

hange the Default Format for all E-mail Messages

Menu Method

☐ Click **Tools** on the menu bar, then click **Options**
☐ In the Options dialog box, click the **Mail Format tab**
☐ Select the appropriate options under the Message format and Stationary and Fonts sections, then click **OK**

et E-mail Message Importance and Sensitivity

Button Method

☐ In the Inbox folder, open and maximize a new message window
☐ Click the **Options button** ⌷ Options... on the E-mail toolbar
☐ In the Message Options dialog box, select the appropriate options in the Message settings section, then click **Close**

OR

☐ In the Inbox folder, open and maximize a new message window
☐ Click the **Importance: High button** ❗ or the **Importance: Low button** ⬇ on the E-mail toolbar

Outlook

Set E-mail Message Delivery Options

Button Method

☐ In the Inbox folder, open and maximize a new message window
☐ Click the **Options button** 🔲 Options... on the E-mail toolbar
☐ In the Message Options dialog box, select the appropriate options in the Delivery options section, then click **Close**

CREATE AND EDIT CONTACTS

Create a Contact

Menu Method

☐ Click **File** on the menu bar, point to **New**, then click **Contact**
☐ In the Untitled – Contact window, click the **Maximize button**, then enter the name, address, phone number, e-mail address, IM address, and other appropriate information for the person
☐ Click the **Save and Close button** 🔲 Save and Close on the Standard toolbar

Button Method

☐ Click the **New list arrow** 🔲 New ▾ on the Standard toolbar, then click **Contact** (*Note*: the New button may differ based on current view)
☐ Follow the steps in the second and third bullets in the Create a Contact Menu Method above

Keyboard Method

☐ Press **[Ctrl][Shift][C]**
☐ Follow the steps in the second and third bullets in the Create a Contact Menu Method above

Add a Contact to Windows Messenger

Menu Method

☐ Start Windows Messenger, then click the **Add a Contact link**
☐ Navigate through the Add a Contact wizard, specifying requested information or accepting defaults as appropriate, then click **Finish**

Modify a Contact

Button Method

☐ In the Contacts window, double-click the contact you want to edit
☐ In the Contact window, click the **Maximize button**, make the appropriate modifications, then click the **Save and Close button** 🔲 Save and Close on the Standard toolbar

ACCEPT, DECLINE, AND DELEGATE TASKS

Delegate Tasks

Menu Method

☐ Click the **Tasks button** 📋 in the Navigation Pane to open the Tasks window, double-click the task you want to delegate in the Tasks list, then click the **Maximize button**

☐ Click **Actions** on the menu bar, then click **Assign Task**

☐ Type each recipient's name in the To text box separated by a semi-colon, or click the **To button**, select the appropriate person in the Select Task Recipient dialog box, then click **To**

☐ Repeat the previous bullet for each task recipient, then click **OK**

☐ Select any other appropriate options, then click the **Send button** 📧 Send on the Standard toolbar

☐ If a message box appears, click **OK**

Button Method

☐ Click the **Tasks button** 📋 in the Navigation Pane to open the Tasks window, double-click the task you want to delegate in the Tasks list, then click the **Maximize button**

☐ Click the **Assign Task Button** 📧 Assign Task on the Standard toolbar

☐ Follow the steps in the third through sixth bullets in the Delegate Tasks Menu Method above

Accept and Decline Tasks

Button Method

☐ In the Inbox folder, open and maximize the message containing the task request

☐ Click the **Accept button** ✓ Accept or the **Decline button** ✗ Decline on the Standard toolbar as appropriate

☐ In the Accepting Tasks or the Declining Tasks dialog box, click the appropriate response option, then click **OK**

☐ If necessary, type the response in the message window

☐ Click the **Send button** 📧 Send on the Standard toolbar

OUTLOOK SPECIALIST SKILL SET 2: SCHEDULING

CREATE AND MODIFY APPOINTMENTS, MEETINGS AND EVENTS

Add Appointments to the Calendar

Menu Method

☐ Click **File** on the menu bar, point to **New**, then click **Appointment**
☐ In the Untitled – Appointment window, click the **Maximize button**, click the **Appointment tab** if necessary, then enter the subject, location, start and end time, and other appropriate information for the appointment
☐ Click the **Save and Close button** 🔲 Save and Close on the Standard toolb

Button Method

☐ Click the **New list arrow** 🔲 New ▾ on the Standard toolbar, then click **Appointment** (*Note*: the New button may differ based on current view
☐ Follow the steps in the second and third bullets in the Add Appointments to the Calendar Menu Method above

Keyboard Method

☐ Press **[Ctrl][Shift][A]**
☐ Follow the steps in the second and third bullets in the Add Appointment to the Calendar Menu Method above

Schedule Meetings and Invite Attendees

Menu Method

☐ Click **File** on the menu bar, point to **New**, then click **Meeting Reques**
☐ In the Untitled – Meeting window, click the **Maximize button**, then click the **Appointment tab** if necessary
☐ Click the **To text box**, then enter recipient names or type the e-mail addresses of the meeting attendees, separating each with a semicolon or to select recipient names from the Address Book, click the **To butto** then in the Select Attendees and Resources dialog box select the attendees and resources from the Name list box, click the appropriate butto for each name (Required, Optional, Resources), then click **OK**
☐ Enter the subject, location, start and end time, and other appropriate information, then click the **Send button** 🔲 Send on the Standard tool

Button Method

☐ Click the **New list arrow** 🔲 New ▾ on the Standard toolbar, then click **Meeting Request** (*Note*: the New button may differ based on current view)
☐ Follow the steps in the second through fourth bullets in the Schedule Meetings and Invite Attendees Menu Method above

Keyboard Method
- [ ] Press **[Ctrl][Shift][Q]**
- [ ] Follow the steps in the second through fourth bullets in the Schedule Meetings and Invite Attendees Menu Method

chedule Resources for Meetings

*ote: In order to schedule a resource, the resource must have its own
ailbox and be included in your Contacts folder.

Menu Method
- [ ] In the Calendar window, click **Actions** on the menu bar, then click **Plan a Meeting**
- [ ] In the Plan a Meeting dialog box, click **Add Others**, then click **Add from Address Book**
- [ ] In the Select Attendees and Resources dialog box, enter the name of a resource you want at the meeting in the Type Name or Select from List text box, or click the name of the resource in the Name list box, then click **Resources**
- [ ] Repeat the previous bullet for each resource you want, then click **OK**
- [ ] If the Microsoft Office Internet Free/Busy dialog box opens, click **Cancel**
- [ ] In the Plan a Meeting dialog box, click **Make Meeting**
- [ ] In the Untitled – Meeting dialog box, click the **Maximize button**, enter the appropriate information, then click the **Send button** ⬛Send on the Standard toolbar
- [ ] Click **Close** to close the Plan a Meeting dialog box

chedule Events

Menu Method
- [ ] In the Calendar window, click **Actions** on the menu bar or right-click the Calendar, then click **New All Day Event**
- [ ] In the Untitled – Event dialog box, enter the subject, location, start and end times, and other appropriate information
- [ ] Click **File** on the menu bar, click **Close**, then click **Yes** in the message box to save the new message

---

PDATE, CANCEL, AND RESPOND TO MEETING
EQUESTS

ccept and Decline Meeting Requests

Button Method
- [ ] In the Inbox folder, open the meeting request to which you want to respond, then maximize the Meeting Request window
- [ ] Click the appropriate button on the Standard toolbar, using Table OL-4 as a reference
- [ ] In the message box, click the appropriate response option, then click **OK**

Outlook

Table OL-4 Meeting Request Options

Buttons	Button name	Used to
✔ Accept	Accept button	Accept the meeting at the proposed time and add it to your calendar
? Tentative	Tentative button	Tentatively accept the meeting and add it to your calendar
✘ Decline	Decline button	Decline the meeting and move the request to your Deleted Items folder

Propose New Meeting Times

Button Method

□ In the Inbox, open the meeting request to which you want to respond, then maximize the Meeting Request window
□ Click the **Propose New Time button** 🕔 Propose New Time on the Standard toolbar
□ In the Propose New time dialog box, select a new time, then click **Propose Time**
□ In the New Time Proposed message window, type a note if necessary, then click the **Send button** 🖃 Send on the Standard toolbar

Update a Meeting Request

Button Method

□ In the Inbox folder, open the meeting request that you want to update, then maximize the Meeting Request window
□ Make the changes to the meeting request, then click the **Send Update button** 🖃 Send Update on the Standard toolbar

Cancel a Meeting Request

Button Method

□ In the Inbox folder, open the meeting request which you want to cancel, then maximize the Meeting Request window
□ Click **Actions** on the menu bar, then click **Cancel Meeting**
□ If a message box opens, click the appropriate option, then click **OK**

Outlook

CUSTOMIZE CALENDAR SETTINGS

Set Calendar Options

Menu Method

- ☐ In the Calendar window, click **Tools** on the menu bar, then click **Options**
- ☐ In the Options dialog box, click the **Preferences tab** if necessary, then click **Calendar Options**
- ☐ Make the appropriate selections in the Calendar Options dialog box using Table OL-5 as a reference, then click **OK**
- ☐ Click **OK** in the Options dialog box

Table OL-5 Calendar Options dialog box

Dialog box section	Used to
Calendar work week	Set work days and hours
Calendar options	Add holidays, change background color, change meeting request options
Advanced options	Select different calendar or time zone, schedule resources

CREATE, MODIFY, AND ASSIGN TASKS

Create Tasks

Menu Method

- ☐ Click **File** on the menu bar, point to New, then click **Task**
- ☐ In the Untitled – Task window, click the **Maximize button**, then enter or select the appropriate information for the subject, dates, priority level, reminder dates and times, and any other appropriate information
- ☐ Click the **Save and Close button** 🔲 Save and Close on the Standard toolbar

Button Method

- ☐ Click the **New list arrow** 🔲 New ▾ on the Standard toolbar, then click **Task** (*Note*: the New button may differ based on current view)
- ☐ Follow the steps in the second and third bullets in the Create Tasks Menu Method above

Outlook

Keyboard Method

□ Press **[Ctrl][Shift][K]**
□ Follow the steps in the second and third bullets in the Create Tasks Men␡
  Method

Modify Tasks

Button Method

□ In the Tasks window, open and maximize the task you want to modify
□ Make the appropriate modifications
□ Click the **Save and Close button** 🔲 Save and Close on the Standard toolba␡

Assign Tasks

Menu Method

□ Click **File** on the menu bar, point to **New**, then click **Task Request**
□ In the Untitled – Task window, click the **Maximize button**, type each
  recipient's name or e-mail address in the To text box separated by a
  semi-colon, or click the **To button**, select the appropriate recipient in
  the Select Task Recipient dialog box, then click **To**
□ Repeat the previous bullet for each recipient, then click **OK**
□ Select any other appropriate options, then click the **Send button** 🔲Se␡
  on the Standard toolbar

Button Method

□ Click the **New list arrow** 🔲New ▾ on the Standard toolbar, then click
  Task Request (*Note:* the New button may differ based on current view␡
□ Follow the steps in the second through fourth bullets in the Assign Tas␡
  Menu Method above

Keyboard Method

□ Press **[Ctrl][Shift][U]**
□ Follow the steps in the second through fourth bullets in the Assign Tas␡
  Menu Method above

OUTLOOK SPECIALIST SKILL SET 3: ORGANIZING

CREATE AND MODIFY DISTRIBUTION LISTS

Create a Distribution List

Menu Method

☐ Click **File** on the menu bar, point to **New**, then click **Distribution List**
☐ In the Untitled – Distribution List dialog box, type the name of the group in the Name text box, then click **Select Members**
☐ In the Select Members dialog box, click a name to select it, then click **Members** to add the contact to the group
☐ Repeat for each member, then click **OK**
☐ Click the **Save and Close button** 🔲 Save and Close on the Standard toolbar

Modify a Distribution List

Button Method

☐ In the Contacts window, double-click the distribution list you want to modify
☐ To add a new member, click the **Add New button**, enter the contact information in the Add New Member dialog box, then click **OK**
☐ To delete a member, click the name in the member list, then click the **Delete button**
☐ Make any other appropriate changes, click **Update Now**, then click the **Save and Close button** 🔲 Save and Close on the Standard toolbar

LINK CONTACTS TO OTHER ITEMS

Assign Categories to Contacts

Menu Method

☐ In the Contacts window, select the contact(s) to whom you want to assign one or more categories
☐ Click **Edit** on the menu bar, then click **Categories**, or right-click the contact, then click **Categories** on the shortcut menu
☐ In the Categories dialog box, click the appropriate categories under the Available categories list, then click **OK**

Outlook

Assign Journal Entries to Contacts

Menu Method

☐ Click **File** on the menu bar, point to **New**, then click **Journal Entry**
☐ In the Untitled – Journal Entry window, click the **Maximize button**, enter the subject, entry type, time, and other appropriate information, then click **Contacts**
☐ In the Select Contacts dialog box, select the appropriate contact(s) in the Items pane, then click **OK**
☐ Click the **Save and Close button** 🔲 Save and Close on the Standard toolbar

Button Method

☐ Click the **New list arrow** 🔽 New ▾ on the Standard toolbar, then click **Journal Entry** (*Note:* the New button may differ based on current view)
☐ Follow the steps in the second through fourth bullets in the Assign Journal Entries to Contacts Menu Method above

Keyboard Method

☐ Press **[Ctrl][Shift][J]**
☐ Follow the steps in the second through fourth bullets in the Assign Journal Entries to Contacts Menu Method above

Tracking Activities for Contacts

Button Method

☐ In the Contacts window, double-click the contact
☐ In the Contact window, click the **Maximize button**, then click the **Activities tab**
☐ Click the **Show list arrow**, then click the appropriate item

CREATE AND MODIFY NOTES

Create Notes

Menu Method

☐ Click **File** on the menu bar, point to **New**, then click **Note**
☐ In the Note window, type the appropriate information
☐ Click the **Close button** ☒ on the Note window title bar

Button Method

☐ Click the **New list arrow** 🔽 New ▾ on the Standard toolbar, then click **Note** (*Note:* the New button may differ based on current view)
☐ Follow the steps in the second and third bullets in the Create Notes Menu Method above

Keyboard Method

☐ Press **[Ctrl][Shift][N]**
☐ Follow the steps in the second and third bullets in the Create Notes Menu Method above

Outlook

Edit Notes

Menu Method

- ☐ In the Notes window, select the appropriate note
- ☐ Click **File** on the menu bar, point to **Open**, then click **Selected Items**, or right-click the note, then click **Open** on the shortcut menu
- ☐ Make the edits you want to the note, then click the **Close button** ☒ on the Notes window title bar

Mouse Method

- ☐ In the Notes window, double-click the appropriate note
- ☐ Make the edits you want to the note, then click the **Close button** ☒ on the Notes window title bar

Forward a Note to a Contact

Menu Method

- ☐ In the Notes window, select the appropriate note
- ☐ Click **Actions** on the menu bar, then click **Forward**, or right-click the note, then click **Forward** on the shortcut menu
- ☐ In the FW: [note text] window, click the **Maximize button**, type the recipient name(s) or type the e-mail address in the To and Cc boxes, separating each name with a semicolon (;), or to select recipient names from the Address Book, click the **To button** 🔲 To... or the **Cc button** 🔲 Cc...
- ☐ In the message body, type the message
- ☐ Click the **Send button** 🔲 Send on the Standard toolbar

Keyboard Method

- ☐ In the Notes window, select the appropriate note
- ☐ Press **[Ctrl][F]**
- ☐ Follow the steps in the third through sixth bullets in the Forward a Note to a Contact Menu Method above

---

ORGANIZE ITEMS

Add and Delete Fields

Menu Method

- ☐ Open the appropriate Outlook tool in the view you want to customize
- ☐ Click **View** on the menu bar, point to **Arrange By**, point to **Current View**, then click **Customize Current View**
- ☐ In the Customize View dialog box, click **Fields**
- ☐ To add a field, click the field you want to add in the Available fields list, then click **Add**
- ☐ To delete a field, click the field you want to delete in the Show these fields in this order list, then click **Remove**
- ☐ Click OK in the Show Fields dialog box, then click **OK** in the Customize View dialog box

Sort Items

Menu Method

- ☐ Open the appropriate Outlook tool in the view you want to customize
- ☐ Click **View** on the menu bar, point to **Arrange By**, point to **Current View**, then click **Customize Current View**
- ☐ In the Customize View dialog box, click **Sort**
- ☐ In the Sort dialog box, specify the appropriate sorting options, then click **OK**
- ☐ In the Customize View dialog box, click **OK**

Filter Items

- ☐ Open the appropriate Outlook tool in the view you want to filter
- ☐ Click **View** on the menu bar, point to **Arrange By**, point to **Current View**, then click **Customize Current View**
- ☐ In the Customize View dialog box, click **Filter**
- ☐ In the Filter dialog box, specify the appropriate filtering options, then click **OK**
- ☐ In the Customize View dialog box, click **OK**

Apply Conditional Formats to Appointments in the Calendar

Menu Method

- ☐ In the Calendar window, click **View** on the menu bar, point to **Arrange By**, point to **Current View**, then click **Customize Current View**
- ☐ In the Customize View dialog box, click **Automatic Formatting**
- ☐ In the Automatic Formatting dialog box, click **Add**
- ☐ Type the condition name in the Name text box
- ☐ Click **Condition**, specify the conditions in the Filter dialog box using Table OL-6 as a reference, then click **OK**
- ☐ Click **OK** in the Automatic Formatting dialog box, then click **OK** in the Customize View dialog box

Button Method

- ☐ In the Calendar window, click the **Calendar Coloring button** 🔲 on the Standard toolbar, then click **Automatic Formatting**
- ☐ Follow the steps in the third through sixth bullets in the Apply Conditional Formats to Appointments in the Calendar Menu Method above

Table OL-6 Filter Dialog Box Tabs

Tab	Options
Appointments and Meetings	Set filter options by searching for a certain word or words in a particular field, or by specifying a sender or time
More Choices	Set additional filter options by specifying category or importance, whether there is an attachment, or message size
Advanced	Define and add new advanced filter criteria

Outlook

Organize Items Using Colors, Rules, and Views

Menu Method

☐ Open the appropriate Outlook tool in the view you want to customize
☐ Click **View** on the menu bar, point to **Arrange By**, point to **Current View**, then click **Customize Current View**
☐ In the Customize View dialog box, click the appropriate button using Table OL-7 as a reference, then click **OK**
☐ Click **OK** in the Customize View dialog box

Table OL-7 Customize View Dialog Box Options

Click this Button...	To open this dialog box...	To perform these tasks
Fields	Show Fields	Select fields to add, create a new field, or choose the order of the displayed fields
Group By	Group By	Select the order by which to group items, and whether to group in ascending or descending order
Sort	Sort	Select the items by which to sort, and whether to sort in ascending or descending order
Filter	Filter	Set filter criteria by searching for a certain word or words, specifying a sender, time, or importance level, specifying whether there is an attachment, specifying message size, or by setting advanced options
Other Settings	Other Settings	Select fonts and size for the columns, and fonts for the row headers
Automatic Formatting	Automatic Formatting	Select rules (guidelines) and assign properties for the view

Organize Items Using Folders

Create Folders

Menu Method

☐ Click **File** on the menu bar, point to **New**, then click **Folder**
☐ In the Create New Folder dialog box, type the folder name in the Name text box, specify the contents of the folder, choose a folder location, then click **OK**

Button Method

☐ Click the **New list arrow** 🔽 New ▼ on the Standard toolbar, then click **Folder** (*Note*: the New button may differ based on current view)
☐ In the Create New Folder dialog box, type the folder name in the Name text box, specify the contents of the folder, choose a folder location, then click **OK**

Outlook

Keyboard Method

☐ Press **[Ctrl][Shift][E]**
☐ In the Create New Folder dialog box, type the folder name in the Name text box, specify the contents of the folder, choose a folder location, then click **OK**

Delete Folders

Menu Method

☐ In the Inbox folder, click the appropriate folder(s)
☐ Click **Edit** on the menu bar, then click **Delete**
☐ Click **Yes** in the Message box

Button Method

☐ In the Inbox folder, click the appropriate folder(s)
☐ Click the **Delete button** ⊠ on the Standard toolbar
☐ Click **Yes** in the Message box

Keyboard Method

☐ In the Inbox folder, click the appropriate folder(s)
☐ Press **[Ctrl][D]** or **[Delete]**
☐ Click **Yes** in the Message box

Move Messages Between Folders

Menu Method

☐ In the Inbox folder, click the appropriate message(s)
☐ Click **Edit** on the menu bar, then click **Move to Folder**, or right-click the message you want to move, then click **Move to Folder**
☐ In the Move Items dialog box, click the appropriate folder, then click **OK**

Button Method

☐ In the Inbox folder, click the message(s) you want to move
☐ Click the **Move to Folder button** 🗐 on the Standard toolbar
☐ Click the appropriate folder on the menu, or click **Move to Folder**, then in the Move Items dialog box, click the appropriate folder, then click **OK**

Keyboard Method

☐ In the Inbox folder, click the appropriate message(s)
☐ Press **[Ctrl][Shift][V]**
☐ In the Move Items dialog box, click the appropriate folder, then click **OK**

Mouse Method

☐ In the Inbox folder, drag the message to the appropriate folder in the Folder List pane using ⍚

Archive Items

Menu Method

☐ In the Inbox folder, click **File** on the menu bar, then click **Archive**
☐ In the Archive dialog box, click the **Archive this folder and all subfolders option button**, then click the appropriate folder in the folders list
☐ Click any other appropriate options, then click **OK**

SEARCH FOR ITEMS

Find Items

Menu Method

☐ In the Inbox folder, click **Tools** on the menu bar, point to **Find**, then click **Find**
☐ On the Find bar, type appropriate search words in the Look for text box, click the **Search In list arrow**, click the appropriate option, then click **Find Now**

Button Method

☐ In the Inbox folder, click the **Find button** 🔍 on the Standard toolbar
☐ On the Find bar, type the search string in the Look for text box, click the **Search In list arrow**, click the appropriate option, then click **Find Now**

Keyboard Method

☐ In the Inbox folder, press **[Ctrl][E]**
☐ On the Find bar, type the search string in the Look for text box, click the **Search In list arrow**, click the appropriate option, then click **Find Now**

Use Search Folders

Menu Method

☐ In the Inbox folder, click **File** on the menu bar, point to **New**, then click **Search Folder**
☐ In the New Search dialog box, choose the appropriate search folder, specify criteria as necessary, then click **OK**

Outlook

SAVE MESSAGES IN DIFFERENT FILE FORMATS

Menu Method

☐ In the Inbox folder, click the message you want to save as a file, or open the message you want to save as a file, then maximize the message window

☐ Click **File** on the menu bar, then click **Save As**

☐ In the Save As dialog box, navigate to the appropriate drive and folder, then type a name for the file in the File Name text box

☐ Click the **Save as type list arrow**, click the appropriate file format using Table OL-8 as a reference, then click Save

Table OL-8 Message File Formats

File format	Message can be opened in	Description
Rich Text Format	Any text editor	Saves the text and formatting of a message to be opened and edited in a word processing program
Text Only	Any text editor	Saves the text of a message to be opened and edited in a word processing program, but does not save all formatting
Outlook Template	Microsoft Outlook	Can be used to create other messages
Outlook Message Format	Microsoft Outlook	Saves the message intact
Outlook Message Format–Unicode	Microsoft Outlook	Saves the message in a format that supports multilingual data
HTML	A browser, such as Microsoft Internet Explorer	Can be displayed on the Web

ASSIGN ITEMS TO CATEGORIES

Use Categories to Manage Calendar Items

Menu Method

☐ In the Calendar window, select the appropriate appointment(s)

☐ Click **Edit** on the menu bar, then click **Categories**, or right-click the appointment, then click **Categories** on the shortcut menu

☐ In the Categories dialog box, click the appropriate categories in the Available categories list box, then click **OK**

Button Method

☐ In the Calendar window, open and maximize the appointment you want to categorize
☐ Click **Categories** at the bottom of the window
☐ In the Categories dialog box, click the appropriate **category check box(es)**, then click **OK**

Use Categories to Manage Tasks and Notes

Menu Method

☐ In the Notes window or the Tasks window, select the note(s) or task(s)
☐ Click **Edit** on the menu bar, then click **Categories**, or right-click the note or task, then click **Categories** on the shortcut menu
☐ In the Categories dialog box, click the appropriate categories under the Available categories list, then click **OK**

Organize E-mail Messages Using Categories

Menu Method

☐ In the Inbox folder, select the message(s)
☐ Click **Edit** on the menu bar, then click **Categories**, or right-click the message, then click **Categories** on the shortcut menu
☐ In the Categories dialog box, click the appropriate categories in the Available categories list box, then click **OK**

Organize Contacts Using Categories

Menu Method

☐ In the Contacts window, select the contact(s)
☐ Click **Tools** on the menu bar, then click **Organize**
☐ In the Ways to Organize Contacts pane, click **Using Categories**
☐ Click the **Add contacts selected below to list arrow**, click the appropriate category, then click **Add**
☐ Close the Ways to Organize Contacts pane

Button Method

☐ In the Contacts window, open and maximize the contact you want to categorize
☐ Click the **Categories button** at the bottom of the window
☐ In the Categories dialog box, click the appropriate **category check box(es)**, then click **OK**

Outlook

PREVIEW AND PRINT ITEMS

Preview Items

Menu Method

☐ Open the item you want to preview
☐ Click **File** on the menu bar, then click **Print Preview**

Keyboard Method

☐ Open the item you want to preview
☐ Click the **Print Preview button** 🔳 on the Standard toolbar

Print Items

Menu Method

☐ In the Inbox folder, click the appropriate message to select it, or open the message and maximize the message window
☐ Click **File** on the menu bar, then click **Print**
☐ In the Print dialog box, select the appropriate options, then click **Print**

Button Method

☐ In the Inbox folder, click the appropriate message to select it, or open the message and maximize the message window
☐ Click the **Print button** 🔳 on the Standard toolbar

Keyboard Method

☐ In the Inbox folder, click the appropriate message to select it, or open the message and maximize the message window
☐ Press **[Ctrl][P]**
☐ In the Print dialog box, select the appropriate options, then click **Print**

INDEX